155.937 KEE
Keeley, Maureen P., 1961-
Final conversations :
helping the living and the
dying talk to each other
32148001414506

3/08

P9-DFP-455

DISCARD

Final
Conversations

155.937
KEE
Middletown Public Library
700 West Main Rd.
Middletown, RI 02842

3 0110 3911 1 1306

Final
Conversations

HELPING THE
LIVING AND THE
DYING TALK TO
EACH OTHER

Maureen P. Keeley, PhD
Julie M. Yingling, PhD

VanderWyk & Burnham

3-28-2008

Copyright © 2007 by Maureen P. Keeley and Julie M. Yingling

Published by VanderWyk & Burnham
P.O. Box 2789, Acton, Massachusetts 01720

All rights reserved. No part of this book may be reproduced or transmitted in any form or by any means without permission in writing from the publisher, except in the case of brief quotations embodied in critical articles or reviews with appropriate citation. Address correspondence to Permissions, VanderWyk & Burnham, P.O. Box 2789, Acton, MA 01720-6789.

www.VandB.com

This book is available for quantity purchases. For information on bulk discounts, call 800-789-7916, write to Special Sales at the above address, or send an e-mail to info@VandB.com.

Library of Congress Cataloging-in-Publication Data
Keeley, Maureen P., 1961-
   Final conversations : helping the living and the dying talk to each other /
Maureen P. Keeley, Julie M. Yingling.
       p. cm.
   Summary: "Final conversations can take place any time between a terminal diagnosis and the loved one's death. The communication needs of the survivors who must go on living are the focus in this book. Direct quotations from 'the Living' merge with the authors' advice about what may work for the reader"--Provided by publisher.
   Includes index.
   ISBN-13: 978-1-889242-30-9 (hardcover)
   ISBN-10: 1-889242-30-6 (hardcover)
   1. Death--Psychological aspects. 2. Interpersonal communication. 3. Terminally ill--Psychology. 4. Communication. 5. Bereavement--Psychological aspects. I. Yingling, Julie. II. Title.
   BF789.D4K44 2007
   155.9'37--dc22
                              2006033950

Manufactured in the United States of America
10 9 8 7 6 5 4 3 2 1

In loving memory of the parents who first led us to consider the importance of communication at the end of life:

Patricia Power Keeley
and
Howard Leo Yingling

Contents

Note on Terminology and Editing

In our first drafts, we found that the words needed to distinguish among interviewees and their dying loved ones and to describe their interactions in context each time became cumbersome to the reader. So we created the following terms, which you will see used throughout the book.

- *FC-talk:* talk or interactions, including nonverbal messages, that occur with the full knowledge that one party to the conversation is dying

- *the Living:* the interviewees; the person who spoke to us about the final conversation(s) after the death of their loved one; the person who will continue living

- *the Dying:* the Living's loved one who was dying

- *spiritual message:* any message beyond the scientifically observable sort (some of the Living considered such messages to be related to religion or faith; others considered them to be metaphysical phenomena beyond rational explanation)

We use the following conventions to identify the Living and their words: Direct quotes from our interviews always appear in type that looks like this. Most interviewees gave us permission to use their given names; a few asked that we use pseudonyms they chose. When two people had the same first name, we differentiated between the two people by using the letters *Q* and *W* after their names. In every case, we place a name in bold letters, for instance, **Gloria** or **Laura W,** the first time it appears in a chapter. The quoted words of interviewees have been edited only when necessary for clarity; nothing was changed in a substantive way.

Preface

"Mom's dying. What can I say to her? What can I do—to stop her from dying, to make her pain go away, to let her know how much I love her, to figure out how to live without her?" This is Maureen's voice, but you too may have asked yourself similar questions upon hearing that someone you love is dying: "What do I say?" "What can I talk about?" "What should I avoid talking about?" "What can I do to walk this death journey with the one I love?" We two authors both remember such questions repeating in our heads as we came to grips with the impending deaths of our parents, yet we were at a loss for any good answers at the time, just as you may feel lost now or will sometime soon.

The last stage of a loved one's life is a final opportunity to say "I love you" and to say goodbye. It is a chance to carry on a relationship until the very end or beyond; a time for growth; a time to let go of any hurt that may have been caused by a difficult relationship. This book is for all who have lost a loved one to a terminal illness; it is for everyone who will lose someone in the future. It is for the surviving partners and for anyone who wants to understand the practical power and importance of communication at the end of life, and to learn how to have a better and more fulfilling final conversation.

You will eventually lose someone through death. Will you think of final conversations as a burden to be avoided or as an opportunity to connect, a gift to embrace? Our hope is that by reading this book, you will understand and experience final conversations in terms of the gifts that remain with us.

Maureen's Story

This book has been a journey that began with the death of my beloved mother. My mother died of breast cancer in November

1998, and during the last four months of her life, I had the opportunity to spend almost nine weeks with her. This gift of time was shared with my family and fellow caregivers: father, two sisters, three brothers, and two aunts—my mother's sisters. I lived in Texas at the time, while my mother lived in Arizona. In a normal year, I was lucky to spend two weeks with my family, visiting at Christmas or during the summer. Yet my mother's terminal illness and my family's commitment to care for her at home during her final months created an opportunity for me, and an urgency in me, to spend as much time with her as was humanly possible.

During one of my visits, I remember writing down two words: "terminal time." I knew that what we were all going through was tremendously difficult because we were so conscious that our time was limited—our time together was terminal. It was hard to see my mother getting weaker, experiencing pain, and struggling with her loss of independence and privacy. It was also heart wrenching to come to terms with my own sense of loss—it began the moment I was told of my mother's terminal diagnosis. At the same time, I was very aware of the fact that I had been given a gift of time with my mother. I had the time to laugh with her, to talk with her, to hug her, to give back to her a small piece of the love and attention that she had given me all of my life. I was able to simply be with my mom. We were experiencing terminal time.

Terminal time created a context in which our relationship became the priority. I lived two states away from my mother, I was teaching full time, I was married with a 15-month-old baby—life was busy, to say the least. Prior to the diagnosis of her fatal illness, all the time that I could give to my mother was a weekly phone call and a yearly visit—two if I was lucky. Terminal time created a window of opportunity for me to give top priority to my relationship with my mother. My mother's terminal illness gave me permission to say no to less important activities; to bring my baby home to share his smile and beautiful blue eyes with his grandmother; and to stop the mad rush of the rat race that most of us call life—even if just temporarily.

When my mother was dying, I was searching for answers about what to say and do, so that I might be better prepared for when I was able to spend time with her. The only information I found were a few hospice pamphlets that said simply that communication was important but gave no detail, and a couple of books that related individual dying journeys. The hospice pamphlets addressed the physical changes that occur when a person is dying and the emotional needs of the dying. What about *my* needs, fears, questions? How could I do this—take the death walk with my mother—and do it well?

After my mother's death and my own journey through grief, I realized that I had received many gifts from the time that I spent with my dying mother. First and foremost, I received the gift of time to talk with her, hold her, laugh with her, cry with her, and simply be with her. Second, I was given the opportunity to talk and share with other members of my family in ways that are not usually possible, because we had slowed down our lives to come together to meet my mother's needs. Third, I am no longer afraid of death, because I trust that it will come when it is my time and that I will be surrounded by those I love—that I will not have to take my death walk alone.

It was at this point, when I could see the gifts I had received, that I knew I wanted to find out more about other living partners' communication experiences during their loved ones' death journeys. Had they found gifts similar to mine during their final conversations? In the process of my research, I found many similarities, and I decided to find a way to share this information about the value and importance of communication at the end of life. I wanted to write a book for all of us who have experienced or will experience the dying process of someone we love.

As a professor, I teach the details of the communication that occurs in families and close relationships. Specifically, I teach people how to communicate more effectively in their personal lives. I have been teaching for nineteen years. For the last twelve years, my research and writing have focused on communication in close relationships during health crises; and for the last three years, on the communication at the end of life. So my life led me uniquely to this project, but I wanted a companion and colleague to share this work. Julie agreed to walk this path with me.

Julie's Story

My father was diagnosed with throat cancer in 1992. After the treatments, he appeared to be better for a while, and we pushed back our fears for several years. But then the treatment took its toll on his lungs, and he began to fail. When his health started to go for the second time, I was in Iowa City, serving as a visiting professor. During the year before his death, I returned home to Rhode Island for Christmas and summer vacations. I spent time talking with him about old times, laughing, eating, and sitting on the beach or watching the sunset from my parents' deck. Dad's oxygen system was ever present, but he only used it in the evenings when he rested. That fall, I returned to my home in northern California, believing that Dad would be able to maintain his steady state for some time. But I got the call I dreaded in November—Dad was in the hospital experiencing breathing difficulties.

Within a week, the family was called home. Unlike Maureen, I did not have the gift of time with my father. His doctors seemed not to know that his lungs were so damaged by the radiation therapy that they would fail quickly.

My two brothers and eldest sister, who all live on the East Coast, made it to his side to spend his last days with him. My younger sister and I, who both live on the opposite coast, did not. As I sat in my cramped coach seat, winging my way to him, I had a sense that he could not hold on. The last leg of my journey was delayed by a snowstorm. I called my family from Dulles Airport, and after I told them of my delay, my youngest brother quietly said, "Julie, Dad died last night." Indeed, I had felt him go. Truthfully, I was angry at first, and I admit I took out my anger on the unfortunate airline representatives who could not get me to Rhode Island. I was angry at being cheated of a final opportunity to say goodbye and express my love for him. During the year and a half before, I had written him letters—one very long one telling him what a good father he had been to us and what a success he had been in all aspects of his life; he had written back, acknowledging what that meant to him, and returning his love to me. But it wasn't the same as being there with him during his final time, when we could both know these would be the last interactions.

I wrote the eulogy, transcribing stories from Mom, siblings, in-laws, nieces, and nephews. And even though I did my best to see him to rest in love and dignity, I still felt cheated. And that's when I was ready to study end-of-life communication.

When Maureen approached me about this research project over four years ago, it struck a nerve. I had been teaching and writing about early communication development for twenty years, and had done some research on communicating with ill children. I discovered, after dealing with the loss of my father, that I wanted to know more about the other end of the development spectrum—the communication that accompanies the shutting down of life as opposed to the growing up. I wanted to know what others had experienced in final conversations, how they had said goodbye, and what they had gained from it. More important, I wanted to share with those who have yet to face the death of a loved one not only what can be gained from the experience, but also how these last interactions can be invited and conducted. My generation needs this information now. Dad would approve. Thus began our journey into final conversations.

Preview of the Book

In this book we will share with you the recollections of the Living about their last conversations with the Dying, and the messages that remained with them months and years after their loved ones died. The book is organized with three goals in mind: first, to introduce you to the concept of FC-talk (defined on page ix); second, to highlight the seven major themes that we found in the Living's stories; and third, to offer some tips for having good FC-talk. Here is the essence of the themes we found:

- *Love* is indeed the most meaningful and common message at the end of life.

- Mundane, ordinary, *everyday talk* is a way to continue living with the Dying until the moment of death.

- *Spirituality* enters into many people's (approximately two-thirds of our interviewees') FC-talk.

- *Nonverbal communication* in FC-talk includes the power of touch and eye contact, and the gift of time to say goodbye.

- The Living who are in *challenging relationships* with the Dying often find some kind of resolution to those difficulties.

- The Living of various ages discover much about *self and identity*.

- As a result of those discoveries, some set a *new course in life*.

At the end of each theme chapter (Chapters 2–8) you will find "Advice from the Living," a list of brief statements using key ideas from what our interviewees told us and our own rich experience in teaching communication. We believe you will find support in these lists for your final conversations. At the same time, we know that every case is unique; every pair of loved ones engaging in FC-talk is different. So every bit of advice may not pertain to your situation. Pick and choose what seems right and true for you.

This book is filled with the voices of the Living who shared their FC-talk with us. We hope that as you read these chapters, you will hear your voice as well. For you who are facing the death of a loved one, this book can give you the courage to have those conversations and to do them better with the advice that we share about communication. For you who have already faced the death of a loved one, these stories will affirm and confirm your own experiences.

Our personal and professional experiences with end-of-life communication led us to this work. We firmly believe that terminal time gives the Living the opportunity and permission to make spending time with the Dying their top priority. We also believe that communication at the end of life brings gifts to the Living that they never expected, and for which they are forever grateful.

Acknowledgments

We appreciate all the sources of support that have come our way during the life of this project. Some of these appear below, some we may have forgotten to name—please forgive us if we have missed you—and some have simply arrived without a name and face to thank. But we are grateful for all; you lifted and carried us through our journey. We acknowledge:

The Dying for their inspiration.

The Living, all our interviewees, for their heartfelt contributions. Even if some stories were not a good fit for this book, the project would not have been completed without hearing everyone's story—they all taught us what FC-talk is about.

Humboldt State University and Texas State University for their support of us during parts of this process. Texas State University provided a grant for transcribing the conversations and for equipment.

Colleagues at both universities and across the country who supported us in so many ways, including bringing us interviews and cheering us on. In particular, we appreciate Darrel and Barbara Piersol for their enthusiasm and financial support; Steve Beebe for his belief and encouragement for us and this project; Steve Duck, mentor extraordinaire, who taught us to write more conversationally; Roxanne Parrott, Valerie Manusov, Jody Konig Kellas, Margaret Wills, and Dawn Braithwaite for helping us to understand how different parts of the conversations worked.

Those who went above and beyond the call: Ken McClure for reading and editing the manuscript as only a former English teacher can do; Sharon Houck Ross for encouragement and direction in early stages of the proposal; Jennifer St. Marie for transcribing the interviews; Melinda Villagran for demographic figures; Aimée Langlois for help with the last chapter; Carissa

Hoopes for gorgeous photos from a gorgeous photographer; Holly Melear for the beautiful painting that brought inspiration for the project; Sandy Ransom for recognizing the potential and bringing us to Meredith; and Meredith Rutter for saying *yes! yes! yes! yes!*

Friends who assisted in less tangible ways: Marie, Valerie T., Karen, Susan, Jennifer, Stacey, Lisa B., Linda, Lisa H., and Heather for the prayers and emotional support; Lynda for the cheer and always inspiring guidance; Dorothy and Kurt for being constants; David and Liliane for their love and understanding; and the Psychic Cowboys (Alan B., Mel, Mark, and Alan V.) for celebrating the publication of this work with their wonderful music.

Our parents, Tom and Pat Keeley, and Eileen and Howard Yingling, for starting us talking and for continuing the conversation; Mark Vassberg for the website, reading, cooking dinner, distracting the kids while their mom wrote, and his love; Ian and Meagan for their patience, good humor, and de-stressing of Mom; Rick Davids for the charts, reading, walking the dog, mutual laughter, and his love; Pat, Ray, Terry, and Mike for floating through life and death with Julie; Gail, Jane, Colleen, Kit, Chris, Jim, Kevin, and Tom for accompanying Maureen during her first experience with FC-talk with Pat, who inspired this project.

We have been honored and privileged to have been the recipients of these stories and to have been the ones who were given the task to write this book. We feel blessed.

Final
Conversations

CHAPTER 1

Real People

Setting the Stage for the Book

There was a shift. You know, we weren't just getting out the crying towels waiting for him to die. It was—what could we do to be with him while we still had him? And that was a major shift. Nothing really changed. I mean the bottom line was that he was still going to die when he was going to die, but it was how I viewed the time and how my kids could view the time. [Ellen]

Have you said goodbye to a dying loved one yet? Chances are good that you will. With medical advancements in the diagnosis and treatment of cancer and other degenerative diseases, we can anticipate "dying time" much more accurately than ever before. A terminal diagnosis is a gift of time and a wake-up call that time is running out. How will you use the time? Will you see the end of life as an opportunity to talk, love, and grow from the experience of talking with the Dying, or will you bring out the crying towel and simply wait for your loved one to die?

A century ago, we witnessed death throughout our lives because people died at home and in the family's care. Now, about 80% of the two million Americans who die each year die in the hospital. We have removed death from our homes and our lives. As a result, we don't know what to do when we are faced with the prospect of helping a loved one have a good death.

Both of us, Julie and Maureen, lost parents to cancer within the last ten years. And we found precious little information to guide us in saying goodbye to these parents—Julie's father and Maureen's mother—as they moved slowly toward their end times. As communication scholars and teachers, we realized that we could help fill the huge gap in what people know about talking with loved ones who are facing death. We asked people who had experienced "final conversations." They told us their stories. We committed to relating those stories to you who want to know: *Why should I engage in final conversations?*

We are aware of how hard it is to watch someone we love die—death is not easy or pretty—however, we are also struck by the gifts that we can experience during this precious time. Many of us live far away from people we love; we are busy working and raising families, all of which makes it difficult to spend much time with those we love. If you have made a commitment to spending time with someone you love, and you are wondering what to say and do, you are not alone. This book is written for you.

The Source of These Final Conversations

We started talking with people in April 2002 about their final conversations with dying loved ones. After a year of interviewing people in two locations (northern California and central Texas) with roots in many regions of the country, we had completed more than 80 lengthy interviews, resulting in more than 1300 pages of transcripts. From these transcripts came the stories we want to share with you.

What Are Final Conversations?

Final conversations, or FC-talk,* include all the moments of talking, touching, and spending time with the Dying. These commu-

---

* See page ix for a brief section on terminology. We are using shortcuts like this one for often-used phrases such as "final conversations" (FC-talk), "the participant who spoke to us" (the Living), and "the dying loved one" (the Dying).

nicative moments potentially begin when you find out that someone you love is dying and continue until the moment the person
dies. FC-talk is not necessarily the "last" conversation that the
Dying had with someone, although in some instances it is.

What is unique about FC-talk is that both people are aware
that one of them is dying. These are not moments that are filled
with the shock of someone dying unexpectedly. They are
moments that can be planned or can occur spontaneously because
you have slowed down your life long enough to sit quietly and
patiently with the Dying. These are moments to be cherished for
the opportunity to say goodbye and to make sure that you as the
Living do not leave any words left unsaid. How many times have
you heard someone say (or you yourself have said), "I didn't get
the chance to say goodbye, to say *I love you* one more time." FC-
talk provides that chance for the Living who are ready for these
questions:

- Are you willing to take the time to engage in FC-talk?
- Why is FC-talk so hard, and how do you get past the
  challenges?
- Do you know how to have the best possible FC-talk?

The answers to these questions will help get rid of some of the
anxiety, fear, and awkwardness that come with communication at
the end of life. If you think you aren't ready yet, read on. You are
not alone.

Americans and Death—Why Is It So Difficult?

Americans are generally taught to deny death, to ignore grief, to
avoid talking about death, and to mourn alone, in private. Death
is shrouded in fear, doubt, loss of control, and feelings of awkwardness and discomfort. Few people know what to expect—
physically, emotionally, or intellectually—about the death process.
Books about the physical aspects of dying can tell us what happens
to the body as it begins to shut down, but most people have never

seen it happen and do not want to see it—they are satisfied with the status quo of keeping death safely out of sight in hospitals. As a result, most grieving is done alone, behind closed doors. The pain of grief is hidden or sanitized until it must be experienced personally. Intellectually, very few people know anything of death's reality because they are discouraged from sharing their questions and thoughts on what happens at the end of life. So death remains in the shadows.

When told of the impending death of a loved one, the immediate experience is shock, denial, and grief. Suddenly, a sense of deep loss is imposed, and an unfamiliar reality must be dealt with. Even as grief and loss hit the unwilling Living one, the demands of providing care, love, and resources also increase. Thus, the partner of a Dying one is experiencing not only emotional stress but physical stress as well.

Death is considered depressing and morbid, yet it is a natural part of life's journey. It doesn't *feel* natural or normal, though, because death has been removed from our view. Our great-grandparents died at home, in their own beds, and their wakes were held in the front parlor. During their last days, the Dying would be surrounded by children, grandchildren, and close friends. Now the majority of Americans die in hospitals, cared for by health professionals instead of family members. There are very few witnesses to the end of life other than those who are paid, such as nurses and doctors.

If the death process is unseen, if there are no examples to demonstrate how to act when a loved one is dying, then how is the Living one to know what to say or what to do? Children learn to walk by watching others move on two feet, and by practicing with assistance. They learn to talk by trying out "baba" when Mom gives the bottle, and they learn from mistakes when Sister corrects the trial word with "bottle!" Almost every human activity requires a model of how to do it for a learner to actually master it. Yet at the end of life, the hidden workings of modern medicine, along with learned negative connotations about death, leave the Living blind, ignorant, and fearful of the inevitable.

Death and taxes are the only guarantees in life, and yet taxes are far easier to talk about. Death has become a taboo topic in our society. Avoiding the topic doesn't make death go away; it only prevents the kind of talk that would make the process tolerable and maybe even rewarding. Perhaps the silence regarding death and dying rests on ignorance and superstition. Perhaps the substitution for ignorance is the magical belief that death cannot happen if it isn't acknowledged. No one would consider this to be sound thinking, but solace and security are strong emotional motivators to ignore sound reasoning.

Coping with challenging tasks is easier if we've done them before, but few of us are eager to practice dealing with death. In our culture death means dealing with the unknown while in the throes of extreme emotional distress and challenging conditions. The emotions may include sadness, fear, anger, denial, even guilt. The challenging conditions are imposed by the harsh reality of terminal illness. This reality may include the physical stress and exhaustion of taking care of the Dying, and financial worries over increased health costs and decreased income from loss of the Dying's assets. Even as emotional stress as well as physical and financial demands on the Living increase, there is a vague expectation that the Living should be able to communicate with the Dying in a way that is satisfying and fulfilling to both, in a situation that is wholly unfamiliar. It's no surprise, then, that the Living not only are uncomfortable talking with the Dying but would prefer to avoid it altogether. It all falls on the shoulders of the Living.

What amazed us is that, when asked, almost everyone wants an opportunity to talk with the Dying at least one more time before it is too late. Even more remarkable is that the experienced Living—ones who have had FC-talks—would not miss an opportunity to do so again. These same Living partners think they will do it better the next time because they aren't as afraid and uncomfortable as before.

The first time is always the most difficult. While FC-talk is not something that can be practiced until the occasion arises, the necessary communication skills can be described and modeled. Hearing other people's FC-talk as you read what the Living told us can give you an idea of what future final conversations may be like for you. There were amazing similarities in people's stories. We draw upon these similarities to show you the skills that will help you communicate more effectively despite the emotions that you will feel and the stresses that will be placed upon you as a companion on the death journey. Each final conversation will be unique, but the similarities bind all the Living.

Why Communicate at the End?

With the anticipation of death, there is time to think about what to say and how to say it. There is time to share stories, hugs, and the natural gestures that help to say goodbye. Communication is the vehicle for such exchange. Communication is a tangible way to connect with the Dying and to leave no doubt about the love that is shared in the relationship. Communication at the end of life is a way to give comfort to the Dying as well as to receive it from them. The frantic pace of life can provide an excuse for putting off the investment of time and energy to complete the unfinished business of a relationship with a terminally ill relative or friend. The false assumption underlying that excuse is that there will be time to do it later. But a death notice means that time has run out—putting death off is not an option.

Specifically, communication during an extended end time gives the Living opportunities: (1) to resolve conflicts and to let go of past hurts, (2) to strengthen relationships by talking rather than by remaining silent, (3) to reach satisfactory closure with the Dying, (4) to confirm and affirm the Living's identity, and (5) to clarify the Living's life path.

As communication experts, we will examine in detail the specific verbal messages and nonverbal actions that occur during FC-talk. Looking at FC-talk from the Living's perspectives will show how their final conversations looked and sounded. This book goes beyond the idea that "all communication is good at the end of life," and shows *what kind* of communication is best. This book will also give you a lot of examples of FC-talk to illustrate what it is and what it can do. These examples are not meant to be blueprints for all final conversations. Rather, the FC-talk shared here provides a first demonstration of what FC-talk is, although each conversation will be unique. You will see examples that will inspire you and models that will teach you. Here, you will find practical communication tools to help you at a time when you will need all the help you can get. And you will find guidelines for preparing yourself to engage in these rich interactions.

Why Look at the Living's Perspective on Communication at the End of Life?

The Dying often choose to shut out all but their immediate family and closest friends. Thus, the Living often are given the time, space, and opportunity to talk with the Dying at a time when no one else is given access. The Living have a unique perspective on the death process and so can reveal not only *what* is meaningful about these conversations, but *why* it is meaningful.

Those who live through the Dying's journey to death are often confused and uncomfortable, and may even feel inadequate because they don't know how to handle the situation. Facing death with a loved one is rough in that it provides many opportunities to see what will be lost; yet there is much to be gained as well. What is gained, if we are open to the possibility, is a forum for listening carefully, engaging thoughtfully, focusing on what is most important, and so ensuring that nothing is left unsaid. Coming together, being attentive, and focusing on the now are at the heart of the communication at the end of life.

The majority of research on death and dying has been done using the Dying's perspective. As authors, we appreciate those findings, yet we feel we must take a different approach. We talk about end of life from the Living's perspective because the Living partner is the forgotten component of the death process. By sharing the Living's stories about their communication with the Dying, we intend to answer the journalistic quintet of questions: who, what, when, where, and why about FC-talk.

- Who, in close relationship with the Dying, participates in FC-talk? Who else is present? Who does most of the talking? Who initiates the final conversations?

- What makes up FC-talk, both verbal (written or spoken) and nonverbal (behavioral or with gestures)?

- When do these conversations occur? Does timing matter?

- Where does FC-talk most often occur? Does location matter?

- Why are final conversations important?

We've included an Appendix in this book to provide a diagrammatic look at the research participants' demographic information and FC-talk data. The following paragraphs are highlights that help provide background for the remaining chapters with regard to the "journalistic quintet" listed above.

Who

Not surprisingly, most of the people who participated in final conversations were family members or the sort of friends who considered themselves to be members of the family. The majority of final conversations occurred when the Living were alone with the Dying. Most people need privacy to open up, to be honest in revealing how they are feeling and what they are thinking. Of those who had FC-talks while others were present, over half were in the presence of other family members and the rest with a nurse or caregiver.

Many things affect who starts to talk: comfort level, needs, opportunity, goals for the interaction, and so forth. Most of the time, the Living thought both partners in FC-talk had initiated the interaction. Thus, the initiation of FC-talk is clearly not the sole job of either the Dying or the Living, but is shared by both participants. One cautionary note: You cannot force FC-talk on anyone, but you can invite it. If the initiation of a final conversation is met with rejection, there may be another opportunity in the future.

What

What FC-talk looks and sounds like can be categorized as we have done in the chapters of this book. You may want to look at the table of contents for the kinds of FC-talk that interest you most and check out the end-of-chapter summaries for our findings on that topic. This process should lead you quickly to the material you most need.

When

The timing of conversations usually depends on the opportunity for conversation. Ultimately, people's busy lives determine when FC-talk will occur. That often means after work or after school. The Living who take care of their Dying may have more of an opportunity for conversations in the middle of the night when the Dying can't sleep or in the morning after rest. The Living who have other obligations, and spend time with their loved ones as visitors, are more likely to have their conversations in the late afternoon or evening. Thus, the timing of FC-talk appears to be related to when the Living are able to visit and the primary role of the Living—as caregiver or visitor.

Whatever the amount of time between diagnosis and death, FC-talk may occur early on or near the end, or anytime in between. A few of our interviewees had FC-talk soon after diagnosis, and even fewer had their FC-talk within hours of death. Between these two extremes were the rest. It makes sense that relatively few FC-talks would occur within hours of death because, as the Dying near death, they usually sleep more, have difficulty speaking, and show numerous signs that their bodies are shutting down. As people near death, their physical capacity for a conversation is diminished. This leads us to suggest that the Living should be encouraged to participate in FC-talk while the loved one is still capable of being an active participant. This is not to imply that the later final interactions are without meaning. These last moments, filled with a final touch or a momentary look, can be extremely meaningful and powerful for the Living.

The timing of FC-talk is related to the amount of contact that the Living has with the Dying. The fewer days you have available, the more intense the time crunch will be. However, if you begin having these talks far in advance of the end, you can afford to spread them out over time.

Where

Where FC-talk takes place usually depends on the Dying's condition at the time of the conversation. The top three locations in order were home, both home and hospital, and lastly, in the hospital. Some FC-talk even takes place over the phone, which illustrates how mobile and spread out our society is today. Usually the most important criterion for where the final conversation occurs depends on where the Dying is most comfortable—we have to go to them. It appears that FC-talk most likely just happens.

Why

FC-talk gives the Living unique opportunities to connect and communicate with a loved one in a way that is not usually possible. To begin to answer this question of why—which will be more adequately addressed in the rest of the book—we want to introduce you to some of the Living's stories because they are the experts. One of them is **Roy**, an elderly, retired lawyer who put it this way: I learned that most conversations are superfluous, superficial . . . and have very little value. But there are rare occasions in which people can communicate on a different level.

FC-talk can be one of those rare occasions. Without FC-talk, the Living feel greater loss and experience regret. Barriers to FC-talk—whether they are cultural expectations, psychological fears, family hang-ups, or busy lives—increase anxiety about both death and the grief that must be experienced. For instance, **Brenda** was forbidden by her mother to talk with her grandmother about her impending death, even though Brenda was her grandmother's main caregiver and the one who was the closest to her in her family. Brenda finally broke down in tears and talked with her grandmother about dying. I was relieved because I could finally now communicate with her. She knew how upset I was about her dying. And I could finally get our relationship back. You know? Because, not being able to express that to her kind of put a gap there that had never been there. I wasn't allowed, so I hid my feelings from her . . . I think you can reaffirm a connection with the person, and the meaning that they have had in your life and vice versa.

FC-talk confirms relationships. **Lori** acknowledged the difficulty of talking about death in America, particularly for strained relationships. It's kind of awkward for you both, but on the other hand, it's so important to say what you have to say. To say that you love 'em, to say that you'll miss 'em, to say that it'll be hard without 'em. They need to know they're valuable . . . that they're still valuable. I don't want anybody to die that I have anything to do with that doesn't know how I feel about them.

FC-talk provides closure to relationships that are coming to an end. **Dana W** stated, I know I was complete. And so that feeling of completeness aided in my grief tremendously . . . I think it's important to communicate. To talk the talk.

FC-talk emotionally prepares people for their impending loss. Every one of the Living acknowledged great grief upon the death of their loved one; yet all concurred that the period immediately following the death was made easier by the FC-talk. They went on to state that in the years that followed the deaths, recalling their FC-talk with their loved ones continued to bring them peace. For instance, **Victoria,** who lost her young husband, said, I think those final conversations and spirit made the immediate period around this time not hard . . . These are the conversations that were the most important to me. And the ones that changed the way I live. FC-talk does not take away the pain that accompanies death, but it does help to prepare us emotionally for the loss.

Clearly, FC-talk is important for many reasons. Perhaps after reading this book, you will have discovered your own reasons to participate in FC-talk with the Dying ones in your life. We hope so.

CHAPTER 2

I Love You

Goodbye

I was able to say goodbye. I was able to say I love you. I was able to say thank you for all the things you did. I was able to tell him how much he meant to me and that was important. Nothing else mattered. [April]

We were heartened to find that love is the most frequent message exchanged between the Living and the Dying at the end of life. Among the Living with whom we spoke, an astounding 99% shared messages of love with the Dying. We have all heard the commonplace "love is all you need." Now, our research confirms that love is what connects us in life and at death. **April** was right when she said that the only thing that mattered to her was to be able to tell her beloved, dying grandfather, "I love you" and "goodbye." While most of us hope for a fast and painless death, we also value the opportunity to say a final goodbye and a last heartfelt "I love you."

The only interviewee who did not talk directly about love was **Darrell**, a no-nonsense, well-educated, successful, 76-year-old man. He told us that the love between him and his 95-year-old mother, Mona, was mutually understood through their actions: *I wrote to my mother special letters about her on Mother's Day and different things. And she had them all. Plus when I was graduation speaker, I brought in my mother and what she had done. The*

University of Iowa has a plaque in her name, and there is a street named after her on the Texas State University campus. So, Mother knew all the history and all the background and everything. The actual words "I love you" were not necessary to them. In this case, actions spoke louder than words. Darrell and Mona remind us that messages of love come in all forms. The important thing is to make sure that the love is expressed in a way that would leave no doubt in the minds of the Living and the Dying. Love is best expressed in a message that the receiver can hear, accept, and understand.

How do you express love? How do you want to receive the message of love? There is no single way to express love. The right way is the one that feels right for the speaker and, perhaps most important, the one that is best received by the listener. Do you know your audience? What is their language of love? How can they best understand your message of love? There are many ways to communicate love, as the Living and the Dying demonstrate in these FC-talks.

Loving the Dying in Close Relationships

A long-time intimate couple are so familiar with each other that they can frame their love messages to be easily received and understood. So it is easier for intimates to send these messages directly, in words or clear gestures, than it is for people who are less closely connected. Love messages are largely direct when exchanged in FC-talk by partners who know each other well. Intimates in FC-talks also make sure that they close their earthly relationships and give each other permission to move on.

Giving and Receiving Direct Messages of Love

Almost all of the Living told us about the priceless gift of being able to share direct messages of love with the Dying. **Grace** lost two beloved husbands to heart disease. Grace's first husband, Carl, died on Christmas day while they were at her daughter's house. She caught Carl in her arms as he had a final heart attack. At that moment, he looked at me. I thought he was going to put his head on the table. I thought maybe he was just tired but actually, at that moment, his heart had stopped. And I was standing by him and caught him in my arms. And I looked in his eyes and I could tell that he was dying. He was gone, just gone. I said, "Oh, I love you, Carl. I love you so much. Don't leave, don't go." But I realized that I had to let him go. I said to him, "It's all right if you have to go." I gave him permission.

I knew he was gone. I also knew that the hearing apparatus lasts longer than the others. So I kept repeating to him that we love him and we were with him. I'm sure that was the last thing he heard. It was very powerful, very moving to me. I felt at peace. I felt that this was his time. I frequently told him that I loved him. I guess what has stayed with me was his ability to accept and to absorb the love messages that I was sending him. I think that gave him a good deal of comfort.

Saying goodbye to a loved one is never easy. Grace had learned from her FC-talk with her first husband, Carl, as she demonstrated with her final message of love for her dying second husband, Steve. Grace's FC-talk with Steve focused on what he needed most from her at that moment: love and acceptance of what was happening. "If you can't breathe, just let go. Just let go. And it won't hurt. You have my permission. You can go. I'll be lonely without you and I love you, but don't fight it. Just let it happen." And that's exactly what happened. His breaths just got fewer and fewer, and I kept telling him that I loved him and I recited the twenty-third psalm. I told him he was beloved by everyone that knew him and that it had been my privilege to be his wife. And that I was so happy that we had that wonderful time together.

Many of the verbal statements of love by the Living were accompanied by nonverbal expressions of affection. For instance, **Mandy** told her dying grandfather "I love you" through actions and words. I grabbed his hand and started touching his forehead and his hair. And I told him that I loved him. Ever since I was a little girl I have really loved him. That we were going to love him forever. And that we would take care of Grandma. And that she was being so strong, and she just loved him so much. He could not respond to me because he had a tube in his mouth. But every time he just looked at me in my eyes and just nodded like he knew. I kept kissing him and loving him and lying in bed with him. And just telling him that I loved him.

The Living also want to hear love messages from the Dying. For example, **William** related his mother's FC-talk with him and his siblings as they gathered by her death bed. We were all standing around her bedside, and she just looked at each of us individually. She told each of us individually how much she loved us. And that's what sticks with me the most. That, and the look that she gave each of us. It made me feel better, 'cause I knew how much my mom loved each and every one of us. I mean, she literally spent her last breath telling us how much she loved us. The biggest benefit is just knowing that the person that you loved got to hear you tell them that for the last time. And knowing that that person was able to also tell you the same thing is also a big benefit of having time for a final goodbye.

Clearly, saying the words "I love you" is important. There is a special power to those words that most people want to feel. **Joseph's** dying father made sure to give him a final message of love, and the message was reciprocated: On the phone, the night before he died, he said, "Son, I love you." And I told him, "I love you too, Dad." Joseph was going to see his dad the next day for their weekly visit. It was Sunday and the family always had family gatherings on Sundays, but his dad died before he could get there. Despite the fact that he was not present at his dad's death, he felt at peace, because they both had had a chance to say a final "I love you."

If there is any doubt about whether love is felt by one partner for the other, there can be a tremendous amount of emotional uncertainty and longing. **Blanca** specifically highlighted why it is important to say the words: Daddy really loved me. And I really loved him. We were able to be cool on that before he died. People struggle way too much on that issue—but if it's **not** clear, it hurts for so much longer.

The message of love expressed to the Dying is often accompanied by a message about the impact that the Dying had on the Living's life. For example, **Jeanette's** message of love to her grandfather, Weber, expressed love as well as the "why" of love—the influence that he had on her life. I spent most of the time just sitting there holding his hand and telling him that I loved him. And I wanted to tell him how important he was to me because my father left when I was little, and he took that place. He was more than just my grandfather . . . So, that was one of the biggest things that I wanted to say—I just had to—I wanted him to know that he'd been really important in my life. And so I told him that I loved him and that I was going to remember him and everything that he'd ever done for me . . . I think it was the first time that I got to tell him how much he meant to me.

Completing the Relationship, Moving Forward

Seventeen years ago, **Ellen** was losing the love of her life. Her husband, Michael, was dying of a brain tumor. He was in his early forties, and he was leaving a young wife and two young children. Ellen revealed that her FC-talk focused on keeping their relationship genuine until the moment of his death and beyond if possible. She wanted to be sure that Michael knew he was loved and that she had completed her relationship with him up until the moment of his death. She repeatedly told him that I loved him, that I would always love him. I really didn't want to live my life without him, but I didn't get to make a choice about it. I would do my very best job to raise our children right. I was just glad that we got to spend the time that we did together. I thought it was a privilege to be able to have shared my life with him. I was grateful for the time that we had and to have had his children.

Ellen emphasized that the message of love had to be clear, leaving no doubts. I think if you're smart enough of a human being, you actually convey to the person that you love them while it has meaning and while it has emotion. This was a conversation [that really mattered]; I mean, we were going to be separated. We knew we were going to be separated. And I just needed to be able to complete with him and to let him know that I've always loved him and that I always would love him. It was a privilege for me to grow up and spend my life with him. I think conversations that you have with people who you know are on borrowed time . . . even though we're all on borrowed time, we don't live like we're on borrowed time . . . I guess what I'm trying to say is that we should all live as if we all know we're terminal. Because we all **are** terminal!

I completed my relationship with him. I didn't walk away thinking, Aauugh, I should have said, I didn't say, I could have said, I wanted to say. There wasn't anything that we didn't really say. And in the final analysis, the most important, the absolutely most important things were all said. Because the person who is left doesn't get stuck holding a bunch of untied knots. It's complete. You're not dragging anything along with it. We both completed the relationship.

We both were able to let each other know that we didn't want it to go that way. But since it was going to go that way anyway, we made the most of that final time. After speaking together, we gave Michael the chance to complete his relationship with his family and his friends. We also gave him the opportunity to tell us anybody that he didn't want to come there. And there were some people, just a few, that he said, "I don't want to deal with them. I don't want to see them." So, it was a new level that a lot of people experienced in relationship to him and his death. Some were shocked that they were able to complete their relationship with Michael [through their FC-talk].

Because Ellen was in love with Michael to the end, she remained open to love and was lucky to find love for a second time. Ellen has now been happily married to Wally for many years.

Ellen isn't the only one who married again following the death of a beloved spouse. **Cathy, Sondra,** and **Victoria** all talked about the importance of FC-talk as a critical tool to assist the Living in moving on past the death. All of these young wives talked about the importance of the Dying giving the Living permission, and sometimes motivation, to continue living life. In these cases, the Dying gave the living permission—even encouragement—to marry again someday. Cathy's husband, Don, was thirty-two years older than she, so he knew that she would outlive him. Don began the conversation with Cathy about marrying again long before their FC-talks, and again when he was dying. Because he knew he was that much older than I, he said that I needed to make sure that I move on. Cathy often dismissed his suggestion while he was alive, but would remember it later. She appreciated his ultimate concern for her and their daughter Christina's future happiness.

Part of the completion of the relationship for these four dying husbands was their unselfishness and release of any personal jealousy of the Living. They knew that life is meant to be lived fully, with love, just as each of these marriages had been lived. For these wives, there was not going to be any guilt or looking back with regret. Completing the relationship honored love itself by acknowledging the love that had been, and by embracing the potential for the love that would be. All four of these women married again.

Sondra's husband, Steve, died of acute leukemia. He had just had four heart attacks in a two-week period. Clearly, he didn't have much longer to live. Steve told Sondra, "I don't want you to fear death. I don't want you to mourn if I pass away." The last thing that he wanted was any fear of that. And he said, "Death is part of life." I'll never forget that. "Everybody is going to die." He told me many times that "the worst thing you could ever do is to mourn my death. Don't mourn me; rejoice because I'm in a better place." Then he said, "I want you to remarry." He made me realize that this is not something that you're going to ever become bitter over. I had always thought previously that if somebody marries somebody, that you show your real love to them [after they die] by never marrying again, and you show that devotion to that person for a long time, even past their death. And he said, "No, you will love." And he told me that "your real love for someone is to want the best for them."

A similar message was given to Victoria by her young husband, Kerry, who was dying of cancer. Kerry was Victoria's first love. They had married young, and she was devastated at the thought of his death. Victoria recalled, We had great passion. I had never been with anybody else beyond casual dating. And I remember sitting in the hospital and saying, "I'll never marry again, there's no way." And he said, "I sure hope you will. I hope being married to me was good enough that it'll make you want to marry again."

Victoria elaborated on the importance of this FC-talk as a love message. When he told me I'd be okay without him, that I could live without him, that I should marry again, he was providing for my family. He was attempting to make sure that we had the best we could, that I would take good care of the girls, that I would have a good life. He was just continuing to be the loving husband and father that he had been all along. He was continuing to take care of us. I have known a lot of women that weren't given that kind of permission, that gift, who really felt uncomfortable with that idea [of moving on to love again]. Her words imply that women who do not receive that gift of letting go can remain stuck in uncompleted relationships and the memory of love—sometimes for the rest of their lives.

Don't Leave Yet!

In some cases, the Living fear that they may never hear the love message they need. The Dying may not be cognizant or conscious any longer, or simply may never have delivered the love message before they entered the dying process.

Returning for a Last Message of Love

Lucia's mother, Engeline, suffered from depression for many years. Engeline's illness had progressed to the point where she was catatonic and was not eating or speaking. Lucia would visit her mother and often take walks with her. Once, shortly before

Engeline's death, Lucia "heard" her catatonic mother express her love. Lucia described one of their walks. She never talked, but I talked anyway . . . it was kind of like she wasn't really alive, but her body was still there. I liked to be around her anyway, even though it was strange. She was kind of like an obedient child or something. "Okay, Mom, you know it's time. Let's take a walk." She'd go get her hat, and I'd help her put her coat on. But she wasn't really there; her eyes were vacant.

On the walk, she would hold my arm. We got through the corner, and then she grabbed my arm real tightly. She never did that. You know? She normally just held on, with a normal tension. But this time it was like a tight tension. And then, she just looked at me, and then she looked up into a tree and pointed up and—I don't know how she saw it, because she always was looking forward—she pointed up to the tree with the bird on the very top. For me it was just like, for a moment, I had my mom back. She used to really love birds. She used to feed the birds. She used to make her own bread, and she would slice her bread on a board and then run one of us kids outside to feed the birds. Somehow she saw that bird, and she wanted me to see it. That's the part that really touched me. I think it is because [prior to this experience] she wasn't relating. She would be obedient . . . but she never asked for anything.

That moment for me was really very special because she had communicated with me. Not only did she see that bird, 'cause I would have missed it—I don't know how she saw it with me there because she's shorter than I am, and I was right next to her. So, for me it was almost like divine intervention, quite frankly.

I talked to her as if she wasn't sick . . . I thought that even if she could hear me and just didn't care—if that's why she wasn't conversing—I still cared. If she doesn't care, it's only because she's sick. And I don't think she didn't care, I think it was something wrong with her to where she couldn't speak. Some of my brothers and sisters said that she just quit caring. So we probably bother her by visiting. But I really didn't get that sense. So I just said, "I'm going to follow my own feeling, and I want to be near her. And I think she wants me to be near her."

But that time [when Engeline pointed out the bird] confirmed that feeling, that she did want me to be with her, she was glad I was there and she wanted to share that . . . She still loved . . . She was sharing the way that she could . . . It confirmed my feeling that it mattered. She loved me . . . I think there's an innate desire to experience true love . . . And so I think she just needed to have that feeling of when somebody just really, really cares—that life has meaning. Even though it wasn't going to turn it around and save her life, but at that moment, I think it was a way for her to confirm that life did have a meaning . . . I think she wanted me to not go away and just think that's what life is—that you just become this catatonic person that people just forget about or something. I even think that God wanted to show me that.

I mean, that's the point that it gets to me. It's like she was . . . at heaven's gate, and God was just saying, "Look." Even when someone is at this state, they can still perceive . . . And that's where I think that love element can transcend just about anything if you really, really care about somebody, and I really, really cared about my mom. And I think she got that; I think it transcended even her. The only reason I can love like that is because she taught me how, because she loved me. I think the thing about true love is that it really validated that feeling—both from her point and from my point of view. And I really did feel nourished. I just felt like I had my mom.

Roxanne's father had dementia and circulation problems for the last years of his life. On Roxanne's last visit, she was trying to unclench his hand as she was feeding him. She shared this story of his coming back to her for a moment to acknowledge her and to share a message of love with her, as Engeline had shared with her daughter. Roxanne told her father, "Loosen up your fingers, Daddy. You're cutting off your circulation." And he took my hand and he squeezed it. And I knew right then that he knew who I was. He was acknowledging me, whereas everybody else in my family had given up on him. He knew it was me on some level. I think he was telling—**I know** that he was telling me, *It's okay. I'm okay. I know who you are, and I love you, and I'm glad you're here.*

Did Roxanne's father really know it was her? The truth is that it doesn't matter. What people perceive *is* their reality. The Living's perception of their FC-talk is what affects them in the moment, and again later when they have had time to reflect on it. The Living's perceptions of FC-talk will become even more important in the years following the death, as they recall those conversations to make sense of the death and their role in the dying process. Roxanne's and Lucia's perceptions of their interactions with impaired parents brought them comfort as they experienced a rare moment of clarity and love. Remember that both Roxanne and Lucia had interactions with their parents that no other person had been able to have with them in quite a long time. We believe that they did have FC-talk with the Dying.

All the same, be aware that all we really have is our perceptions of interaction. None of us has a video camera in our head to record every experience. And if we did, we would be very surprised: Almost never do we recall exactly what occurred in every detail. Our brains are set up to experience what is valuable to us, to make sense of it by comparison to past experiences, and to remember *that version*—our own sense-making version—of the interactions we have. What we perceive is colored by our past experiences, biases, and beliefs. Communication is a more complicated process than simply signaling our needs and feelings. We can perceive what we want to perceive ("wishful thinking," some would say), or we can perceive another's intentions accurately because we have such depth of experience with them ("good intuition," perhaps).

So, are these last messages of love from the impaired Dying a result of "wishful thinking" or "good intuition" on the part of the Living? We can't say, but you can perceive for yourself. (We visit the role of perception in FC-talk again in Chapter 9.)

Finally, Love Expressed

Lori's father, with whom she had been very close, had died a year earlier than her FC-talk with her mother. She cared for her dying mother the entire year after her father's death. Lori and her mother had a strained relationship for most of their lives. Lori told us, *She was not a loving person. She was very jealous of me and my dad. And she hated me basically all my life . . . but I think that she came to understand that I loved them both. Just before she died she could barely speak. I had always told her I loved her. I told her that a lot; and somehow, she got out, "I love you." It took her about five minutes to do it. But it meant so much to me. It was the first time that she'd said it in so long. It was the first time that I think she ever meant it.* For Lori, it was worth the wait. That priceless memory helps her to put away some of the pain from their relationship.

Messages of love are not always easy to exchange. Some people have a much harder time expressing love than others. Understanding where the Dying are coming from can help the Living reach out to them in a way that will be accepted and understood. **B.J.** talked about the importance of telling her dying mother-in-law, Sylvia, how she felt about her. *"You know, Sylvia, you've been an incredible mother-in-law . . . I'm so lucky. You've never interfered in our lives. You've always been supportive of us even though I know you didn't want me in the beginning. I've come to love you, and I know that you love me." And she said, "Absolutely. I feel the same way about you. You've been a great daughter-in-law." She didn't elaborate because she wouldn't ever do that. That just wasn't who she was. She permitted me to tell her how I felt about her—when she normally didn't go there . . . And she then told me how she felt about me the way she could. And, thank God, I knew who she was so that I could receive that from her and not say, "Oh, you know, that crabby old woman, she never did say she loved me. She never once in her life told me she loved me." But I knew she loved me . . . and what she said was enough, you know, she didn't have to say the word "l-o-v-e."*

B.J. understood from the reciprocity of the words "I feel

the same way about you" that Sylvia meant to send her a love message.

As All Else Fades . . . Love Becomes All

Sandra came from a very traditional, Hispanic family in which men were macho and rarely revealed their feelings to others. Perhaps that's why her FC-talk with her surrogate grandfather (her fiancé Ronnie's grandfather) was so powerful for her. Rudy, at 85, had lived a long life and made a long and loving marriage. He was dying of leukemia and gathered members of his family for this message about love: "I have to say this. I have to let this out." Ronnie and I were holding hands because it was just so painful to see him this way because he was such a strong, stern man. He had never talked about his feelings before, much less ever sat here telling us what he was about to tell us.

We didn't know what was coming, but you felt it. And then he said, "You know when you go through life there's so many things you can go through, but when it comes down to it, the most important part is having somebody to share it with. Because when you are at the point where I'm at—and you can't even get up and go to the restroom by yourself, and you can't feed yourself, and you can't change yourself, and you can't wipe yourself—I don't know how I would've made it without Alice.

"And I want you to know something—you should always appreciate everybody in your life. But at the same time, I know that school is important and work and everything else, but don't get caught up in the routine. Let yourself love somebody because that's the most important part of life. I've been through a lot of things, but the most important part of my life is loving the person I'm with, and the most difficult part is sharing this part with them."

All of us had tears running down our faces. I think that's the first time that he'd actually said that in front of his wife and thanked her. And Grandma—tears were just running down her eyes. And Rudy, I had never seen Rudy cry. Rudy was crying. He told us, "I wish ya'll the best of luck, and whatever happens, just remember that the most important person is the person that's there until the end. That's the most important person in your life."

This message of love took on extra value because it came from a man who was not accustomed to talking about such personal matters to anyone. Rudy's impending death had removed any barriers to intimacy and to expressing his love for his wife and family. He wanted his family—the young and old—to learn from his life and to hear his thoughts on love. Nothing but love mattered to him any longer. Sandra was not use to seeing this kind of emotion from a man who had lived his life according to the cultural norms of machismo.

Similarly, **Patti's** father, Joe, talked about his love and marriage with his wife of fifty years. Patti described her father's eyes sparkling, talking about true love, and reminiscing about the time that he and her mother first met. When he was winding down from his excitement of talking about his sweetheart, he told us, "I am one lucky man. Not many men on this earth can say that they've done everything that they wanted to do. And not many men have been as loved as I have been." He told us he was ready to die. He said, "I have lived a whole life. There's nothing else that I would like to do except spend more time with you. But just know that I'm a happy man."

I was rubbing his hand, and he said, "Honey, please don't do that." His hand, his skin was so thin it would tear and I didn't know. I couldn't stop touching him. He told me he loved me. He told me that my husband and I had done a wonderful job raising the kids, that they knew how to love and that was really the most important thing. And that made me feel really good. I hugged him. We just sat with him quietly. Didn't really say much more. And I just told him I loved him and gave him a hug. And looked him in the eyes and he told me he loved me. And that was it. I left that day. A week later he passed.

Laurie Q needed to tell her father, Raymond, that he had made a difference in her life, and that the most important lesson from him was how to love unconditionally. "Dad, I just want to let you know how really important you've been to me. You have always had such a spiritual influence on me. You brought a lot of understanding to the world and helped me understand it, and I appreciate that. I also really appreciate that you moved around a lot. That, for me, was neat to be able to go to different places and to see different people, and to know that the church was always there and love was always there, and that no matter what, we were gonna be okay. It was a lot because of what you did . . . Then there's something that you did, that I don't think anybody else could've done as well as you did. Somehow you were able to share and pass on a love for people that's unconditional. No matter who they are or what they've done, they deserve the respect and the love just because they're there." He had an openness and love for people. No matter what their educational status, nothing else matters, as long as they've been honest. He passed that on to me. I thanked him for that. That was so important. Now I have passed it on to my kids; they tell me that.

What sticks with me is that I knew that he loved me. I don't think there was any question about that. I remember watching him. It was significant to watch him, to talk with him and know that he was declining, and know that **he** knew he was declining. And I never really worried about that. I knew that there was a path that he had to be on. And so it was significant that I could watch that path and wonder about it, but I didn't worry about him in that path, that journey to death. And that's significant.

Nothing More to Say
A Good Goodbye

It was time for **Herschel** to say a final goodbye to his son, Douglas. The night before he died, we had this final conversation with him where basically about all we could say was, "It's okay. It's okay, son. We know what's happening and it's okay." Because he knew he was very close, and of course we didn't want him to give up, but we also didn't want him to go through any more suffering. Just saying it was okay and saying goodbye to him was the most meaningful to me.

Dana W was 12 years old when her father was dying. He knew that he was dying. Realizing and acknowledging the fact that he was dying, and not knowing when that was going to be, he had come to terms with it. He was comfortable with that. He was able to be totally comfortable with me and not hide anything. He didn't have to hide anything or be false at all . . . And because he never knew when the last time would be, there were just lots of hugs and kisses and just lying there next to him. There were a lot of "I love you's." "I love you . . . I love you . . . I love you," and back and forth.

It was a good goodbye because I think the final conversations solidified that really positive, healthy parent-child relationship. They reaffirmed that, yes, we're different than most 42-year-old fathers and 12-year-old daughters, but he's still my dad and I'm still his daughter. And that really focused on enhancing the relationship because you couldn't really know when he was going to die. We had to continue maintaining and building the relationship. And so we did that. Even though most father and daughter conversations don't consist of "I love you" and "I will always remember you." The FC-talk was maintaining that strong relationship and keeping it solid.

Death Does Not End the Connection

Remember the story about Ellen and her relationship with her husband, Michael, who died of a brain tumor? It was very important for her to tell us that her relationship with Michael did not end with death. In fact, she and many of the Living have told us vivid stories of their continued connection with the Dying long after they have passed away. Ellen began this part of her story by telling us about a message that she and Michael exchanged during their FC-talk.

I clearly remember telling him over and over again, in many different conversations, that he was going to be taking all of our love with him, and that he wasn't going to be alone . . . It was just my belief that we will all meet again someday. Those people whose souls have been interconnected here [will meet again]. Michael, I know, didn't want to go. Michael defied whatever the doctor said. I mean, Michael's surgery was in August and they said that he's just not going to live very long. They said that he might live until Halloween; then it was Thanksgiving, Hanukkah, and Christmas. Michael didn't die until February twenty-eighth. Michael was a strong-willed person, and I just truly believe—I saw it with my eyes—he just wanted to be connected to us. I know that he heard us even after it was impossible for him to talk to us.

I told him that I needed him to somehow, somewhere along the line, make contact with me. Just based on—I don't know what. Just based on that we had been in a relationship here. I told him that he would always be with me no matter what, no matter where. I told him that I would make sure that the kids never forgot him . . . I told him that I would carry him with me wherever, that the kids would do the same. But I still told him that he should find a way to communicate with me. I didn't know how . . . it's just a leap of faith. I just said you just have to do this.

Some time had already passed and I was in agony. I missed him so much. It was just so hard. I can't even remember if it was after the first year, because after the first year when society expects that you've recovered—quote, unquote, recovered—that's really when it gets hard because that's when you realize, Oh my God, that you geared yourself up and you made it through the first year, but there is no prize here. This is just life, and you just gotta keep going. It's not getting better; this is just the way it is.

Finally, Ellen felt Michael's presence. She felt he was communicating from somewhere beyond the world as we know it. Ellen described two such visits: I think the first thing that happened was I had an experience in my car. I used to be in outside sales. I was driving around with the radio on. And I wasn't thinking about Michael. There was nothing going on in my mind that was connected to him at all. And all of a sudden, I felt Michael's hand touch my right shoulder. First of all you have to get that Michael was 6'5 1/2". I am small-boned, I am 5'2". Okay? So when he would have put his hand on my shoulder, his hand covered my entire shoulder. It was his touch. I mean, I was married to the man for a long time; it was Michael. It's a good thing I didn't get whiplash; I immediately turned my head to the passenger side seat, because that's how strong the feeling was. Of course, nobody was there. And it was like, *Oh my God. What was that? What could that be?* It was part of my education that communication beyond death is really possible.

And then I think the next thing that happened was the dream. I went to sleep one night, and in the form of what seemed like a dream—in the same sanctuary where our daughter had been bas mitzvah and where I had put up a plaque, a memorial plaque for my father and Michael. And the room itself happens to be a very, very calming, soothing place. And in my dream, I was in that space, and Michael and my father were there with me. No words were spoken, but it was just the sense of well-being. The sense of, "We're okay. And you need to know we're okay so you can be okay." And when I woke up in the morning, I felt great. And I couldn't believe it. And I just kept saying, "Ah, you know, but was it a dream? Was it only a dream?"

I had been seeing a wonderful therapist who knew Michael and who had worked with both of us when Michael was sick. I told her about it whenever my next appointment was with her. She was so calm, and she just looked at me and she said, "Well, what makes you think it was a dream?" And I said, "Because I don't know if those things really happen." And she said, "Well, why not?" It was great. It was like, *Oh my God. Maybe this really is not just this feel-good dream thing. Maybe this was really their souls connecting with mine.*

And that was the beginning for me. If he's really attached to me, maybe I could really do this. That was the beginning of my understanding about the connection that love can create.

Ellen went on to describe numerous experiences such as these. Once she opened herself up to recognizing the messages from people who have died, she recognized them more easily.

Cathy also wanted to stay connected to her husband, Don. Don had a bad heart and couldn't hang on any longer. Cathy described the part of her FC-talk with Don that occurred just moments before he died. I talked to him about how much I loved him, about the great things he had done, that I am going to miss him, and that this is the way it is supposed to be. And I said, "Don, you're going to be the one who is going to find out the real answer here. You've got to let me know. You've got to make sure that I end up with you. You've got to make sure. I don't know how that happens, and I don't know what the answer is, but don't, don't, don't separate, don't. You need to make sure that you save a place for me. You can see me anyway, because I don't believe it's over. I want you to do that. Can you hear me?" And for some reason, even though he wasn't supposed to, he evidently was coming out of the coma. I don't know. But I had his hand, I was holding his hand—in fact I was lying on top practically—and he squeezed my hand.

Then, I knew that was done. So I took his hand and then I said, "Okay this is it, don't be afraid." And I kind of tried to just walk him through it. But I remember when the blood pressure—we've always had this thing about 11:11 or 1:11, whether it is on clocks or whatever—I remember seeing his blood pressure. I just remember seeing the ones all across the screens. And I said that's it. And then right after that he went. He died. I cried and I hugged him. Although I was wrecked, I did get a sense of the infinite possibilities of life and the life after my life. It's not over. It's never over. Many years after his death, Cathy continues to feel her connection with Don.

Benefits of Love Messages

Confirming and Affirming the Connection

The Living need to know two things for sure: that they are loved by the Dying, and that the Dying realize they are loved by the Living. As Lori put it, FC-talk let me know for sure that he loved me as much as I loved him, that that closeness in our relationship was every bit as important to him as it was to me, and that he looked forward to those conversations as much as I did. It was just his way of spontaneously, emotionally showing how he felt about me. It meant a lot. My life is different because my final conversations with my dad let me know that I will always be loved. I will always be admired and supported even if he is not here.

Jarrod agreed and summed it up in this way: Knowing that you're loved is so important—from somebody that you revere so much—it plays such an integral part in your life. Not only do you love them, but they love you. It's a reciprocal thing.

Kasey confirmed that messages of love remain the most memorable and valuable over time. She recalled clearly the love message her 27-year-old sister, Angela, crafted for her. What I remembered most is just how much she loved me. Kasey recalled a letter that Angela wrote her during her final days: She'd put this letter on my end stand. I remember I got in the shower, and then I came out and there's this letter on my end stand. It was a letter telling me that no matter what happened, to just remember how much she always loved me. She would always care about me. It was past tense like she was already gone. I was kind of upset with her. I told her, "I love you and thank you so much for the letter, but I hate it when you talk like that. That's so negative." Angela said, "Well, it's just something that I want you to always have."

Ensuring That the Living Do Not Feel Abandoned

Completing the relationship lets the Living move on with their lives while still cherishing the love they shared with the Dying. Victoria's reflection on her marriage and on their FC-talk showed that positive assessment: I think we've done good, Kerry and me, and the fact that we had the final conversations. I'm proud of that marriage. I'm proud of the way we walked the whole walk. Neither one of us abandoned the other and neither one of us was selfish.

Showing Love as a Way to Live . . . and Die

Life is about who you love, how you love, and the choices that you make in your life for love. These love decisions also empower the Dying at the end of life. A life that is lived with fear and regret

I LOVE YOU 33

leads to a death journey that is filled with the same negative elements. **Sam** discovered that when life is slowly being stripped away, all that is left is love. What I learned from my mom and her death was that the things that are important in the last years or months of your life are the things that are important. If you keep that in mind, if you think in terms of—is this something today that's going to make me better prepared to face this transition in life? . . . In other words, the outcome of life is how you die, and if you face your death with regrets, with bitterness, with fear, or with loneliness, because of all the choices that you made in life, then that is how your final months and days will end as well.

You can use that as kind of a measuring stick for your life: What are the things I can do today that are going to prepare me for facing my own death, maybe with excitement or anticipation of something new? Feeling satisfied in the choices and the way I've lived my life up until then—surrounded by people that care about me and love me. You know, those are the things that are important.

Victoria also elaborated on the importance of love in life. We might not be alive tomorrow. I try to remember that; I try to remember that I'm in the process of dying. Even though I expect to live in my body for many more years, I believe it's important to remember that we are all dying every moment. I don't want to leave anything unsaid, any lessons untaught, or freedoms unexercised. This is part of the thing about not living out of ego—to live out of love.

Leaving Nothing Left Unsaid: Closure

When everything has been said—the "I love you" and the "goodbye"—there is a peace that comes with closure in the relationship. The Living and the Dying have the opportunity to move on without regret. With the closure that accompanies messages of love comes a lesson, and that is to love those in your life well, and to tell them often. If there is someone in the world whom you love, but you have been too afraid or too proud to admit it, consider the love lost in every moment, and don't wait. These messages of love at the end of life are a reminder that time does run out, and the opportunity to express love can be lost.

April talked about the closure that she experienced with her grandfather, Bill, and what she learned from FC-talk focused on love. *When you love strongly enough, it just hurts that much more to let them go. But it was inevitable, and we knew it was. That's probably why I didn't cry for so long. I knew I had told him that I loved him. I knew that I told him goodbye. It didn't bother me because there was nothing left unsaid. I learned to love and love strongly. That was the best.* We recently heard that April, a young mom with five children, died last year. April's husband, Greg, told us that she had a peaceful death surrounded by those she loved. April had learned her lessons well from her grandfather regarding the importance of exchanging messages of love. She undoubtedly left no doubts about her feelings for her loved ones. Goodbye, April.

Melissa Q described simply how her message of love with her grandmother, Florence, gave her relationship a respectful and loving ending: *For me it was closure. I got to tell her I loved her, she got to tell me she loved me. I got to see her one more time.*

Summary

What the Living Learned from Messages of Love

The Dying often need and want to share final messages of love with the Living. It's no surprise, then, that the Living have this same need. At the end of life, people often experience a strengthening of their relationship and an increased sense of connection. Why does this occur? The Living and the Dying usually spend more time with one another; they talk more; they make each other a priority in the midst of a chaotic and hectic world. Slowing down and paying more attention to the relationship often leads to a clear benefit: a stronger relationship and a deeper connection.

We can conclude about messages of love, one, that people crave them and, two, that people prefer the messages to be sent directly. First, we all need to know we are loved. The Living want to express their love to the Dying definitively. But they also want to hear a message of love from the Dying. Impending death brings urgency and intensity to the message of love.

Second, the message of love must be explicit, whether verbal or nonverbal—"I love you," or a hug, a kiss, a caress, a look. Implicit messages of love are not reliable enough. Actions may have several meanings. For example, cooking for someone could be a "labor of love" or it could be a job, a duty, or a personal pleasure that has little to do with who receives it. We simply have to express love so that the expression cannot be understood in any other way. Cathy agreed: As much as we would like to say that in a relationship you don't have to say things—we say, "I know you love me. You know I love you"—but if these things had not been said, then I would be stuck.

Communication is the most tangible and real way that we have to make a life, to survive and thrive in our relationships. Everything we say has the potential to affect someone's life. Therefore, Cathy was right in that the responsibility of every sentence is enormous. Everyone needs to walk out of this room today and pretend like it might be the last day with somebody they love, and say those wonderful things that you want to say. Because, for me, saying "I love you" to those I love helps me get through life. It's just crucial!

The experienced Living have taken the lesson about exchanging messages of love with the Dying into all of their relationships. They have learned that saying "I love you" to their intimates is important every day. Because the truth is, no one knows for sure when will be their last day.

Advice from the Living

- ♥ Tell the people you love that you love them. Tell them often. Tell them now. Tell them before time runs out.

- ♥ You can't say "I love you" too much to the Dying or, for that matter, to the Living.

♥ Just because you say "I love you" doesn't mean the receiver will say it back to you. Telling someone that you love them always entails taking a risk; you make yourself vulnerable. But without becoming vulnerable, you cannot experience the full gift of love. It's worth the gamble.

♥ It's okay to express what you feel, especially when all pretense has been stripped away. Never, ever be ashamed to cry over someone you love.

♥ Death is a great triage nurse for love. The dying process fails to nurture pettiness and triviality, and then only love remains. Love, the highest of human emotions, is nurtured to the end. Count on it.

♥ When you love someone so much that you think you can't live through their death yourself, that's when you really have to make yourself participate in FC-talk. To be able to say what needs to be said does help the Living cope. FC-talk helps the Living make the transition to a life without the Dying.

CHAPTER 3

Everyday Messages

Taking Care of Business

Maybe we'd watch a movie. We'd have dinner and go to bed. And that's what everyone does every day. And that was all we were supposed to be doing. [Ryan]

When you hear the words "final conversation" you probably think of deep and intense messages of the sort you don't hear every day. Although some FC-talk may be that, few can maintain such depth for long. Some necessary FC-talk is about mundane concerns, from small talk to shared interests, rituals, and histories, to tying up loose ends.

I'm Not Dead Yet!

Ryan had known Tere since he was a youngster. Ryan wanted to learn Spanish, and Tere, a Mexican immigrant married to Wally— a local man—was willing to teach him. Shortly after Ryan's graduation from college, Tere was diagnosed with cancer. He visited and spoke with Tere as often as he could until her death six months later. During one visit, Tere, as she often did, had asked about Ryan's life: *"What are you doing now?" And I think the feeling is, you know, "Who cares what I'm doing?" I could be getting married, and that doesn't matter in the same way that what's going on with her does. But I sort of thought about it, and she's not dead yet. And it mattered tremendously what I was doing, because throughout the* time we'd known each other in our life, it mattered what the other was doing. And she's not dead yet. So it still mattered.

The Living expected highly intense and important last messages, but many of the conversations were about the usual topics they'd discussed every day. It was as if the Dying were saying, "I'm not dead yet, so let's continue to live as we always have." Each partner who agreed to such "normal" conversations knew full well that these everyday moments would not last forever. **Cathy** noted that most of her conversations with her dying husband, Don, were everyday but more so. For the most part it was just everyday, but it's like heightened conversations. It's like everyday, but intensified. Because you don't know which day is going to be your last.

Grace felt that daily routines were continued out of mutual respect. I read the paper to him. And we discussed things. But he didn't have much interest in it, really. It was more his politeness to try to keep the conversation going than anything else. Grace and her husband had a long history of talking about the daily news and sharing their views on what was happening in the world. To continue this routine affirmed that they were both the same people they had always been. The only difference was that one of them was dying.

Maintaining a relationship relies a great deal on keeping the interaction easy, comfortable, and predictable. **Judy W** spoke with affection about Sam, her stepfather for fifty-eight years. Judy lived at a distance from him and her mother, but their relationship remained comfortable and solid from visit to visit. That didn't change with his last illness. We just kind of picked up our relationship. We shared an interest in politics and what was going on in the world. We read a lot. The war in Iraq was high on his list of things to be concerned about. And he just talked in general about what was happening: How are my kids? What was going on? And it wasn't like, "I'm here to watch you die." It was . . . like we just picked up.

Judy's example highlights how easy it can be for people to "pick up" where they left off—their relationship or their previous conversation—by talking about topics that are comfortable and predictable for the two of them. Topics that have always been easy to talk about are not only enjoyable for both the Dying and the Living, they are also a way to maintain normalcy—to connect in a nonthreatening way. Perhaps these tried-and-true topics are also a way to acknowledge that the Living is choosing *to actively share and to continue creating a life* with the Dying, rather than simply acting as an observer of the dying process.

Consistent with that idea of living life rather than observing death, the Living emphasized that the experience included the cherished opportunity to live out the remaining days with the Dying as they'd always lived their days. As much as the Dying were able, it was important to do the activities that they had always done with each other. Again, Ryan spoke of his last visits with Tere: To me, the time there interacting with her and interacting with Wally—there's no question of what I should be doing. This is what I should be doing. And it's not as mysterious or even so big and profound as you might want it to be. You know, we were all just there, and in the morning we ate breakfast. And during the day, sometimes I would help Wally work on things around the house, or I would talk with Tere. A couple of times we took the boat in the river. And other times, we would drive the roads into the hills. Tere could still ride in the car, so we'd drive into the hills. And so there would be activities. And then we would have lunch and there would be other activities, and maybe we'd watch a movie. We'd have dinner and go to bed. And that's what everyone does every day. And that was all we were supposed to be doing.

By acknowledging that the Dying one is not dead yet, the Living one sends a powerful message: You are alive today, I am alive today, and in the end, that's all that is important. Quite simply, you matter to me, and this relationship matters to me. Ultimately, this demonstrates that what people often take for granted in the normal bustle of life becomes precious when their assumption of life's continuity comes into question.

In general, the Living agreed that everyday messages and interactions served important purposes for both partners in this final dance of relating. Many of these everyday messages are pleasantries between loved ones: shared interests, rituals, and memories; others concern practical decisions about the future of the family, stories about the past, or feelings about the present. Ultimately, during FC-talk, everyday messages help the Living maintain and preserve their relationships with the Dying.

Maintaining the Relationship for Now

Small Talk, Pleasantries, and Simple Joys

Perhaps the most overlooked of our conversational habits are the automatic pleasantries that people use to keep interaction fluid, and in these cases, to demonstrate respect and comfortable care for the Dying, as well as to maintain the relationship between the Dying and the Living. **Laurie Q** expressed this ease with Raymond, her father. For me, it wasn't a problem going in and talking with him. I'd say, "Well, how are you doing today? Here's what we're doing today" and "Well, here's what the weather is like today" and "Gary went home today" or "Joe came in last night—you probably remember." Just little chit-chat things. Nothing really intense. Very relaxed, I think. Sad, but relaxed.

The FC-talk experiences of two daughters (both named Dana) with their dying fathers demonstrate how the easy, routine, mundane conversations can act as a way to maintain their parent-child relationship until the very end. When her father was dying, **Dana Q** reported that he continued to ask the same sorts of daily questions that most dads ask their 19-year-old daughters in order to maintain some degree of normalcy in their father-daughter banter. They would speak about how my day was, and how his day was. And what I had been eating. If I had actually been working out. Like little things. And making sure that I'd always done my homework on time. Or if there was anything I needed. He was always asking about my friends: How were they doing? And when were they going to come up?

Dana observed that both she and her dad became more aware of these small gestures as her father's health failed. She felt that the everyday, routine talk served as a reminder that the relationship was healthy, despite the fact that her dad was fatally ill—indeed, *in spite* of that fact. Her dad was dying, but he still wanted her to know that he cared about her life.

Dana W's father, Michael, also showed his interest in his 12-year-old daughter's daily life. Dana thought their everyday messages were her dad's way of still *being* her dad until the moment he died. His brain tumor, and the resulting months in the hospital, had robbed him of most—if not all—of the ways he had previously carried out his role as "Dana's dad." Their pleasant small talk about her homework, tests, and daily happenings was all he could do to show her—and perhaps himself—that he was still "Dad." He always said, "Remember, study for the math test" because it was not only a final conversation, but I was also leaving for the day. So, he was always saying things like "Don't forget" and "Remember" and "Work on your diorama" and "Do your projects."

Dana W, now an adult, recalled the multiple goals their everyday messages served. As a 12-year-old girl, she thought that each FC-talk might be the last she would have with him. She wanted to be sure she told Michael that she loved him and how important he had been in her life. Dana was looking for the *profound* to remember, versus the mundane she was hearing, such as "Don't let that word trip you up on the spelling test." Dana clearly demonstrated Michael's awareness that the profound moments need a solid foundation of consistent, daily, concerned interaction. Dana and her dad show us that the Dying and the Living are working with different assumptions. The Living member of the relationship is preoccupied with anticipating the profound messages they assume that the Dying member wants to share. Meanwhile, the Dying typically is more aware of the time remaining, and wishes to maintain and even improve the bond between them before crafting the more profound end-time messages.

The Dying are aware that not all messages can or should be profound. The majority of messages that create and maintain relationships are routine, easy, and predictable. It's far too exhausting, stressful, and unrealistic to think that the majority of the messages exchanged in our relationships must be profound and memorable—this remains true even at the end of life. Surprisingly, it's often the everyday talk that becomes the most memorable to us simply because it occurs frequently in intimate relationships.

For instance, think about a common interaction in your own life—something that you probably take for granted. Now imagine that it is taken away. How do you feel? If snuggles at night with your child ended right now, or if you couldn't share that morning cup of coffee and chit-chat over the paper with your spouse, or if your loved one wasn't there at the end of the day to ask you how your day went—wouldn't you miss it? When the Dying are gone, it will be these communications that are missed because they were regular bonding events. Their absence will become the daily reminder of what has been lost. Relationships are made up of these small, ordinary moments. Our lives would be fairly empty without such small acts of love.

Small gestures are exchanged as unspoken love notes during FC-talk—the message is carried in the gifts of extra effort and attention. For instance, **Susan** recalled one special gift that her mother, Molly, appreciated during her final days. As time went on, we fed her what we could. You know, what appealed to her. She had always had a very small appetite and it got even smaller. And in the end, she lived on what they always called zebra pudding. It's chocolate wafers layered with whipped cream and then iced over with whipped cream. And you slice it on the angle so it looks like a zebra. And she loved that. I think my sister said that she was making it twice a week.

Small talk, pleasantries, and simple joys are possible because the two involved in a close relationship *know* one another in a way that most people cannot. To know each other well enough to ask about a test that day, or to make a favorite dessert, are powerful ways to maintain a relationship because they confirm the knowing. Such a common knowledge base includes shared interests and activities.

Shared Interests and Activities

Shared interests take the attention off illness and allow the Dying to enjoy the simple pleasures of companionship. **Darrell** had a long and close relationship with his 95-year-old mother, but they did not engage in one last and profound conversation. Instead, they continued to discuss the stock market over cocktails in the afternoon. Mother had a very practical mind. We watched the stock market together, had the cocktail as we had for years in the afternoon, watched the stock market. And she'd scream about the low or the stock that was not doing well. And fortunately, she didn't get to see the real drop . . . But there wasn't any last conversation or anything with Mother; I was with her the day she died.

Like many fathers and sons, **Herschel** and Douglas didn't talk much about feelings, but they maintained their bond in familiar ways. When asked about their final talks, Herschel said, A lot of 'em here [in the nursing home] were just kind of social and talking and you know, you couldn't talk about how you feel too much, but you could talk about other things. And we did. We talked about lots of things. We watched TV, a few TV shows together, and we did some reading and things of that sort.

Judy Q and her grandfather, John, shared passions for family history and collecting coins. When the state quarters started circulating, Judy was studying on the West Coast and could get the Denver-mint quarters, while John on the East Coast saved them from the Philadelphia mint. Judy described one of the last times she was able to see John before his death: So when I would go back East, I'd bring all my coins with me and we'd check out the little D's. And that probably was the most meaningful because he would just get so excited over that. I mean, I was definitely the grandchild that went and talked to him about our family history. We'd look at photos. And you know, I really liked collecting coins. I have quite a few, and he does too. So that was a bond that we had that was just really close. And the last time I did that with him, which I think was the second to the last visit I was there, he was so excited.

In their married life, Grace and Steve were in the habit of discussing the news and current events. The only difference now was his difficulty with breathing. And we talked about trains, and we talked about news . . . We subscribed to the *New York Times*, and he would read that. And he was interested in what was going on, but he mainly was interested in any development of light rail and things like that. So a lot of our final conversations in that last month were about what could be done to facilitate transportation around Austin and to restart passenger routes in the East . . . Of course, right on the eastern seaboard they're grand, but you get inland to Pennsylvania and there's none at all. So we talked about that, and talked about lobbying and what we contribute to as railroad passengers and that sort of thing. And mostly it was all upbeat; it wasn't much about his health.

In addition to a new take on an old shared activity, an interest could be a new one—to be shared for the first, and possibly the last, time. **Cara's** grandfather, Jed, left an impression with his grandchildren by sharing an enthusiasm they hadn't seen before. I sat down next to his bed. And he was up on a high floor to where you could see over to that little life-flight helicopter. He was in the Army, so any kind of plane he really enjoyed. So, he was like, "Oh, yeah, go look out the window," and, you know, "Isn't that a neat view?" And so my sister and I were lookin', and he said, "Yeah, I get to see 'em fly off." And he was telling us about how he thought that was neat.

I guess it was just meaningful because he was wanting to let us in on one of his interests, and just seeing his face when he was telling us that . . . his face was just like a little kid. I mean, he was a very strong man. And seeing him like that hurt me. But it just meant a lot, him showing us the helicopters. And if he could've, he would've gotten out of bed with us and stood at the window. He was like, "Oh, look at the view." And I'm so glad that he was up there. Because he just loved going on trips and seeing the view. So being able, for him, to show us one of his interests and how much it meant for him; and for me to be there . . . It means a lot to me.

Occasionally, especially when age or infirmity brings a cognitive impairment, the Dying may include a loved one in a remembered or fantasized activity. **Greg's** grandfather, Albert, took him on a virtual fishing trip. And Greg was happy to accompany him. Sometimes he was off in la-la land, and he wanted you to go with him. And you did. I sat on the couch for hours, fishing. You know, you're casting downstream. He caught it. You get up. It was harder on my grandmother to watch this, because "Albert, you don't . . ." "Grandma, leave him alone. He's happy." You know?

Shared Rituals and Private Codes

Shared rituals are mutual meanings for things about which long-term partners or relatives can assume an understanding. Without preliminaries or negotiations, they act or converse in the same way they always did. For instance, Judy W not only talked politics and news with her stepfather, she performed the same rituals they'd started long before. We got in the same routine we had for years and years. I had not lived there for thirty years. And when I'd go to visit and get up to make coffee, watch the news, read the paper, we'd talk about what was going on.

The Living said that they relied on these comfortable ways of interacting, which gave reassurance that the relationship hadn't changed even if the physical well-being of one of them had. Since failing health can change the nature of the activity between the Living and the Dying, familiar ways of talking can stabilize the relationship. For instance, **Brenda** cherished the "same old" ways with her grandmother. I think a relationship can change . . . Luckily ours didn't, except I became more of her caretaker, but the loving nature and everything stayed there . . . I liked the notion that it was the same. It was my grandmother; it was the same old, same old.

For many, the lack of intensity was a comfort. In **Leeann's** experience, an old familiar ritual took on a new meaning that was profound for her. It was in the midst of familiar family activity that she found her comfort on the night her dad died. No more could be done for him, so they brought him home from the hospital. After checking to see if he was hungry (he wasn't), she suggested a drink. She had brought her dad's favorite liqueur. The family members gathered to share a toast to Dad, to life, and to his new adventure. Leeann then went on to describe the remainder of the night for her and her family: And then we watched TV that night—you know, his favorite shows he wanted to see. So we watched and he laughed. Really, he had a really infectious laugh . . . and even if you didn't think it was funny, you had to laugh. And you could hear it throughout the house. It was a really great laugh. And so he was laughing even though he was really sick.

While reminiscences typically were extended conversations, other mutual memories were so ingrained in the relationship that they could be referred to briefly, in shorthand code between the partners. Private codes are typically brief words, phrases, or behaviors that are used instead of the more complete sentences, explanations, or actions that most people have to use during an interaction to fully understand the gist of the conversation. Private codes include a shared look, a private term, or anything about which two people have a mutual understanding. The fact that others don't know the secret code makes it all the more meaningful. Cathy told us about two instances of the private meanings she shared with her husband, Don. In the first case, it was a code expression about family solidarity that she then explained to her daughter. I passed it down to Christina: "When we hit the wall, we will all hit together." I mean these are things to carry on . . . "When we hit the wall, we will all hit together." [LAUGHTER] And then there was . . . "In ten years, we will have money." [LAUGHTER] And these are things that Christina should know, these kind of things [that Don and I shared]— I want just to keep that alive.

Cathy and Don shared a love of music that also became part of their private code. Cathy tried to explain: There was an opera playing. It was just a Saturday, but we had it on the radio. We played it real loud—always. I was cleaning and he was in the back room, and we met in the hallway. I was going to tell him that the soprano sharped—Don Giovanni. I know, that means nothing. But you didn't have to say all that much . . . I mean, he knew what I was thinking. The fact that Cathy and Don shared a moment in the hallway by wordlessly acknowledging a flaw in the opera illustrates their mutual and private understanding. The fact that they never actually said a word about the sharped note, but simply looked and smiled in a knowing way, meant to Cathy that they could read each other's minds. Sharing a private code is mind-reading in the best sense of the word

Shared activities, rituals, and private codes serve to maintain relationships. But everyday talk also preserves relationships long after the Dying are gone. Sharing personal and family history, and completing unfinished business, preserves the remembered relationship with the Dying for the Living and other members of their network, especially young family members.

Preserving the Relationship into the Future

Shared Memories: Integrating Our Past Together

Mutual memories are enjoyed, savored, and tucked away to cherish. In addition to the sheer pleasure of sharing memories, the Dying and the Living both get the chance to relive their shared experiences and review their times together. The Living find relief, comfort, and humor in the reminiscences.

Laurie Q and her mother cherished this particular talk with Raymond (her dad) before his death. I went up to visit, and I remember sitting around the table with my mom and with him. And we were just conversing about the past and remembering things. I don't remember communicating anything particular to him at that time, but I remember the conversation and how critically important it was. That even though he wasn't feeling well and wasn't getting around well, that we were able to sit around and relax and just talk about things. Especially trips that we'd made and places that we'd lived—just different memories about those kinds of things. And he would share some. And that was good that he was able to think and share.

Easy talk is often all that is left when physical activities are limited. **Laurie W** fondly recalled the pleasure of sharing memories and sharing laughter with the Dying. The joy created by this kind of FC-talk helped Laurie focus on what her mother wanted them to remember about her. One evening, my brother and his wife and I sat with her, and we all talked about family times and things we remember. It was actually very happy. There was some laughter at times. The things we remembered are the things that she would have wanted us to remember.

The Living frequently spoke about the importance of laughter and humor during FC-talk. Very often, these happy talks were about silly things, unimportant at first glance; but in reality they were conversations that not only recalled old memories but created new ones for the Living.

At the age of 21, **Tory** watched her 19-year-old brother die of a brain hemorrhage resulting from the chemotherapy treatment for his cancer. She took every opportunity to be with him and keep his memory alive in her. She recalled one timeless session. Seeing him lie in my bed that day . . . We'd just kind of lie there and reminisce about our childhood, things we would do.

When he was kid, he would bang his head against the wall or hit the wall and make it seem as though my sister and I were beating him up. And you could hear him yelling, "Mom, the girls are hitting me. Mom, they won't leave me alone." And our mom would get mad at us; we'd get grounded. We wouldn't be able to watch TV. And we were like, "You're getting us in trouble. We're not getting in trouble for nothing. You know, you say we're hitting you, let me hit you now." And it was funny because we were laughing about the day that my mom discovered him lying about it all. And the day he climbed on top of the roof because he was getting a football and broke his leg. And I mean it's just funny how we just sat there—and it was just for a couple of hours—but it seemed like it was an eternity as we went through the things we did together.

Tory described a feeling of time stopping—which is what she desperately wanted to do to prevent his dying. The feeling of time stopping returns to her from time to time when she recalls and retells this story. During her interview she began to laugh, and we could see her recapture that moment and its feeling.

Such memories not only cement the history of the relationship for the Living, but for some, the sharing of joyous memories also helps to begin healing a troubled relationship. **Holland** had a difficult relationship with his alcoholic mother, Pamela. Even though he felt anger and resentment during their last times together, the exception was a shared happy memory that brought them peace. He stated, We were reliving some fond memories of the river, and she was laughing and I was laughing. And I think it was the first peaceful conversation I had with my mother in seven years.

In a more positive parent-child relationship, **Linda** used shared memories to acknowledge the role reversal that age and infirmity bring to the parent-child relationship. She shared her impression that it was natural and right for her to nurture her father. "It's okay, Dad. It's okay." I'd say things like, "It's an honor to take care of you. You wiped my butt when I was little." And I would joke with him. I'd say, "Oh, c'mon. I mean, you must remember you had to wipe my butt when I was little." Linda's example demonstrates the fact that humor exchanged during shared memories can also be a way to reduce embarrassment, and to lessen the discomfort of challenging situations that are part of the end of life.

Housekeeping: What's Left to Complete

Most of the Dying seem to feel the need to "clean house"—to pick up loose ends and complete their duties to life and the Living. This is a different sort of everyday talk in that it's a new need, yet it's still a continuance of ongoing concerns. These house-keeping duties seemed to fall into two categories: orders for the Living to fulfill, and family information to pass on.

To-do lists: "No weeping angels" Some of the Living were given directives from the Dying about business matters and other details that would make life easier for the Living after the death. For instance, **Jim's** father was concerned with financial arrangements. He would show me their spreadsheet of everything they own, and wanted to tell me what they were worth and how they got their trusts. And he'd never talked to me about that exclusively before. Similarly, Cathy's husband left her with practical information, such as a list of what I am supposed to do for the next income tax, and then we went through "Here's what you do in case of . . ."

Others of the Living received specific directions about who to contact and what to do with the loved one's estate or with their remains. **Laura Q** reported some initial discomfort with this kind of talk. I really think that her knowledge that she was getting sicker kind of turned into these conversations where we covered kind of new ground that we never covered before . . . like lists of people to contact or repairmen. You know, where I keep this list, and who does what, and how you can get a hold of 'em? And originally I thought, *Oh, I just want to blow this off*, because I thought this was too spooky. You know? But then I thought, *Well, she's being practical*.

Some of the Living were relieved by the information and direction given by the Dying, because they knew that it was going to make life a little easier for them after the death. Others of the Living agreed to participate in the housekeeping talk and tasks as a way to give the Dying some comfort and peace of mind. For instance, Darrell finally felt he needed to put his mother's concerns to rest so they could both move on to enjoying each other's presence. She said, "Well you bought this house for me, and the car, and all that." She said, "I think you ought to sell the house." And I said, "Well Mom, we won't sell the house right away. We'll keep it as long as you need it or keep your things in it and so forth." And as I looked at the house and all that, she said, "Let's go over the will again" with her attorney. And we did. And then she said, "Now let's go down and make sure that the banks and the stocks and all that are in the right form." And I said, "Well, we've got all that done." And I said, "I think we should just eat and enjoy and watch TV and do the things that we can do."

A few of the Living even managed to find the humor in having to deal with the macabre. **Emily** recalled a time with her best friend near the end of her life. I said to Jeanette, "You wanted to tell the doctor something." She looked; I said, "Your body." [LAUGHING] She says, "Oh, yeah." She says, "Doctor, I want to see about giving my body to science." And he got all flustered. And, of course, it just tickled the two of us to death. You know? We were just about to come unglued, because of his reaction. And he says, "Uh, mmm, uh, mmm, uh, uh." She says, "Well what's the matter? Do you have too many?" He says, "Yes, ma'am, we do. We have all the cadavers that we can handle." [LAUGHING] But he says, "I would suggest that in San Antonio . . . that you do it there." Which she did.

In some instances, the Living who knew that they had limited time with the Dying would bring up the subject of the Dying's wishes. This was the case for **Jack,** who traveled far to spend time with his dying mother and felt he had no time to lose. Maybe the most interesting sort of conversation we had during the summer was this . . . I said, "Well, Mom, when you die, what do you want?" She says, "Well, I want to be cremated like your dad was." And I said, "Well, what do you want me to do with your ashes?" "Well, put them with your dad."

Dad's ashes were east of our house about three hundred yards, near a little spring that was over there that Mom and Dad liked a lot. My dad's ashes were just in a can. They'd just been stuck in the ground for a bit. Nothing real permanent. So I said, "Yeah, I know where they are. But where do you want to be exactly?" And she said, "Oh, anywhere." I said, "Well, why don't you come pick out a spot?" She said, "No, you do it." I said, "Mom, come on." She was walking with a cane occasionally, anyway. "All right." And so we walked out there and up through the woods through this valley. And she walked around, and she looked around and wandered back and forth, and said, "Right here." And I said, "Okay. That looks like a good spot. That should be easy enough to do." I put a rock there to mark the spot. And so, I said, "That's done."

I said, "And we'd like to put up a marker here too, you know, for you and Dad." She says, "No. We don't need a marker." And I said, "Mom, we . . . we'd like to put a marker up." She said, "No. You don't need a marker." I said, "Mom, we'd really like to do it." So she stopped and she said, "Well, all right. But no pink granite and no weeping angels."

Then Jack had to broach the subject of his return home and his concerns about her being able to take care of herself in his absence. I said, "Well, I gotta take off and go back. You know, if things get to the point where you can't take care of yourself, you can always get somebody to come in and help you with stuff." She says, "Not on your life. Nobody is coming into my home to do work that I should do. And I'm not going to have anybody going through my things. When I get to the point where I can't do it anymore, I'm going to go into a rest home." My mother was really organized. She took care of everything. The details of things. "Furthermore," she said, "we're going to say our goodbyes now. I do not want you coming back here with me dying in a bed. You can come back for my funeral and not before."

Jack's mother was not a woman to tolerate nonsense. And her legacy would certainly not include weeping angels. She wanted to be remembered by her son as a strong-minded, vigorous woman.

Passing down the family history A different sort of gift to the Living lies in sharing lore about the family before that information is lost to succeeding generations. **Sam** and his sisters videotaped their group exploration of family photographs. As we talked, he began to realize how important it was to have created this record to keep. My parents kept photo albums of all of our lives . . . they probably have forty photo albums. And we used to go through those and reminisce. And we kept a video record of all this. So we have videotapes of us looking through the photo albums, and her looking at different pictures and saying, "I remember this" or "You don't know who this person is; this was your aunt who died." So, we chronicled it. I don't know why . . . You know, I was going to say I don't know why we did it, but I do know why. And it was truly a valuable thing. We realized at the time that the interactions that were going on were really important. And it wasn't just that we were videotaping some kind of major event. We were videotaping the mundane, unimportant things on the surface, but there were some real valuable things happening during that sharing. You can see little microcosms of my family on it.

In contrast, Darrell regretted not having asked his mother more about the family photos. Every now and then, I'd say, "Mother, who is so and so in these pictures?" But since I grew up much closer to my mother's side of the family—grandparents out on the farm— I knew most of them. And every now and then I'll think, *I didn't ask Mother about that*—about that person or that family deal. Now that my dad's gone and my mother's gone, we've got all these pictures. My cousins and I don't know what the hell to do with them all, because our kids don't have any real tie-in to any of that. That still bothers me, what to do with all these pictures. I don't know what the hell to do. I'm trying to get my son tied into it, but he doesn't know these people. And we need to make first cousins' kids know. It's something we'll have to sit down and work out in the future. It's not a major thing, but when a family is going on with a different generation . . . they don't remember who on earth they are. Mother and I talked about that, but not much. She wasn't too concerned about that.

Those who did talk about family relationships felt fortunate in having the stories to carry on. **Breanna** was grateful to her grandmother for sharing some of the larger family dynamic before she died. I remember sitting there on the couch, and we just kind of had that casual conversation that meant so much to me. We talked about what all the members of the family were doing and, like I said, she had always taken care of everyone. She was telling me about one of my uncles, who's an alcoholic. She'd been trying to help him get a job after he'd been out of treatment. And just about other cousins and just kind of casual and everything. But also I remember the whole time thinking how lucky I was to be talking to her.

Family histories, whether they are the result of many years of gradual interaction or a last-minute scramble to record precious information while it's still available, can be important to the Living and to the Dying. In part, family data are a valued legacy to the Living; in part, these bits of information, opinions, and viewpoints are the last personal expressions of the Dying.

Problems with Everyday Messages

The Living experienced many kinds of everyday talk, from sharing simple pastimes to receiving family lore for future generations. All this talk served the relationship between the Living and the Dying, both maintaining it in the present and preserving it for the future. But some of the Living found it difficult to engage in everyday talk with the Dying, even though they saw the need.

Avoiding the Difficult

Some of the Living felt that everyday conversation simply took up precious time and energy that could be better used to get to the profound or difficult messages they expected. For instance, Brenda was waiting for the profound message that never came. She missed her "last words" from her grandmother. I remember very distinctly feeling that everyday talk was problematic during the time that she was getting sicker and sicker. I was waiting for her to give me some kind of words of wisdom or impart some advice to me. And it never happened.

Others felt that small talk served as a stage on the way to the important issues. **Patti** felt that everyday talk served a purpose during her father's progression toward death. But once that stage was past, the communication was on a direct emotional and non-verbal level. Everyday talk was just showing that we need to talk.

And the relationship was still there. Actually, even more so, almost even more pure because a lot of the uncomfortable issues about him dying—he was not going to be here long—meant that there'd be a lot of small talk, avoidance almost, of the issues. And then that was gone. That was surpassed, and we weren't using words anymore. For Patti, the everyday talk was necessary to reestablish their relationship, to help them avoid some discomfort, to get to the pure feeling level of their bond, and to feel that again before he died.

On the other hand, in Cara's case, as her grandfather lay dying, Cara felt that other family members were preventing the important talk from occurring. But my aunt . . . When she and my grandmother were sitting in there talking, they were talking about how my grandmother needed to buy another purse. And it just makes me sad to think that when he was dying, he was probably wanting all of us to talk to him and reach out to him. And here we are talking about buying purses. I mean, that's stupid. Was Cara's grandfather waiting for profound talk from his relatives? Maybe, and maybe not. But Cara thought so.

Negativity

Some of the Living reported that as illness progressed, the Dying one became more difficult. As **Melissa Q** told us, her grandmother just grew more "mean" as she grew sicker. She got kind of testy when she got more sick. I guess you could say she would get mean more than she used to. Or maybe I was just getting older, and I recognized it more than being a little kid. I don't know. But my mom would testify to that too. That she just grew a little bit more mean.

Although these negative feelings could be the result of increasing discomfort, they also may be the outcome of knowing that time was too short to mince words or suffer in silence. One more possibility is that this example demonstrates a truth expressed by many of the Living and identified in books about people who are dying: Most people die the same way that they lived. If the Dying ones were crabby and negative when they were healthy, then they are most likely going to be crabby and negative during the dying process. Impending death does not make people sweet just because they may expect to be at heaven's gate asking for entrance. People's true personalities are often most evident during everyday talk and routine interactions.

But there may be another reason to appear negative. A few of the Living felt that the Dying became more negative in order to force a release of the important messages. In this way, as in others, the small talk is functional, even though it may be an irritation. **Katherine** guessed that this was true of her mother's negativity. Hard to know . . . On the one hand, I always thought that she was intentionally being so difficult to make us go to that emotional place. Because we would have days where we talked about the weather, we talked about the food, and we watched TV—real surface. And then she would throw these fits. It would force the emotionalness to come out, as ugly as it was. Although I had been preparing and setting up for it, thinking, you know, I need to orchestrate this so that we can have this closure on our relationship, I didn't know how to get us there. And so in a way, I would say she did.

Sam agreed: The impactful [FC-talks] were when she was hurting or afraid. It often takes a push to get to the hard places to heal, but the healing may be worth it.

Sometimes it was the Living who indulged in negativity, becoming annoyed at the loved one's failure to continue their normal routines. Laurie Q found herself becoming irked with her father's failure to maintain his health. He couldn't walk very far; he got very short of breath. He'd come back with great victories when he'd walked a half a mile or something, and report that to me. And I really was sort of annoyed at this, this diminution of his ability and of his focus in life and his ability to write and so forth. He did have some consulting jobs after he retired, but he found them very, very difficult to do. So that sort of annoyed me. He'd been such a tremendous achiever in the past, and he was so brilliant, that I couldn't imagine what was happening in his life. So I guess I was sometimes annoyed . . . And at any rate, I think some of my conversations with him were sort of self-serving; trying to protect myself from the inevitable by making him take more responsibility for it. And that, in a way, makes me feel sort of bad.

So, everyday talk is not all positive, not all easy, but apparently it is functional. It serves to lighten the heaviness of dying, to seal the bond between the Dying and loved ones, and to integrate the experiences they have had in sharing their lives.

Benefits of Everyday Messages

Cementing the Bond

Most of the examples mentioned earlier in this chapter make the case that one of the prime purposes for everyday talk in these conversations is to maintain and preserve the relationship between the Living and the Dying, or to heal their damaged relationship. To move too quickly and exclusively to deep and profound messages would risk changing the nature of the relationship. People know this intuitively. Melissa Q put it in terms of the family network of relationships. She recognized that it's all about family and knowing that we weren't going to treat Mom any different. And everything was going to be okay . . . that the family was still going to be there and do the normal thing.

Lightening the Load

Many of our respondents realized that upbeat messages and humor helped them get through the difficult times. And they reported that both the Dying and the Living found peace in light-hearted messages. **Erin** learned how good it is to laugh sometimes, and that laughter could definitely help when you're struggling through certain things. I remember . . . my cousin Anita was pregnant at the time, and she had just gotten married and her last name was Potts. And I remember my grandmother and my mom and I sat around thinking of names for her baby that would be funny with Potts. And it was like Clay Potts, stuff like that. And we were being so silly. These conversations really helped me learn that laughter is good . . .

Then there were those who could laugh at their own deaths. In this case, it has to be the Dying one to introduce the gallows humor. Leeann reported earlier that her family watched TV and laughed the evening before her father's death. Then, as the evening came to a close, he said he was ready to go to bed. We pulled him up out of the chair and got him onto the bed, and he said to me and my sister, "Anyone got any hemlock?"

Clearly, it's humor that gets both the Living and the Dying through some of the rough moments. Laughter shared is itself a physical release of the pent-up stress that all participants inevitably feel. Do you recall the old Abbott and Costello comedy routine, "Who's on first?"* If you do, you're either a senior citizen, a humorist, or a classic-movies fan. **Maureen** recalled an incident with her mother that was very much like that old routine. Pat, Maureen's mother, was taking a walk around the hospice—where she resided temporarily for some palliative treatment—with Chris and Colleen, two of Maureen's siblings. They would walk a bit and Pat would ask, "Where are we going?" Chris and Colleen would answer, "To your room, Mom." They'd walk a few more steps and she'd ask, "Where's my room?" And they would answer, "Just up ahead." This went back and forth, round and round, for quite some time until all three broke down in uncontrollable laughter. In fact, the three of them laughed heartily every time they recounted the story to Maureen and other family members. The rest of the family didn't really understand the joke—it was one of those instances where "you had to be there." But everyone appreciated the humor and loved to see how much the incident tickled Pat, Colleen, and Chris. Everyone else ended up laughing too, each time the story was told. And the laughter felt good.

---

* Abbot wanted the rundown on a ball game. He said, "Who's on first?" Costello, knowing that the name of the guy on first was Who, replied, "That's right." This continued in the same vein with "What's the guy on third?"

Centering a Life

Our informants pointed out the function of centering—pulling a life into focus—before we considered it. For both the Dying and the Living, the discussions they had of shared history and good times together served to integrate their life experiences—to solidify who they were and who they had become together. Sam probably put it best when he said that it was in the reminiscing. You know, it felt a lot like an integration of my life in a way. I mean, the only people that knew me when I was a kid are dead now pretty much. My sisters are a lot older than I am. And so they were out of the house when I was still very young. And you know, for them to tell me—my mom, my dad were horrible historians—so my mom, for her to actually reminisce with me about when I was a child, and to really give me that before she left, it was like she made a point of giving me that. And undoubtedly, although she did give that gift to Sam, at the same time she was giving herself the gift of summarizing her life.

Summary

What the Living Learned from Everyday Talk

How to "do" FC-talk varies for different partners as well as for the various stages of the dying process. However, we did note a general theme in the difference between the Dying and the Living. The Dying prefer to start with specific details about the relationship or the day's events. On the flip side, the Living need to state the important generalities, the big picture. The Living, who are left with memories, want some general framework to identify their relationship with the Dying. The Dying, who are leaving, feel the need to clear up the specifics and integrate them into a coherent story while they have time. Many of the Living reported wanting profound messages that could immortalize their relationship. What they often received were the detailed reminiscences or reminders of the everyday nature of their bond.

Dana W was the one to call our attention to this discrepancy between the agenda of her Dying father and her own needs as the Living child. I went from more general to specific, and his were more starting with the specific and the details, and moving out to the more general, to the I-love-you-always-and-forever type phrases. I mean, I knew that he just wanted to continue that associative bond with his daughter on a level that I would recognize. I wanted to make sure that I said all of these important, possibly life-altering things.

For the Living, like sisters **Nancy** and **Mary Jo,** there was a heightened awareness of the general importance of relationships. The sisters were left with the impression that the relationships that we have here today are not a given. Nobody promises you tomorrow. And you better make sure that you're right with everybody . . . everybody, every single day.

The Living were grateful for the normalcy of everyday affection. **Sarah** found that her expectations of "big talk" were unfulfilled, but she discovered that she got what she needed anyway. You know, it sounds great, but nobody gets really intimate or has any deep conversations. So I thought that I would've been nervous that he would reject that kind of talking and be like, "Sarah. Let's not talk about that." You know? And I'd be like, "Papa, I really wanted to talk to you." But don't get me wrong, every time I saw my grandfather we kissed and hugged so tightly, I've never hugged anybody that tightly in my life, and we did it every time we saw each other. And I always said, "I love you, Papa." And he'd say, "I love you, Sarah." That we were very free with. That happened every time. We never changed.

Ryan told us that he was struck with the continuity of life's progression, including death. It's just that things are still going on. It's still spring and flowers are still gonna grow. And then it's gonna get uncomfortably hot. And then it'll be fall and it'll start to rain. And that natural progression . . . I don't think that we value it until it seems suspended. He went on to acknowledge that the Living are always looking for answers to the "big" questions, for profound messages to surround the dying process. I guess we're always saying, "Well, what is our purpose here? Why are we born? To what end should we live?" And all these mysteries. I don't recall after my initial confusion at the newness of the situation, I don't recall questioning anything.

Despite any disappointment they may have felt, the Living did learn an appreciation of the gifts of everyday talk in preparation for death—their loved ones' and their own. Susan put it this way: Death is a part of life. It's not to be feared. We're all going to get there some day. And I have the choice to go into my dying time . . . with a positive attitude. Everybody makes the choice of how they're going to do it. They can go kicking and screaming, or they can go with acceptance and try to find the best parts of themselves to give to the people that they love. My mom showed me very much how to do that and that it doesn't have to be scary . . . that if you allow the people that love you to take care of you and to give you their love, you can in return give back to them.

Advice from the Living

♥ Be prepared to start with the little issues—small talk— before you get to the big or profound messages.

♥ Recognize that everyday talk is what keeps relationships going—and what you will remember after the Dying one is gone.

♥ Know that your loved one may need everyday talk and reminiscences for their own closure, peace, and acceptance.

♥ Death *is* a part of everyday life. Be true to the beauty of the relationship you have created as long as it endures, and cherish its memory beyond the failure of the body.

CHAPTER 4

Grace Happens

Spiritual Messages

*I think that when people communicate authen-
tically with another human being, the sharing
and the love that's possible in relationships is
one of God's miracles.* [Ellen]

The meaning of life comes up often in conversations when death
is near. When people are out of hope, they pray for miracles and
look for answers. When people are confronted with a terminal illness, they search for meaning by exploring their spiritual beliefs.
The Dying talk about God, their faith, and their beliefs. The
Living want to ease the suffering of the Dying as well as their own
anguish, so many pray, talk about being together again in heaven,
and share their spiritual and religious beliefs. When medical science offers no hope, spirit and faith provide soothing words for
people to embrace as death approaches.

Witnessing faith up until the moment of death, sharing spiritual beliefs in the final weeks of life, and experiencing spiritual
events are all moments of "grace" at the end of life. Grace is a positive encounter with a divine or transcendent reality. The Living's
FC-talk we recorded included various spiritual or religious issues,
which we'll call "spiritual messages." The Living considered these
spiritual messages blessings in their lives.

People of all faiths, and even those without a specific religion,
very often encounter and question a transcendent reality when

they find themselves beyond the limits of all rationally explainable experience. In the midst of these experiences, people tend to turn to their frames of reference (such as Buddhist, Catholic, Christian, Hindu, Jewish, Muslim) for explanation and insight. In our world, people turn to many belief systems as a way to understand their experiences. And while people can become constrained by the language used to describe religious beliefs and spiritual experiences, we hope that everyone reading this book will see past the specific language used in our interviews to understand that spiritual messages are possible for anyone open to them.

Approximately two-thirds of the Living said that spiritual messages were part of their FC-talk. Spiritual messages were sometimes brief comments in the midst of many different topics, but at times they were also the focus of the entire final conversation. On the whole, people who spoke about spiritual messages with the Dying felt validated and comforted, and discovered a need for community.

Witnessing Faith

Testimony from the Dying

Many of the stories that the Living shared with us focused on the Dying's faith. These spiritual messages were meaningful declarations of faith from the Dying, which gave the Living comfort and reassurance, and strengthened their own faith.

Karen recalled that the most profound final conversation she and her father shared concerned his unwavering faith in Jesus and an afterlife. *The most profound thing was his declaration . . . He said, "You don't need to worry about me." He said, "I'm going to heaven." His speech was somewhat impaired, but I remember him pointing upward, and saying, "I'm going to heaven. Jesus is my savior, and he is yours too. And don't you ever forget it. I'm going to heaven and I'm going to be fine." That was so meaningful to me. He was 47 years old . . . He was a young man, and he was leaving three children. He was leaving a 3-year-old. And that was the thing that he wanted us to know most* of all . . . I think because it was so profound for him and so real for him at that moment. He was living his faith right in that moment . . . He was about to claim the victory, and he wanted us to know. He was ready and unafraid. He was really just waiting—waiting for it to come.

Now married and with two small children of her own, Karen highlighted for us the continuing impact that her FC-talk with her dad has had on her own life: I had a very religious upbringing. We'd always gone to church and been very involved. My dad was very devoted and very dutiful. He was an elder with the church. We went to church every Sunday. My parents never said, "Oh, let's sleep in— never, never, ever did they say that. I think that was his final and most important opportunity to be a witness to his faith, to his family. And especially to my brother and me. It was very fulfilling and very reaffirming. It was such a strong declaration. It was very intentional and very purposeful. It has always had a big impact on my faith and my spirituality. It really made the promise of salvation so real. It was very comforting to see the way my father handled it. He was so sure, and he was so confident . . . "Jesus is my savior and I'm going to heaven." And there wasn't an ounce of doubt in him . . . I've always kept my faith. A lot of times people go through periods of doubt . . . I never really had that. It was a lesson of faith, that the promise is real.

Karen's story demonstrates how spiritual messages give comfort to the Living and often confirm their faith. This type of FC-talk may also securely place the Living on their own personal paths of faith.

Susan felt relief in her mother's direct statements about Jesus because it was the first time she had heard her mother declare faith in a way that was similar to Susan's own beliefs. This gave Susan some peace. One day the minister came, and my mother wanted to talk . . . She said to him, "I believe in Jesus." Growing up, I never heard her talk about Jesus. She talked about God. It was more God, the Father; but she didn't talk about Jesus. So when I heard her say that she believed in Jesus, that was something that was important to me.

While Susan had a strong belief in Jesus Christ, she wasn't convinced that her mother had. Susan's grandmother had been the Christian teacher for Susan, more so than her mother.

Lori talked about the comfort she received from her FC-talk with her father because it reinforced their shared beliefs. During our last conversations, he always told me to trust in God, and to believe in myself, and to know that no matter what happened, I'd be okay, that I'd be blessed . . . He always had a lot of words of comfort. And often God was a big part of the comfort.

Karen and others like her were open to testimonies of faith and didn't feel "put upon" or "preached to" by the Dying. Not every participant in FC-talk would have wanted this sort of spiritual message, nor should it be pressed upon anyone. It's important to note that while Karen, Susan, and Lori's stories arise from a Christian perspective, it is the declaration of faith that is important in FC-talk, rather than the particular religion. All religions have specific beliefs about the afterlife and how the faithful will get there.

Testimony from the Living

Gloria's son, Robert Jacob, was diagnosed with leukemia. He died within six weeks of his diagnosis from a brain hemorrhage caused by chemotherapy treatment. From the very beginning of his terminal illness, Gloria relied upon and talked about her faith—with her son and with others. In this example, Gloria employed faith to fight her fear. I knew that I had to not show Jacob that I was in fear. He was a terrible momma's boy, terrible; he was my crier. Up until he was 19, he was my crybaby. When I walked into the hospital . . . everybody was there, and I prayed to God just to give me the strength not to show him that I was scared. And I saw him, and he started crying . . . "Mom, what am I going to do?" I said, "Well, what do you think we should do, Jacob? What is it that I have taught you? What have you and I always talked about?" And he said, "You always told me to fight for what I believe in." I said, "You and I are like that.

You know that, right?" . . . "Yeah," he said, "but I'm scared." I said, "That's okay. It's okay to be scared. I'm here to help you." And then, I don't know how I sat there . . . but I did. I sat in bed, and I held him . . . And so, we sat there for a few minutes, just really quiet. And he kept holding my hand real tight. I said, "You know that God is a very powerful part of our lives. I have always tried to teach that to you." And he said, "Yes, Mom, I know." I said, "So grab a hold of him, Jacob. Grab a hold of him and don't let go. Remember when you were little, you told the Bishop, 'I'm going to grow up to help Jesus.'" I said, "Well grab a hold of it. Jesus is here to help you." I said, "And don't let go." I said, "And don't lose that, because you and I, we have a long road ahead of us." Gloria's demonstration of faith would be vitally important to Robert Jacob's journey, and later, to other members of her family when they were angry with God and questioned their faith.

Sometimes direct testimonies of faith to the Dying won't work or won't be welcome. **Maureen's** mother is one example. Pat was afraid of dying, as many Dying are, because she didn't know what was going to happen. Was she going to be safe, protected, and still somehow connected to all of her loved ones after she died? Pat's three daughters, Kit, Colleen, and Maureen, are very spiritual people who believe in an afterlife and have faith in a higher power. Pat wasn't the kind of person who wanted be preached to, and her daughters would never dream of trying. But Pat had been waking up with nightmares and feared dying would be the end. Being a private person, Pat wouldn't talk directly with her daughters about her beliefs or fears. Kit, Colleen, and Maureen wanted to help ease their mother's fears and suffering, so they began talking with each other in Pat's presence about their belief in guardian angels and an afterlife. Pat rarely participated in these conversations, but listened in silence. The three daughters told each other—and their mother—stories about spiritual occurrences they had heard about or personally experienced.

Maureen recalled, One night when I was with her, Mom woke up from a horrible nightmare. The nightmares were becoming more regular. I put my arms around her and told her that it was a nightmare, and to ask her guardian angel to come protect her, to be with her, and that God wasn't going to let her be hurt again.

Pat lived weeks longer than anyone expected was possible. Her three daughters believe that in part, Pat lived until she could work through her fear of what lies on the other side of death. It's possible that Pat waited to die until she believed that an afterlife exists, and that God would be there to protect her. Because of one last experience with Pat, Maureen believes that her mother was finally able to surrender and trust in something beyond this life. The night before she died, Pat was in a coma. I sat holding her hand and praying. My twin sister, Colleen, was asleep on the couch beside us, and the rest of the house was silent and asleep. I heard fast, high-pitched whispering; I turned around and asked Colleen what she had said. Colleen had not said anything, and had not heard the whispering that I had heard. Again, I turned to my mother, held her hand and again began to pray. For a second time, I heard the fast, high-pitched whispering. I turned around in time to see Colleen sit straight up and ask me, "That wasn't you?" No it wasn't. And this time there were two people who heard the whispering around the bed. Both sisters believe that they heard Pat's angels talking with her, telling her that it was okay to let go of the pain, and showing her what heaven looked like so that she would have no fear. Pat died the next afternoon.

Faith Challenged, Faith Found Again

Other direct spiritual messages in FC-talk seemed to be a final lesson about faith from the Dying to the Living. **Jarrod** was very close with his grandmother and visited her every Sunday for the last eight weeks of his life. Sometimes, he would share a private Mass with her, and other times they would simply talk or pray together during their FC-talk. Most of the conversations were about God. She was never like this before she had cancer, but she always wanted me to pray with her when I got there—right when I'd get there on Sundays. And sometimes Father would come in and have a little Mass for her when I was there.

Jarrod found it fascinating that his grandmother wanted to pray with him because, he said, she was mad at God for doing this to her. Jarrod remembered talking with his grandmother one Sunday about his parents' new house on a lake. She was upset that she would never get to see it. Jarrod recalled that she said, "I will never make it out of this hospital. I'm going to die here. This is it, I'm done. Why would God do this to me? Why would God take this from me? Why would He, when I have so many grandchildren and great-grandchildren? And now, I'm not going to be able to enjoy this." That's what was scary because I'd never heard her be angry. So angry—so mad at somebody or something—at cancer and at God. That was a really tough day.

Jarrod's grandmother's anger at God is fairly consistent with research about dying that suggests that as part of the death journey, many of the Dying question their faith. Specifically, the Dying often need to explore their religious and spiritual belief systems in the face of death as they search for meaning about life and death. Jarrod went into detail about his FC-talk with his grandmother on the day that she seemed the angriest with God. We prayed a lot that day. She wanted to pray. We would say our Our Fathers and Hail Marys, but then she was coming up with all these other prayers that I'd never heard her say before. I don't know where she was coming up with them. I don't know if it was the cancer that was getting to her somehow . . . but she was coming up with prayers. And she would say, "Don't you know this prayer? We taught you this in CCD [class for Catholic children]. You should know this prayer." But they were things that she was making up—the prayers would involve people in our family.

Week after week, Jarrod's grandmother asked him to pray with her during his visits. Witnessing his grandmother's doubts, anger, and search for answers impressed Jarrod. Observing her anger, seeing her dedication to prayer, and realizing that she had singled him out to pray with her led Jarrod to conclude that God was sending him a direct message through the one person that he might listen to—his beloved grandmother. I think a lot of it was God talking to me through her . . . telling me that this was going to be all right. And that this is something you're going to have to go through at this stage in your life. And it's just another step that you're gonna have to take to get you closer to Me—which is God . . . He couldn't tell me directly because I wouldn't have listened to Him. Because I didn't want to listen to Him, I would've blocked Him out. Not that God doesn't mean anything to me, but it was more personal coming through her . . . because of what she meant to me . . . I think it was the prayers, and I think it was the touch. Jarrod and his grandmother held hands while they prayed together—something else that differed from their interactions prior to these FC-talks.

Praying with the Dying led many of the Living to the knowledge that God was present for them. Jarrod explained the outcome of his spiritual message FC-talks with his grandmother: I think it did lead me to be spiritual. I've always been spiritual, and I think that's what helped me. I know that's what helped me, to do it all with her, because she was so spiritual. These messages of faith remained potent for many years following the death of the loved one.

Tory talked about the challenges of faith that she faced as she walked the death journey with her brother, Jacob: Talk about having my faith questioned soooo hard . . . In the back of my mind, I doubted; but I didn't want him to know that. When Tory had to face the fact that her brother was brain dead, and they were about to turn off his respirator and let his body go, Tory was very angry with God. We were all in the room, and we were crying and sobbing and just in disbelief, and Gloria just stood there, and she held his hand and she just cried very softly, very quietly. And I was so angry. They were going to turn off the machines. The chaplain came into the ICU room, and he asked us to pray. I said, "I'm not going to pray. I'm not going to pray to a God that allows this to happen." I was so angry with God for the longest time. Gloria took me and just slapped me, and said, "You're going to pray, and you're going to do it now." She said, "It's not about you. It's about your brother." And I was so angry . . . like, this lady is crazy. I'm so upset right now, I'm so pissed that I'm going to hit her back, you know. And I didn't. I found some kind of strength to do it, to please her.

Tory continued, She was right, it wasn't about me. So I think it's made us closer . . . I didn't think we could get closer. But we did. Tory added that in the end, her relationship with God was also strengthened. Today, she is a devout Catholic with a strong faith. Her mother helped her realize that only through her faith in God could she live through the loss of her brother.

Experiencing Spirit

Spirituality refers to the experience of transcendent realities rather than the practice of any particular religion. Spirituality as discussed in our interview examples assumes that there is more to life than what we can see or fully understand. It is experiencing the unknown that opens people up to considering a divine or transcendent reality.

The Spiritual Experiences of the Dying

In their FC-talk, some of the Living learned about spiritual events experienced by their loved ones at some point earlier in their lives, but not revealed until the end. These stories often had a profound impact on the Living, because of their knowledge of, and respect and love for, the one telling the story; and because it contradicted their sense of the world prior to the final conversation. For instance, **Roy** was an 85-year-old retired lawyer from Texas, who evaluated the world using logic and hard evidence. Roy was also an elder in his church, had a strong faith, and had viewed religion from a traditional perspective for most of his adult life. He recounted a story that his mother shared with him during one of their FC-talks, which confirmed his faith, expanded his spiritual beliefs, and gave him comfort. Roy's mother told him about something that had happened to her ten years before. The story concerned Roy's father, who had been dead for twenty-five years, and a sealed door to her bedroom. She had never told this to anyone before her FC-talk.

Roy recalled his mother's story: [My deceased father] walked out of a door in their bedroom [which had been sealed. My mother said,] "I know it was him. He came over to me and got me by the arms and lifted me up and he held me in his arms, and he told me, 'I have been permitted to come see you. And everything is wonderful with me, but I had to come to tell you that I love you. I'm permitted this one visit.'" And then he held her in his arms; he turned and walked away. She felt him, she saw him, she heard him . . .

When she told me that story, I knew that she knew it was true. I'm a rationalist, and I'm skeptical. But I knew that she knew that happened, and because she told me it did happen, I believe it did. It was meaningful to me because she had chosen to tell me the most important thing that had ever happened to her. And she considered it that. She knew that my daddy loved her. She knew that all the time, but this confirmed it for her . . . I think it has affirmed some other [spiritual] episodes that I had read about and heard about— heard my friends talk about. There are things which happen after physical death, or maybe even during physical life, that are things of the spirit and not of the flesh. And that reality may be spiritual and not material.

Roy explained that this experience with his mother had made him more open to the possibilities of the spirit. Thinking about the possibility of something beyond the rational was heartening to him. While Roy and other people like him were reassured by stories about the spiritual experiences of their loved ones, others recounted witnessing their loved ones in the midst of a spiritual event. Few direct words were exchanged between the Dying and the Living in these cases, but the Living reported experiencing a profound scene. One especially powerful example came from sisters **Nancy** and **Mary Jo,** who observed their mother seemingly reconnecting with others who had died before her. The sisters described an experience that they shared while sitting next to their dying mother. It not only validated their own religious beliefs, but gave them tremendous comfort because it confirmed for them that their mother was going to heaven.

For seven hours on Monday, Mother, who had not been talking, swallowing, since Sunday, with her eyes closed and not recognizing us sometimes, opened her eyes, looking up, was holding her hands up, shaking people's hands, hugging people, nodding her head, saying "Hi," and smiling. Once she said, "Mama." She even did the motions of taking the Lord's Supper. She took the bread, and chewed, and swallowed, and nodded her head. Then she took the cup of wine . . . and drank it, and swallowed, and nodded her head. She was having a wonderful time seeing all those people in heaven. It was truly amazing . . .

Around 7:00 p.m. the nurses came in to turn her. When they would touch her, she would hurt and get grounded back to this earth. Nancy and I were holding her, and Nancy and I started asking her if she saw . . . and we named all these people, about twenty-five. If she had not seen them, she made no motion at all. If she had seen them, she nodded yes and smiled, eyes were closed. She had seen seven of the twenty-five we named, including her mother, my daddy's mother, and her twin brother that died soon after childbirth . . . After the nurses finished with her, she settled back down. In a little while, she began all the motions and "Hi's" again just as I described earlier. It was amazing.

Witnessing their mother's experience at the end of her life, Nancy and Mary Jo felt comforted and felt that their beliefs were validated. They stated their specific religious beliefs, and described how this FC-talk had confirmed their faith. I am a true believer in Jesus Christ and God and everlasting life in heaven with them, but, I tell you, this has made me an ever-stronger believer. [We were given] the absolute confirmation that there is a heaven, and that we all are able to go there if we believe in Jesus and accept him as our Lord and Savior.

Susan witnessed her mother, Molly, talking with her deceased grandmother. The conversation was first observed by the night aide caring for Molly; the aide thought that Molly was speaking to her. Uncharacteristically, Molly snapped rudely, telling the aide that she wasn't talking to her, but to her own mother, who had died many years earlier. Susan recalled, My mother, the lady who never was rude to anyone, said, "You shut up. I'm not talking to you." The aide said, "Really, who are you talking to?" And Mom said, "I'm talking to my mother." The aide said, "Really, what's her name?" "Her name is Margaret." "Well, where is she?" "She's right there sitting on the end of the bed." Well, the next day my sister called me and told me this. And I felt as if God had put His hand on my shoulder and said, "Don't worry, I have her." [It comforted me because of] the fact that she saw my grandmother sitting on the end of the bed. My grandmother was the one that took us to Sunday school. Mom didn't go, but our grandmother was the one that took us to church and read her Bible. And so, for my grandmother to appear at my mother's bedside was very comforting to me. I felt like she's okay. She's going to the right place.

Susan then described her mother's final moment of life and what all of these experiences had taught her. Mom opened her eyes, smiled at [my sister], and then she was gone. So, you know, there was peace about it. It was by watching her get ready that she showed me it wasn't scary, that it was okay, and that she had a peace.

Bill recalled watching his fiery, red-headed, Celtic mother communicating with angels. Unlike the Dying in the previous stories, Bill's mother made her pre-death connection with transitional-spirit angels rather than with departed family members. Once at the dinner table, once when she was sitting in her recliner, and once when she lay down, but she wasn't asleep. She told us about her angel. My sister and I were sitting at a table with her, and she said, "Well, I just saw my little angel again."

In that transition phase one time . . . I got her into the bed, raised the bed up, and I was doing something, and I looked around there, and she was shaking her head "no" . . . She said there were boy and girl angels around her several times . . . and she was telling them, "Not yet."

So, that makes me perceive things in a clearer way in relationship to spiritual relations. Her vision of these angels helped my perception of the spirit world get stronger. Even though she had no formal education, she had the perception that Martin Luther talks about—that the only real existence is between this of humans and the spirit world. She knew these things. That helped my perception of this spiritual seeking path . . . It has enabled me to look more towards that side and move towards it, since I don't have to think of it in the forms that I used to think about it in. That's how her vision of the angels helped to strengthen my view of my spiritual beliefs.

The Spiritual Experiences of the Living

Not only the Dying experienced the nonmaterial world. The Living also gave accounts of their own spiritual experiences near their loved ones' final moments. **William** recounted a story about the moment of his mother's death. He had just returned home from the hospital. I remember receiving the phone call from the hospital saying, "Hey, you need to come back up here. Don't rush, but your mother's taken a turn for the worse." And I remember just falling to both of my knees. I went limp. But at the same time that I hit the ground, that my knees hit the ground, I felt a wave come through me. And it still gives me the chills now. It was just a wave that picked me up . . . It just kind of lifted me up. And the thought came through my mind like she was there, saying, "It's going to be okay. You're going to be okay. I'm all right. I'm okay. You're going to be fine. Just pick yourself up." . . . That was the message.

When I got to the hospital, my brothers and sisters were all outside waiting for each other before we went up. I remember stepping off the elevator, and we didn't know for sure that she had passed. But when I took a step off that elevator, I felt that same . . . that same energy come through my body and tell me, "Okay, you're going to have to face this, and you have to be strong for everybody else around you.

You're going to have to be strong." . . . There's no doubt in my mind that it was my mother's spirit. I believe that she took her last breath at that moment that I was first lifted up by that energy—it was her talking to me.

Some of the Living requested that the Dying send them a sign from heaven that they were still with them and in some way watching over them. Others told of appearances in a dream by the loved one who had passed away. The Living also told stories of things appearing with no plausible explanation (collectable coins, flowers, pages of a book, a card, or a Bible opened to a spot in response to a question). **Jennifer Q** told one of these remarkable stories. Her paternal grandmother was dying. Jennifer had gone with her father to say her goodbyes and to have a last FC-talk. Her grandmother asked her about her great granddaughters (Jennifer's four daughters) during the conversation. I said, "When you get to heaven, keep an eye out on my girls." She said, "I will. I know I haven't met Parker, but I love her. I'll be their guardian angel." . . . That was neat because she was saying she's going to be their angel.

A few months after her grandmother's death, Jennifer Q felt she had proof that her grandmother had indeed kept her promise and was keeping watch over her daughters. One warm day, Jennifer's three youngest daughters were at home: Parker (age 3), Alex (age 6), and Houston (age 14). Ordinarily, Houston was out with friends, so this day was an exception. Their father was in the front yard working, and Jennifer was away at the store. Parker always swam in a "floaty" bathing suit—she jumps in and she's buoyant—all of a sudden she thinks she can swim. Well, she'd thrown one of her Barbies in the pool and jumped in thinking she could swim, thinking that's how it always was when you jumped in even though she didn't have on her floaty. She had her clothes on. She jumped in to save her Barbie. And my 6-year-old, Alex, was out at the pool with her and thought that she would get in trouble if she got in the pool with her clothes on. So she's standing by the side of the pool. Alex was just standing on the side of the pool going, "Swim, Parker, swim." And

Parker is drowning. And she is trying to swim . . . but she was drowning. Alex was holding her hand out, and she couldn't quite reach her. She couldn't get to her, and she was just screaming, "Swim, swim!" And Houston just happened by, and looks out the window and sees that Parker has fallen in and she's under water. So Houston runs out to the back yard and pulls her out of the pool, and she is throwing up and choking.

The next morning, Parker went to her day care, and the day care lady said she was talking about a dream or something . . . When she got home, it was at night, and we're sitting by the pool. And I was holding her, sort of like a baby. I said, "Well, Karen said you had a dream. What happened?" And she said, "Yeah, I dreamed about Grandma Cleo." I said, "Really?" And she said, "Yeah, she flew in my window." I said, "And then what?" And she said, "I flew out with her. And we went up there where she lives. Where all the stars are. And then the sun came and got her." I had chills and thought, *That is the closest thing to an angel—a sign,* especially because I specifically said, "Watch out for my kids." And I don't know why, I don't know what prompted me to say something. Because it's kind of like saying, "Well, you're going to die soon. So when you get to heaven, watch out for my kids." That's kind of a weird thing to come out and say to somebody . . . And she said, "I will. I love those kids. I'll watch out for them. You know I will. I'll be up there watching out for them." I just thought it was so amazing. And for Parker to know about heaven and lights and stuff like that; it's never been explained to her. I felt really comforted by that. Like, *Oh good. They have someone watching over them.*

Jennifer Q explained that while Parker had never met her great-grandmother Cleo when she was alive, Parker recognized and identified a picture of Cleo as the one who had taken her flying that night. Jennifer expanded on the meaning of her daughter's experience. *I think the main thing is feeling close to God. On the way over here actually, I was thinking: What are certain things that stand out in your mind in your life that you remember? "Wow" . . . a thing that makes you, at your core, feel close to God or something* other than of this earth . . . a greater being. And just after [Cleo] died, that experience with Parker really stuck with me. I mean, it was so . . . I just couldn't get over it. I just felt like that was a true angel.

During **Melissa Q's** last visit with her grandmother, less than a day before her death, she told Melissa, "I feel funny." This message became profound for Melissa because she began to believe that about that point in time, she was between worlds. I think she was dying; she was spiritually between worlds . . . And I think that's evidence of it. I mean, "I feel funny"—it's not, "I feel sick," " I feel cold," "I feel bad," "I hurt"—but she said, "I feel funny." And that, to me, is a justification of a transition; there is some sort of a transition.

This evidence of a transition made by her grandmother would gain greater significance in the months to follow. Melissa told us that she had questions about spiritual messages. She then shared a story about her departed grandparents coming back to talk with her, with the specific goal of helping her to have faith and to find her spirituality. I was standing by this tree, and I had an experience. My grandfather came to me. I don't know how to explain it in words . . . But I really think that my grandma and my grandfather came to me; and I think specifically my grandpa did, to prove to me that there is a spiritual world. He's like, "Melissa, there's something out here—you have to believe in it." My grandma and grandpa were both there; it's like they won't let me ignore it. They won't let me, and it's not that I don't believe in spirituality, I just have a really hard time with Catholicism and the religious aspect of it . . . But that was meaningful to me, because again, I think that it was just a reassurance by them that they were there, and that it exists. And that I need to stop—not ignoring it—but I need to figure out how to deal with this. If it's not through religion, it's through something else.

All of these examples illustrate the fact that the Living's spiritual messages have the potential to comfort them during the dying process and long after their loved ones die. Faith in God or a higher power, and belief that death is not the end but another beginning, are frequent topics for FC-talk. The common experience of sharing stories and experiences regarding spiritual messages suggests that the act of communication with others affects the continuation of their lives as social beings. Communication, the medium for sharing spiritual messages, also creates a sense of community that serves both to cradle the Dying and to support the Living.

Creating Community

What is "community"? Ideally, community is a local network of people who provide the opportunity for interaction, recognition, and acceptance, and the chance to participate by serving and caring for other members of the network. The convergence of energy that is created by communication, within the space and time of community, allows members to connect with each other and be forever changed by the experience.

If this is so—if community is how we satisfy our social needs, and how we grow, change, and understand our world—then how is community best achieved at the end of life? True community can be achieved only through communication. Communicating with the intention of creating community is accomplished through deliberate choices by the members to be open, to interact with clarity, and to be vulnerable. Thus, community and communication are especially necessary at the end of life. The Dying depend on their loved ones and caregivers; the Living depend on each other and on the Dying's last contributions to the community. Interdependence is the essence of community.

People often want a witness to the most important events in their lives—and death is the last important event in people's lives. To accompany the Dying ones along their final journey is an act of love and faith by the Living, and a privilege because it means that the Dying trust them. Life's moments are meant to be shared. The more difficult the time, the more important it is to share with someone. Witnessing the death process can teach the Living to fully participate in the precious gift of their remaining time.

For community to be formed through FC-talk, the Living must make a deliberate decision to be fully present in the death journey—by communicating with the Dying. Communicating, being fully present, means being honest and open while talking with the Dying about the things they need to discuss. It also means being concerned not with the past and future, but with just the two speakers in the present. Being fully present may mean sharing a comforting touch with the Dying. Being fully present may mean sitting in silence with the Dying if that's what is most needed. Besides caring for the Dying, the Living who spoke to us expressed the need to help their family and friends as they were dealing with their own sorrow and fears.

Many of the experienced Living have felt compelled to carry forward this responsibility of creating community, to occasions when they meet a person who needs a companion on the final journey. Three types of FC communities have been created by the Living we interviewed: (1) midwife to death, (2) Living support, and (3) spiritual path.

Midwife to Death

This group of the experienced Living felt strongly that people should understand the significance of their FC-talk. Their experiences were life-changing events that persuaded them that no one should ever die alone, that death is not to be feared, and that people—the Dying and the Living—can truly create community through communication. Just as the presence of midwives at birth makes the birthing process easier, these Living spoke of the need for the Dying to have midwives at death to assist them in a gentle crossover from this world to the next. The first person to use the phrase "midwife to death" was **Victoria.**

Victoria's young husband, Kerry, was dying of cancer, and he was leaving her with two young daughters to raise alone. The doctors told us that we just had a few days. That night, he woke up at the same time that he had been waking each of the last few nights, and he called me to come over to the bed. He said, "I'm seeing something I need to tell you." He was not particularly drugged; we seemed to be able to manage pain with just my being present. He said, "Let me tell you what I'm seeing and what I want." So he talked me through this vision. He said, "I'm walking up a mountain, and it's really a beautiful forest, and the air smells really pure and clear, of white pines. It smells really good. I'm walking up the trail. The forests are green and silver. And I'm walking to the silver trees hearing the laughter of children. And I get to the top of the mountain. And there are stars. I've never seen so many stars." And then he said, "All I have to do is step off into the stars, and there is God. But I can't do it. I'm not going to do it . . . because I've never told Mark, my best friend, that I love him. And I'm not going to do it until I do that."

Then he came back down the mountain, and he said that they had told him that what he would be doing next would be midwifing people who were dying. And that I should be doing it from one side and he would be doing it from the other. And that whenever anybody was afraid about dying, I was supposed to tell them to ask for Kerry . . . Then he said, "Oh, this is so cool. I've had such a good life, and I'm really excited about what comes next."

After her FC-talk with Kerry, Victoria believed that people often need someone present to help them cross over. She said that by being fully present with her husband at the end of his life, she felt that his death was made easier for him; but perhaps just as significantly, his death was also made easier for her. Because his death was so peaceful, and because she saw that he was ready to go on to the next dimension, she gained tremendous strength to deal with her loss in the first weeks following his death. After her husband died, Victoria became a midwife to death. She went into private practice as a counselor. One of her main areas of expertise is grief counseling; she has helped many families deal with their own death journeys.

In a similar story, **Betty Lynn** shared her view that God wants people to be involved in the death journey, placing them where they need to be at the right time. Betty Lynn and a friend decided at the last minute to travel four hours to visit Ruth (Betty Lynn's surrogate mother) and her husband, C.C., at their ranch for the weekend. When the friends arrived at the ranch, they found a note telling them that C.C. had been in an accident. C.C. was dying from wounds after being kicked by a horse. Betty Lynn began her story: *Well, this one weekend—it's as my minister says . . . a coincidence is God working anonymously. This weekend was full of God working anonymously.*

Betty Lynn described the spiritual experience that would eventually help C.C. die. She knew that Ruth would need care during this process, and she also knew that C.C. needed reassurance that Ruth would be all right. *You could tell Ruth was torn up. It was just obvious C.C. was going to die. So we went in that evening about 9:00 p.m. to say goodbye. I was the last one to say goodbye. I took his hand and said, "See you soon." I said, "It looks like you're in a lot of pain, and we know you're hurting, and I just need you to know that you need to do whatever it is you need to do. And if that's to leave this earth, just know that I'll take care of Ruth. Because I know that you love her, and I know that you're going to want her to be taken care of. That's why you married her. But you know if you can't stay here with us, it's okay, because I promise you I'll take care of her." Then just a little bit of a squeeze of his hand, and that was about it.*

Right after, we went home. And, you know, you just never sleep when you know someone's fixing to die. We got a call about 4:00 in the morning, and again—where the coincidence is—no one else heard the phone ring but me. I went and answered, and they said, "This is the hospital, and he is not doing well. We don't expect him to live, and you need to get back up here." So about 4:00 in the morning, we jump in the car and just make this mad dash again. And we get there a little bit after 5:00, and Ruth goes in to see him, and comes out and says, "He's not doing well." Evidently, what was happening was his heart was stopping, and they would give him something, and the heart would run until the meds were gone, and then it'd stop again.

But he was still alive, technically speaking. I was tired. In the family room there was a recliner, and I lay back in the recliner and just had my eyes shut. I was hearing other people talk, and I was there, but I had my eyes closed. And I felt I could see, even though my eyes were shut.

All of a sudden I could see the ceiling in the room I was in, and this light came and just settled in on top of me. And I could feel this spirit in me; just a part of me. I wasn't scared, you know. It was just like this was normal. I'm Church of Christ background—you shouldn't be feeling these things. But it didn't bother me. I just lay there, and I smiled and said to myself, "C.C., it's okay. You can go. You can go." And in about fifteen, twenty minutes of that acceptance, still my eyes shut, and I'm just sitting there smiling and just kind of holding this presence in me, and just saying, "It's okay, you can go. You can go." I could see it, my eyes still shut. I could see it come up above me, and just for a split second, it just hovered there, and then it went out the window of the hospital. And within about two minutes, three minutes, I heard them call Code Blue. And it was for C.C. He was gone.

It was so neat, because he was a part of me for that few seconds, and it felt peaceful. It was as if I knew what he was feeling at the time and thinking at the time. He wasn't thinking a lot; he was just thinking, "I've got to go." And I just knew, I knew what to say. I didn't say it out loud, I just said it in my head to him, to my body, and I said, "It's okay. You can go." But to feel him come above me and feel that lifting. That was just unbelievable, to see the light go out the window of the hospital. All that was done without a word said. Not a word said. But I knew what was happening, and I wasn't scared and it wasn't weird. But that sticks with you. That sticks with you when you've had that kind of an experience.

Betty Lynn shared what this experience had meant to her: It gave a lot of peace, I think, to all of us, especially for me, to know that I helped him turn loose. I helped him go. I helped him leave this earth. [I was hesitant at first] to tell people what had happened, because I thought that they would think, *Oh, she's crazy!* You know, those things don't happen. People don't become spirits, travel this earth. You can't believe in ghosts. But then, the more that I told the story and shared it with people . . . it was like I was putting certain people in my life to hear it. And they would say, "Oh yeah, I believe that. I know that happens." And they would tell me about their grandmother dying in another part of the United States and then coming and saying goodbye. That helped to normalize it.

But it was just one of those things. You know, we weren't supposed to be there that weekend. And we were. And that's why. We were there so that I could tell C.C. to go ahead and go on, and to support Ruth.

I realized that it's okay to die. It's okay to die. There is a God, or whatever you want to call the higher power. For me, it's God. There is a life hereafter. There is a place for us to go. We aren't just living here as a dead-end thing, as when we die, it's over with. There is a God, or someone smarter than all of us, that is directing all of this. And, you know, it took away a lot of that fear of dying. It just made dying a part of living, a part of that process. A continuation, whereas before, like most families in the United States, we'd never really talked about death and dying.

This is something that is ongoing in my life now. Where every now and then, someone will pop up and I help them die. I will help them say goodbye, help them detach from this earth. Death is just the next step. And I don't know where it goes to. But C.C. was ready. And he willingly went out that window. So he must have seen something beautiful over on the other side. And that is what I believe. I believe there is life hereafter. We are going somewhere else. I don't know what it's going to be, but we're going. And I want to be ready to enjoy when I get there. Enjoy life today. Live for the moment. And when it's your time to go, say, "Oh, it's been a fun ride. We're going now. See ya."

Betty Lynn and Victoria expressed clearly that the Dying often want someone to accompany them on their death journey, and it's an honor to be chosen. It means that the Dying one is comfortable with the Living one, and recognizes that the Living one has the strength and courage to take the walk. Once a Living one has served as a midwife to death, he or she is changed. The more experience people have with death, the less uncertainty and fear they feel when confronting death again. To provide community as a midwife to death is not a role for everyone. That's okay because, at the end of life, there are many essential roles.

Living Support

Another powerful story about the need for community at the end of life is **Bev's** story about her mother and her maternal Aunt Lucille, who was dying. Bev's aunt was dying of lung cancer, and Bev had gone to the hospital with her mother to say goodbye to Lucille. Bev's mother was having a difficult time talking to her beloved sister, and Bev tried to help her mom say goodbye so that Lucille could die in peace. Bev's story begins here with her opinion about how Americans deal with death. People shy away from terminally ill people, and I don't think it's right. Because somewhere deep inside, they know what you're saying to them . . . whether they let you know or not. And I just felt like it was my obligation, my responsibility to say, "Hey, go for it."

Bev wanted to talk to her mother about what she thought Aunt Lucille needed to hear from her sister in order to finally let go. Lucille was in great pain at this point in the dying process. My mom and I left the room. This was really late, and there was nobody else around. And we sat down right outside of her room, and I told my mom, "Look, you need to go back in there and tell her. You need to say goodbye to her." And she got up, after a few minutes thinking about it. She asked me, "What am I supposed to say?" And I said, "Whatever you feel." You know? "Say goodbye." Mom was gone for twenty minutes. She came back out. Then we both went back in and sat with my aunt . . . I was half asleep. Something woke me up. And the next thing I know, she's dead. She's gone. But I could feel that presence. When I woke up, I could feel that presence leaving the room. And before my mother could even say, "She's gone," I knew it. And it was just seconds—half seconds.

Lucille died within one hour of her conversation with Bev's mother. Bev explained to us the significance of the FC-talk, and what it meant to her to have helped her mother assist at Lucille's death. It was quite an experience . . . I experienced something that I had learned—but didn't believe . . . I took a risk, and that risk worked. I just felt I was supposed to do that . . . I felt that I was there for a reason. And that reason was just to bring them together. I was kind of in that triangle . . . I think good things came to my mom because of it. I think she was a nonbeliever; she's a believer now. She also listens to her daughter a little bit more: "You know, you were right!" I also think it brought us closer on a spiritual level . . . a heart and soul level. It's something that we will always be able to share, because we experienced it together. I couldn't sit there doing nothing. I was told to do this particular thing. And things will work out, it will smooth out. But to sit there wondering when is it going to happen, when should you go in there and have a conversation . . . It's not what you say, it's that you say it that counts . . . I think it is important. It's very important.

Death is hard, and the Living often need strength from others to get through the rough times. By seeing a need, and by listening to her intuition and her heart, Bev helped her mother have an FC-talk that helped her aunt die more peacefully. Communication created a strong end-of-life connection between Bev and her mother. It also opened her mother to new possibilities, setting her on a new spiritual path. Witnessing the extraordinary at the end of life can be miraculous.

Spiritual Path

The Living who saw themselves as part of a community that was created through shared spiritual messages believed that God had chosen them to be present at death—not just for the death of their loved one, but for other Dying who enter their lives. As opposed to any specific religious ritual that may be shared at the end of life, community created through spiritual messages focuses on the acts of sharing, meditating, praying, and other practices that open people to transcendent realities. The stories of Victoria, Bev, and Betty Lynn are strong examples of FC-talks using spiritual messages. These messages did more than help the Dying or the Living walk the death journey; they also put these sincere and skilled Living ones on a new spiritual path. These Living, identifying with the community of the Dying, felt blessed because they believed that they were doing God's work.

Betty Lynn, the woman who had the spiritual experience with C.C., eventually became a lay minister at her church. For many years prior to her FC-talk with C.C., she had been in the agriculture business. Subsequently, she returned to school and earned her master's degree. Betty Lynn became a licensed, practicing counselor, feeling strongly that God had called her to help people who need someone to assist at death. She shared with us the story of someone in need: Valerie was in her early forties and dying from a lung ailment. She was in a nursing home, lying next to people in their eighties and nineties. Valerie was brought into Betty Lynn's life through a mutual friend, Valerie's best friend. Betty Lynn became the one with whom Valerie talked, especially about her fears of death and about spiritual messages. When I met her, she was on her little motorized wheelchair. And on the back of it, a sign said, "Grace Happens." And the name of her motor was "Gracie." She and Gracie went everywhere.

Betty Lynn spent time with Valerie, often talking about her eventual death, and talking about her life—whatever she wanted to talk about. It was like therapy sessions. But she taught me about the higher power, and that she wasn't afraid to die, and it was just wonderful. We cried together. We laughed together. She'd tell stories of her childhood, and then she would talk about dying . . . I remember going and just feeling totally comfortable, feeling all those feelings of happiness, sadness, regrets—just going with her through all of her feelings. There were times when she would talk about being so sad because she was going to die. And then she would talk about being happy because she was going to die and go be with her God—she was such a wonderful Christian woman.

Betty Lynn recalled learning these lessons from Valerie: Talk about death. Talk about what's happening. Don't let it become this monster that is going to invade you and then take you away from here. Feel all the feelings. Don't just stuff them away and not have them. Live life. You know, because there is always grace. Grace happens. Betty Lynn learned the phrase from Valerie, but said she thought that grace happens whenever people take the chance and let God work miracles through us. Betty Lynn felt strongly that FC-talks—especially spiritual messages—show that grace does indeed happen.

Benefits of Spiritual Messages

Providing Comfort

Spiritual messages provide comfort to the Living through direct affirmations of faith and experiences of spirit. The Living who told us about spiritual messages expressed a feeling of comfort from their FC-talk, which had reduced some of their distress about losing their loved ones; these conversations were filled with hope and the expectation that they would meet again one day.

When the Dying and the Living communicated openly about spiritual messages at the end of life, they found that FC-talk gave them great hope that there is an afterlife. By definition, comforting communication soothes distressed feelings through words and/or actions. Specifically, spiritual messages provided the comfort for the Living. While many different types of FC-talk may give comfort to the Living, spiritual messages were acknowledged as a primary source of comfort.

Creating Community

Communication creates community, and spiritual messages create community for the Dying and the Living. The idea of community rings true as a means of bringing people together spiritually. Three likely outcomes of community are created through spiritual messages.

First is community as midwife. Most of the Dying need somebody to walk the path toward death's door with them because it's hard to leave loved ones behind, and it can be very scary to die. To be reassured by those they love the most that they will be all right after they die truly makes it easier to go. They need to hear that it's okay to die, okay to choose not to hurt or struggle anymore.

Second is community as support for the Living. Some people need help and encouragement to have an FC-talk with the Dying because it can be difficult for the distressed and unskilled. Everyone can use friends as they prepare and grieve. Having a community means that people will be around to support the Living as they assist their loved one.

Third is community as spiritual path. Many of the Living felt a sense of community at the end. Many believed that their presence at death was a calling from God, and some have chosen to answer this call in the future. The community created by FC-talk can become an ongoing special network. Such a community can continue long after the loved one has died. All of the members of that community have experienced something difficult, amazing, and powerful together by witnessing the passing of a life. The resulting bonds are deep and strong.

Gaining Validation

Spiritual messages offer validation of the Living's faith and spiritual experiences. The Living believed that, because they were fully present for FC-talk, open to conversations concerning spiritual messages, and accepting of the spiritual experiences that occurred, they received gifts: a stronger or renewed faith, or a new faith in God and an afterlife. Almost 70% of the Living participated in FC-talk that was specifically related to spiritual messages. They were left with the belief that they would see the Dying again, and that God—or whatever they perceived as a higher power—had been present during their FC-talk.

Summary

What the Living Learned from Spiritual Messages

Testimonies of religious faith, discussions about spiritual beliefs, and witnessing spiritual events are all moments of "grace" in life. Recall that grace is defined as a positive encounter with a divine or transcendent reality. Thus, as grace happens, comfort is shared, community is created, and spiritual faith is validated.

Comfort shared through words and actions is possible only in the tangible world of communication. For the people we interviewed, community was created because the Living took a chance and, through FC-talk, participated in the death journey with the Dying. Validation through spiritual messages removed doubt from the Living's hearts and minds in a way that only faith—a firm belief in something for which there is no proof—can accomplish.

Many of the Living drew firm conclusions about profound end-of-life events for which there were no logical explanations. In the end, the Living who experienced spiritual messages came to believe that the body is merely a vessel for the soul; that when the body is used up and can no longer go on, the soul of the Dying is released to experience eternal life.

Advice from the Living

♥ The Dying may choose their moment of death. They may wait until they are alone so as not to burden their loved one; they may wait until everyone is present; or they may wait until they are with just one special person. Remember that this is their choice, and it's not for the Living to judge, feel bad about, or try to force.

♥ Pay attention to the Dying; they will reveal their needs, interests, and fears about death, about the afterlife, or about

God. Your job is to slow down and be quiet enough to read the signals.

💜 If you think you can be a good midwife to death, then be open to it and offer your help. Ultimately, the Dying will choose those with whom they feel most comfortable. This is not a time to be jealous; accept the Dying's wishes.

💜 Talking about spiritual messages can be very powerful and often private. Be prepared to find private times.

💜 Don't preach to the Dying if it isn't wanted. It's not your place to share your own ideas about faith or religion with someone who is not open to FC-talk concerning spiritual messages.

💜 Relax your analytical mind, and release your fear of the unexplainable—if only for now—so that you can experience grace with the Dying.

💜 Don't stop the spiritual experience because you believe it can't happen. Yes, perhaps the Dying one is hallucinating. But it may be that the Dying are more aware and open to extraordinary experiences because they are closer to another reality.

💜 Accept the message for what it is—a gift from the Dying. If you disagree with their beliefs, this is not the time or place to argue. If you agree, then confirm this.

💜 The Living need community at the end. Be there for one another. Be gentle with each other, listen, and watch. You will tell each other what is needed.

CHAPTER 5

Beyond Words

The Power of Nonverbal Communication

*I would've had a harder time dealing with it if I
didn't get to see him, touch him alive, hug him,
and rub his head. [Jim]*

Although words create much of the intellectual meaning of FC-talk, final conversations are not really about the intellect. The Living told us that nonverbal actions were emotionally significant for them. Nonverbal communication gives the Living and the Dying a way to share, without words, their messages of love, comfort, closure, and more. What exactly counts as nonverbal communication? Nonverbal communication is every unspoken act between two people that has meaning for them. This chapter illustrates the power and purpose of nonverbal communication at the end of life.

There are many ways that people can communicate with each other without using words:

- *Eyes, face, and body* communicate in combination to express feelings such as love, anger, or frustration.

- *Voices* can hum, cry, sigh, and so on to modify words or convey specialized meaning for partners. Even silence can be significant.

- *Touch,* such as kisses, hugs, gentle pressure, or holding hands, can signal love, affection, or recognition.

- *Proximity*—simple presence—sends a message of caring, and essentially creates the opportunity for FC-talk.

- *Time* set aside to be with and care for the Dying conveys a willingness to rearrange life with the Dying as top priority.

- *Tokens of love,* such as flowers or gifts, and *material possessions,* such as photos, jewelry, or stuffed animals, can trigger memories for FC-talk; they help to create a soothing environment for both the Living and the Dying at the end of life, and act as reminders in the Living's future.

See Me, Feel Me, Hear Me, Touch Me

Eyes: Windows to the Soul

The Living often talked about the gift of a final connection with the Dying in the form of eye contact at the last moment of life. **Pinky** got to the core of why the eyes are often so compelling for the Living and the Dying: I remember looking at her in the eyes, and there was this real heart-to-heart communication. **Victoria** shared specifics with us about the power and meaning of a final look between her and her husband, Kerry: I just walked over and took his hand, and he opened his eyes and looked at me and died. And there was a real sense of peace . . . at the very end, just having him look at me one last time. There was a tremendous love and tenderness in that look.

Maureen's mother came back from between worlds to say a private goodbye to Maureen's father, Tom. Maureen recalled the story: Pat had been in a coma for a day and a half. Tom had been holding her hand, kissing her cheek, and sitting by her side for two hours, when suddenly Pat came out of her coma and looked at him. Tom stood up, kissed her, and said, "Pat, I love you and you are surrounded by love." Then she took one last breath and died. A window had opened momentarily, and she had come out of her coma to say goodbye to her beloved husband of forty-six years. Pat's private goodbye through a last shared glance between the two of them was a powerful message of love for Tom that continues today to be a precious memory. A final look exchanged between the Living and the Dying is not uncommon, and is remembered and cherished by those who are fortunate to know that final connection.

Eye contact can also tell the Living that they matter, that they are significant to the Dying. **Ruth** told us about the eye contact her father made with her during one of their FC-talks. He made eye contact with me, and that was important because he was talking to me like I was a real person—not like I was his little 5-year-old. He was telling me, "You're going to be all right." Ruth explained that her father's direct eye contact with her made all the difference in the world to her becoming an accomplished adult today.

The eyes can send messages other than love or acknowledgment for the Living; they can also provide hope and leave a strong impression on the Living. **Debbie** spoke about the importance of the look on her grandfather's face and in his eyes: When he looked at me, it was like he had this glow on his face . . . It was like we connected . . . It was something I'd never experienced with him before. His eyes were watery, and of course, my eyes teared up. And then I knew I'll see him in heaven one day.

The Face Conveys Emotion—The Body Conveys Intensity

Emily was with her best friend, Jeanette, during one of Jeanette's chemotherapy sessions when something happened that scared them both. After the frightening event was over, they sobbed in each other's arms. Emily understood the situation through Jeanette's nonverbal communication. She described the intensity of the moment and the meaning that the nonverbal interaction had for her. I was holding her when she was taking chemo. And one of the IV lines ran out. She looked up at me, and I could see a little fear. It ran out of her hand. It was finished. And I think back then, they didn't have them where you can turn it off naturally. I was afraid of the infiltration. So I calmly put her down. I mean, but the look on her face! I had already rung the bell, but no one came. So I went to the door and said, "Ms. Grant's bed STAT!" I saw the fear in her face and heard it in her voice, and I felt like I had to do something to relieve that fear. I didn't know how to get anyone in there quickly except that—I'd heard that on TV. It got results. They got in there quickly! [LAUGHING] And I saw the relief on her face again. She didn't say anything . . . It was a relief for me, and a release for her, and we both really did cry—like sobbed. I mean, neither of us ever had in each other's presence before. And I think the crying helped both of us. I really do.

It was very peaceful. Very peaceful to be able to do that in front of each other—that you could do that with someone and not feel any embarrassment whatsoever. We always laughed heartily together, and we certainly cried heartily together too. I mean, our souls truly met that day. I know that. It was very emotional. I think it was good for both of us. I really and truly do. We needed that. Tears are good. They are healing, and they are loving.

While the Living often described times when they shared their tears with the Dying, Emily revealed that some of the Dying can't cry with all of their loved ones. Although Jeanette finally cried with Emily on the day when they were both frightened, Jeanette typically didn't cry easily with others, including her husband. Some people are naturally private—crying in someone's presence might be uncomfortable. People are sometimes afraid to cry with the Dying or with other family members because they don't want to cause more grief to their loved ones; they hope to spare them more sadness and stress. Yet crying together can heal, and can bring two people even closer. Crying makes both the Living and the Dying more vulnerable and, therefore, more open to love. Being vulnerable with someone requires trust.

The Living should know that crying openly is not for everyone. When it comes to communication—nonverbal and verbal—it helps to know your audience. Who do you want to cry with? Who can you cry with? What are the circumstances? Where are you—is it private, safe, appropriate? How do the Living and the

Dying typically respond to the expression of strong emotions? It's amazing how much people can learn by being observant. For instance, Maureen's mother, Pat, was a very private and stoic woman. One night while Maureen was with her mom, Maureen began to cry, and Pat didn't like it one bit. Pat made it clear to Maureen through her disapproving glance, tone of voice, and question "What are you crying about?" that she was not happy with Maureen's show of emotion. Maureen left the room until she was calm again. Pat didn't mean to be harsh or critical. She was just being honest—she didn't want tears that night. At other times, Maureen reports that it was okay to cry in front of Pat, but not often.

There is no right response concerning the appropriateness of tears. There is merely the promise that, with increased awareness of one's own nonverbal communication and others' reactions to it, there will be fewer missteps, and more positive than negative moments of interaction during FC-talk.

Voice: Sounds from the Heart

Waltraud's father was dying in Germany, and she was living in America, so she made frequent phone calls home to her parents. She expected her mother to answer the phone, but her dying, silenced father surprised her once. I made one of my regular phone calls to my parents. It was either mother who would answer the phone, or nobody. Daddy just let it ring, since he couldn't talk anyway. This time, however, after a while, somebody picked up the phone. It wasn't without effort, and I sensed that it must be Daddy since I heard a murmur. "Are you there, Daddy?" "Hm." "Mama isn't at home?" "Hm." "I love you!" "Hm." And then I thought I heard him humming. But I wasn't quite sure. So I listened carefully. Could it be? "Daddy, are you humming?" "Hm." I pressed my ear to the receiver and, sure enough, I recognized the melody of the song Daddy was trying to "sing" for me—"Ach, ich hab' in meinem Herzen da drinnen"—a song we had sung many times together. It is a romantic, melancholic song from the fairy tale opera *Der schwarze Peter* (The black Peter) by N. Schultze. The first stanza roughly translates into "Oh, deep in my heart, I feel an awesome pain. All of my flowers I want you to have. And I shall think about you beyond my grave. Oh, deep in my heart, I feel an awesome pain." While Daddy was humming, I was singing quietly along. "Daddy, thank you for singing this song for me." "Hm." "I love you." "Hm, hm, hm, hm." I knew what he was saying. Four days later, he was dead. Daddy didn't die with his song still unsung. And I am still listening to it. I am forever grateful. A simple tune, carried on a familiar voice, with a uniquely shared meaning for both the Living and the Dying, can convey caring through reminiscence.

Jules also recalled a final connection with her dying grandfather that came only in the sound of his voice. I got there on a Friday afternoon, his hospice room, and he was pretty comatose. They said he hadn't been saying much. But when I got in the room, I just said, "Grandpa, I'm here." And he didn't say anything. I said, "It's Julie Pulie." That's what he called me when I was growing up. And he kinda laughed. He just went "huh." Everybody in the room started laughing except me, and I started crying. This was his way to reach out to me. He moaned and then his hand went up in the air. And I stroked it. About every ten minutes. I said, "Julie Pulie is still here." And he always did that grunt. The family, his wife and the others that were there, said, "He knows you're in the room." That's how he talked to me. Those final moments—it was neat 'cause just my sister and I were able to get something out of him that other people couldn't. He didn't say anything to anybody. It was his way of connecting with us in his last hours. A simple sound that would seem insignificant to a stranger told Jules that she was acknowledged and valued.

Touch: To Connect and To Let Go

Touch might seem fairly straightforward. But there's a big difference between a pat on the cheek from a dear relative and a slap on the shoulder from a relative stranger. The key factors that influence the meaning of touch include the *type, location, frequency,* and *length of time* that the touch is held, and most important, the appropriateness—whether or not the Living has permission to touch the Dying. The Living told us not only how important touch was in connecting to their loved ones, but also how it facilitated their willingness to let them go.

Victoria shared her story about holding her husband as he lay dying. Kerry said to her, "I want the luxury of being held to earth only by your love. Not to be connected to anything else" . . . That afternoon, I just cuddled up in the bed with him, and he was crying, and then later I went in and we didn't talk because we both felt like words would hold him. And there wasn't any reason to hold him to earth any longer. Kerry would die later that night, but their afternoon of holding each other helped them to share their love and to ease his pain.

Blanca remembered dancing with her dad, Louis, and the special meaning it had for the two of them. Daddy could dance to anything. Each of us has a way that we connected to Daddy on something. And dancing was mine. Nobody else loves—**loves**—all the way, from head to toe and out, dancing as much as I do. And Daddy was that way. If there is good music, you want to dance. I totally remember that he was in blue jeans and a denim shirt. I asked him to dance. I said, "Do you want to dance to a tape?" He says, "Yeah." Because it's always hard for both of us to listen to good music and not dance to it. Mama was worried that I'd wear him out. I said, "Daddy, I don't want to wear you out." He says, "No, no, I'm fine." And he couldn't dance as long, but we got to dance. And in that dance, father and daughter connected in a joyful way that was familiar to them both.

Others mentioned the role of touch in confirming that their dying loved one was still understanding and responding to them. As you will read in Chapter 6, **Holland** had a very difficult relationship with his mother, but finally found a way to connect with her. Holland began speaking to his mother, knowing that she could not respond verbally. In fact, this was the first time that Holland could talk with his mother when she couldn't cut him off, disagree, or argue with his comments. He was telling her that he loved her, and that she had done the best job she could as a mother. The squeezes from her hand were reiterating that she was understanding, even if she wasn't able to explain or . . . verbally express what she was feeling. And while they very well could've just been muscle spasms at coincidental spots in our conversation, I felt—I know, without a doubt—that she understood what I was expressing to her. Thus, where the two could never quite connect through words during their FC-talk, Holland finally found a way to bond with his dying mother in a way that was a necessary first step in his healing the wounds suffered during their relationship. Touch can heal.

Susan also held her mother's hand during their FC-talk, and she spoke to us of the meaning that simply holding hands with the Dying can have for the Living. I remember as a small child holding her hand, and then getting to that stage as a young teenager where, oh my gosh, you would never hold your mother's hand! And how it had come full circle where it was comforting to hold her hand. I remember her hands were always cool and dry. FC-talk is often about the Living coming full circle with the Dying, and it's often most strongly noticed in nonverbal communication. The touch, the dance, the caress remind us of where our relationship has been, and how far it has traveled.

Stan also came full circle with his mother, Sylvia. He talked about the symbolism of carrying Sylvia to her eventual death bed. The most meaningful event probably that took place—it was one of those that I knew at the time was quite meaningful—it was very interesting. She had a sort of hospital bed at home, but we needed one for her that was higher. She was in the back of the apartment in her bed, and when the other bed came, I carried her from there into the other room to the new bed. It was clear to me that this was symbolic; the symbolism of this was not lost on anybody. She only weighed eighty pounds, but she weighed eighty pounds. And you know, I'm not a big strong guy, so it was sort of my last chance to really carry her in some fashion. "Carrying" a parent is another kind of role reversal that, as we'll discuss in Chapter 7, allows the child to nurture at the end.

For all of the Living who talked about touch, the meaning of touch seemed more important than other types of nonverbal communication, and in some cases, even more important than some of the talk. The Living noticed the kind of touch, its frequency and how long it lasted; and they felt the peace and comfort that came with the touch. **Erin** and her grandmother talked a lot about hugs and that touching meant a lot. It just seemed like it was intensified more. For Erin and others, touch was a very intimate way to communicate "it," and "it" meant many things: love, connection, and even the sense of impending loss that both the Living and the Dying experienced. For some people, and at some times, it's easier to communicate the intensity of these feelings through touch because words simply are not enough to describe everything that is being felt or thought.

The most important FC-talk Maureen had with her mother, Pat, was through touch. Maureen often had to lift Pat from the couch or bed, and then slowly walk with her to where she needed to go. But every time Pat put her arms around Maureen's neck, the lift turned into a hug. As Maureen lifted Pat, they would stand still for a moment to steady her, and then look in each other's eyes and hug—every time. Maureen thought that everyone lifted Pat this way until her dad, Tom, pointed out to her that in fact, this only happened between Maureen and Pat. It was Maureen and Pat's way of sharing their love, their connection, and even at times, their sadness about their impending loss of each other. For Maureen, whose mother was fiercely independent and did not easily let others "do for her" when she was well, this touch spoke loudly and clearly about Pat's trust, love, and acceptance of her. The lift became a hug, and a hug became an unspoken symbol of the strength of their relationship. Maureen can still feel her mom's arms around her neck and the connection of their eyes.

People shared with us that they simply couldn't touch the Dying enough. **William** illustrated that the frequency of touch was as important as the type of touch when he observed, We just did a lot of holding hands and hugging. Through touch, it's possible to communicate love, loss, and even fear. The Living really wanted and needed to touch the Dying as much and as often as possible, if the Dying could tolerate it. Some of the Dying are very sensitive to any kind of touch, so it's best to check on sensitivity. It's almost as if the Living are trying to get all the touch they can get, to "fill up on the touch" before it's gone. Wouldn't it be nice if that were truly possible?

B.J. talked about sitting quietly with her dying mother-in-law, Sylvia, and her husband, Stan, with all three of them holding hands until Sylvia felt peaceful enough to let go and to end her fight against her worn-out kidneys. I decided I was just going sit with her and hold her. So I sat down beside her and held her hand. And then, after about fifteen or twenty minutes, Stan did the same thing. And within fifteen minutes, she was dead. I mean, it was so amazing. And it just felt so right to be with her that way and to hold her. I finally understood what it meant when someone passes, because I felt her body relax from her head down to her feet, because we were holding her. Touch shared by B.J., Stan, and Sylvia is more impressive considering what B.J. told us—that when Sylvia was healthy, she was not a touchy-feely person; she avoided most attempts at touch. Touch at the end of Sylvia's life meant to B.J. that she really loved me. And that she really trusted me.

The Meaning of Space and Time

Proximity: Being There Simply Feels Better

Stan lived halfway across the country from his dying mother, Sylvia. As soon as my sister called me and told me that Mom had renal failure, and that they were going to have to make a decision, I got on a plane that afternoon. He and his wife, B.J., were with Sylvia as she took her last breath. He wanted to be with her because it felt right to him, and because it was comforting to her that I was there. I'd had a friend ask me, for his own reason, "What does she want from you?" And I said, "She just wants me to be there. It makes her feel good." And that was clearly the case.

Dana W wanted to be physically close to her father, Michael, as he lay dying in his hospital bed from a brain tumor. That's where they both wanted to be—as near as possible to each other for as long as possible. When he had the strength, I was in the crook of his arm. You know, not cradled, but like he was a big guy with his arm around you. There was a lot of that closeness. And because of that closeness in proximity, I was always on the bed until I got older and he got sicker. Then I would stand next to the side of the bed where there was room near his head and neck area and his upper body. I would stand there. And sometimes I would lay my head on the pillow next to him, but standing outside the bed; kind of reaching over and talk to him there, that way. But I was never having the final conversations while sitting in a chair. For Dana, sitting beside Michael was not close enough for father-daughter intimacy.

Kasey was in school about three hours from where her sister, Angie, was spending her last days. She remembers arguing with her 26-year-old sister, who was dying from cancer, about wanting to come home to be with her full-time. It was painful to be so far away from her and connect with her only through the phone or on the weekends. We had the big conversation about how she did not want me to come home. She didn't want me to stop school and to come home, because at this time she knew she wasn't doing well, but she was sticking around. We didn't realize that she would die within a week of this conversation. I mean it was literally a week that she was just gone.

There are so many things I wish I'd done differently. I felt like at the time I was doing everything right. I just wish I spent more time with her. Or that I wouldn't have acted like it was something that was gonna go away. It's not very common that someone gets cervical cancer and passes away within a year. I mean, it was a year and two *months. We just never expected it to happen that quickly. If I had not been in so much denial, then maybe I could've been there a little bit more. Or realized that the last time was so much more important.* In spite of how difficult it is to watch someone you love dying, it's often harder to be far away from the Dying because there will be no second chance. Proximity does matter. Closer feels better, even when it's hard to witness the death journey. As Julie discovered (see her story in the preface), it's painful, disappointing, and sad to miss the last opportunity to see your loved one. When the Living can stay close to the Dying, or at least visit them often, they have more opportunities to connect in FC-talk and complete their goodbyes.

Time Matters

Especially relevant to our examination of nonverbal communication in FC-talk is the amount of time spent with the Dying, and the willingness of the Living to give time to communicate love and care. **Jennifer W** was at her husband's side nonstop for the last 72 hours of his life. **Lori** sat next to her father and held his hand for hours at a time. She also quit her job to take care of her ailing parents for two years. **Katherine,** a busy single mother with two teenaged sons, talked about the difficulty, but importance, of spending hours every evening with her dying mother—especially in light of the fact that for her entire life, she'd had a strained relationship with her mother. One of the most common regrets expressed by the Living was not spending sufficient time with the Dying.

The Living, both men and women, consistently expressed the desire to spend more time with the Dying. Some of the primary caregivers recognized that they were exhausted during those long days and nights, and wondered aloud how long they could go on living in the shadow of death. **Ellen** described the feeling: *I would have to say, just being with him, sometimes it was very hard. Sometimes it was very, very hard for me. When a person dies of cancer or a debilitating disease, when you're losing more and more of* them, you raise the bar of what you're willing to put up with just to be with the person. And sometimes it's very difficult. Yet what is the alternative? Is it better or easier to avoid spending time with the Dying? Perhaps in the moment, avoidance seems attractive. But not one of the Living we spoke with regretted time spent; indeed, the opposite was true. They wanted more.

Cathy was losing her beloved husband to heart failure and didn't know at first if she could accompany Don on his death journey. I think for a while I distanced myself. And we even talked, at one point, about separating. I said, "I am not going to be able to live through your death. I don't know how; I am not going to be able to do this." We thought about separating when I was doing my PhD up here . . . because he was in the valley for a while. And I remember calling him up and saying, "Am I out of my mind? Of course not. You know this is crazy! You know I **can** do it." But it was very strange. I didn't want to live through his death. My mother doesn't go to funerals. We didn't really like the death thing. And it was really essentially his idea. Thinking back to how that even came up, he said, "A good idea would be that we separate. I'll live right down the street." Because he didn't want me to have to take care of him until he died . . . [The FC-talk helped me] change in that way. I had to learn to accept death.

I knew that he knew that I was up to doing it. So I think a lot of that came out of the final conversations. It would be different if I had not had that; if I hadn't been able to say those things, spend that time with him, and have those last few days and make that transition—I think it would be a lot different. Cathy demonstrates that spending time together does matter, no matter how difficult it is. Time together helps the Living, in the long run, cope with death and the loss of the loved one.

A few words of warning: First, the Living can't force themselves on the Dying. Ultimately, who the Dying want to see is up to them, but you'll never know unless you try. Second, the Living need to watch for signs that their visit is taxing the Dying one's strength, and it's time to end the visit. Third, the caregiver of the

Dying one has the power to say who gets to visit, for how long, and even when the visits may occur. Respect the caregiver's authority; only one person can guard the gate.

The majority of the Living acknowledged to us that the gift of time benefited them as much as the Dying; they wanted as much time as possible with the Dying until their time together literally ran out. Time spent together became an unexpected gift.

The Importance of "Stuff"

Tokens: A Little Something

Dana W's father, Michael, wanted to be sure that she knew how important she was to him. He wanted her to always have a token of his love and, throughout the years to come, an affirmation of his view of her as a wonderful daughter. Michael gave his 12-year-old daughter a heart necklace with her first diamonds. Dana described her gift and what it meant to her: It's a little, thin, gold rope necklace. Probably a sixteen-inch gold rope necklace. And it's not even that big. Here on the right side are a couple of little diamond chips. I wear it all the time. That has the most meaning and most value of almost all my possessions because my father gave it to me so that I could remember him. I wear it whenever I have something of importance, ever since I was 12. And back then it was big tests, or it was getting into college, or the SATs, or getting a job when I was 16. You know, I wore it to those interviews. And I was able to finger it and touch it, and think of my dad. I wear it all the time . . . when I took the GREs, when I was interviewing to go into grad school. And I know when I look into PhD programs, that heart will be on . . . Oh, and on my wedding day. Absolutely.

Laura W felt that having a possession of Aunt Ceini's was a way to carry a part of her aunt's spirit into her life. There is one thing that I really cherish. This ring was hers. She always wore this. I specifically put it on today. And whenever I do—I mean sometimes I'll just wear it to wear it—but whenever I do something for honoring her, I will wear it. Because it has some essence of her. So I wear it, I touch it, and I play with it. Sometimes, things seem to have the Dying's energy or spirit captured in them. In fact, if the Living believe that, then it's true for them—and what a fortunate gift!

Symbolic Possessions: Perfect Beds and Canned Peaches

Tory told us a story about her perfect *Better-Homes-and-Gardens* bed, which had once been so important to her that it had to remain perfect once she'd made it for the day. Then her brother, Jacob, was dying, and the bed became a source of comfort and love instead of a source of pride. *Jacob would always come to lie on my bed because I had the fluffy pillows and the nice comforter. I normally wouldn't let anybody lie on my bed. I'd say, "Don't touch it!" because in the mornings, I'd make up my bed and then tell everyone, "Now, don't mess it up!" When Jacob was dying, I didn't care. [When someone you love is dying,] you have a new perspective on life, new priorities. So I let him lie on my bed. He was lying on the comforter that I worked so hard on that morning, but it was okay. And I gave him all the pillows he wanted, and I kind of wrapped him in the comforter itself. And I kind of lay there with him.* Tory, now in her unique way, keeps Jacob's memory alive. She was reflecting on her old, fanatical concern for her perfect bed: *For somebody who was very organized . . . I have never made my bed since then. Just never been made. If it's made, it's because my husband did it.* When asked why, Tory replied, *I don't know. I feel like if I make it up, his spirit is gone. I feel like if I make up my bed, I'm covering up his spirit.*

Gloria talked about coming full circle with her son, Jacob, as she fed him his last meal. *Jacob's favorite food is peaches. And he used to love to put the can of peaches in the refrigerator because he couldn't have fresh. So I went into the room, and he was just out completely. I said, "I'm here. Do you want something to eat?" And he says, "Yeah, but I don't know what." I said, "Well, come on, let's go to the kitchen. Grandma said that you have been in this room all day." So he got up and walked to the kitchen with me, and he sat down. "I'll have peaches, Mom. I know there's some in the fridge, Grandma put* some in." So I open a can of peaches. I put them in a bowl, but he couldn't see them still. His hand was totally loose. I said, "Jacob, this isn't normal." He says, "I don't know, Mom, don't worry about it. Just, I'm just . . . feed me. Please." And I did. I spoon-fed him his favorite meal.

Within moments of finishing his peaches, Jacob had a brain hemorrhage that was a result of the chemotherapy treatment he was undergoing for his cancer. The family didn't know it yet, but Jacob was brain dead. Gloria had to decide within days of this final interaction to finally let Jacob go; she made the decision to remove the respirator that was keeping him alive. Gloria reflected on what it meant to her to feed her son his last meal: I felt like he was little bitty again. I felt like he was little when I would feed him when he was a baby. And I felt good that God allowed me to experience that final moment with him . . . He even said that he was a little embarrassed that I had to feed him. And I said, "I love to feed you." And he was crying. That was a very special moment for me. I guess that's the feeling of being a mom. Motherhood is—I know I knew this, but it was evident at that time—it is the good and the bad, the sacrifices. I think this experience was telling me to be a mom is special. And to have a child, to be able to share this with him, was a very strong indication to me that my role is what it should be, that I was there for a reason. All these years, from the time he was born up until then, this is what I was destined to do. And that my role as a mother was important to him and to me. I was the one to be there to experience that. I don't think it ever was so strong as at that very point. And I thanked God at that time for allowing me to be the one to feed him, to give him his favorite food.

Tokens of love, perfect beds, and doing favors for the Dying: they all seem to be about *things.* The importance of possessions or tokens may be minimized because people don't want to focus on material things—yet these things are really about feeling special, or making the other person feel special. This world sometimes feels superficial; yet these examples show that tangible things can hold powerful meaning for people. Look around and see what's special in your own life. Most people realize that things held, felt, or seen are intensely significant for both the Living and the Dying. Special tokens or possessions can keep precious memories alive for the Living in ways that nothing else can. It's affirming to touch a treasured necklace during a test; or to look at an unmade bed— and remember how a perfectly made bed became more perfect when it brought comfort to the Dying. And from that day forward, it brought comfort to others.

Benefits of Nonverbal Communication

Revealing Truth

Nonverbal communication can reveal a lot about the Dying: not only their feelings, but also near-death awareness and level of pain. It can offer the Living information about the Dying and the dying process. Nonverbal communication can also provide the Dying with the truth about how the Living are coping with the death journey. **Ryan** talked about the impact of nonverbal communication at the end of life, as it revealed the truth to both the Living and the Dying. *One of the biggest nonverbal things is simply being able to look at someone in the diminished physical state. Just try to see them. Maybe we're disgusted, or maybe we're afraid, and we look away. Or maybe we're just full of pity. But no one wants to be looked at that way. People, even when they look very good, very attractive, they really want to be seen for who they are or who they think they are. And it's that situation even more so in Tere's case, with her being ill and looking the part—looking unhealthy, looking like she's dying. I think that's probably one of the most powerful things. Just being able to look at her. To give the same reaction I always did, like the confused look when I don't understand. When they say something stupid and mean, they want to be glared at. And when they say something funny, they want you to laugh. And they want all the things that have been. At least, that's my feeling. And especially* nonverbally: I think that we all have the sense that nonverbally, we're more honest.

Making Contact When Speech Is Gone

At the very edge of life, during the last days and final hours, the Dying often are dealing with a wide variety of symptoms, such as shortness of breath, dry mouth, and overwhelming sleepiness. Their bodies often are shutting down, making them physically incapable of verbal communication, so totally dependent upon nonverbal channels of communication. The Dying are very often in and out of a coma at the very end of their lives as well, which can lead to greater reliance on nonverbal messages. Thus, nonverbal communication can bring information and consolation to the Living because the Dying can communicate with them even when words are no longer physically possible.

Laura W described this experience in FC-talk with her Aunt Ceini. I sat next to her bed and held her hand. I don't remember her as a super touchy-feely. She wasn't distant, but that just wasn't her. I guess she had a more sort of masculine communication style. But, you know, she was so quiet, and she couldn't talk, so the only way to really communicate was through touch. Just being physically close to her and holding her hand was all that we could really do.

Ellen's husband, Michael, had a brain tumor and no longer had the ability to talk. But even in his final days, he made sure that Ellen knew what he wanted and liked—or in this case, didn't like. Michael died February twenty-eighth. On February fourteenth, Valentine's Day, I came in with a bouquet of balloons. You know the red heart, "I love you" balloons? And Michael was truly [limited]; I don't think he was even seeing very much anymore. And I remember standing by his bedside and singing, "You are my sunshine, my only sunshine. You make me happy when skies are gray." And Michael got a look on his face and started waving his arm around like, "Don't sing anymore, don't sing. Don't sing. I know you love me, but don't sing." I mean, it was just so funny.

Revealing Emotions

Nonverbal communication can often help the Dying and the Living reveal what may be too difficult or impossible to say in words. Strong emotions are not always easily shared, especially if people have been taught to hold back their tears and other strong feelings. Why would people hold back from sharing their emotions with one another—especially at the end of life? Because of fear. People are often taught that sharing their emotions will burden others or that sharing their feelings will make them too vulnerable.

Jim told us that his family didn't share their emotions easily in the past—especially Jim's father, Tom, who was dying from pancreatic cancer. In my own family, Dad's reticence, and my reticence to push the limits of his reticence, was an obstacle. He did not talk about his feelings. It was really hard—I mean, he just wouldn't have it. Jim's reflection that his family was reluctant to talk and share deep thoughts and feelings highlights another reason that nonverbal communication is a valuable way to connect. Sometimes it really is easier to say things through actions rather than words. Specifically, Jim talked about the simple sweetness of a kiss: The night before he died, I stayed up with him all night. He was in his living room and hospice stuff was all around. He'd wake up kind of moaning, and I would get up and pat his head and give him morphine pills. And one time during that, he reached up and pulled me down and gave me a kiss on the cheek. Really, really sweet. I really cherish that memory. I think that was the last interaction we had that I **know** that he knew I was there.

Confirming Relationships

The Living sometimes communicate nonverbally because they simply don't have words to adequately describe the depth of their love and grief. **Patti** told us about her last days with her dad, Joe. I was rubbing his hand, just loving him, and thinking all these things, but I didn't know how to say them. We just sat with him quietly, didn't really say much more. I just told him I loved him and gave him a hug; I looked him in the eyes, and he told me he loved me. And that was it. I left that day—that was on my way out the door. And we left probably an hour and a half, two hours after I thought I was ready to leave. I just couldn't leave my dad. A week later, he passed.

Carol's dad, Ronald, communicated his love for her in the only way that he found comfortable. If we were sitting watching the race, or whatever, if we were just together, every time we were together he would take my hand, and he wouldn't let it go. I think it's just that he wasn't good at talking. He wasn't good at telling people how he felt. But it was his way of telling me that he loved me without having to actually say that. What's important is that Carol felt loved, and she accepted her dad's message in the way that *he* could best communicate it.

Comforting and Connecting the Living with the Dying in a Tangible Way

"Being close" must be conveyed in a very literal way at the end. **Jarrod** explained why the nonverbal—in this case, holding his grandmother's hand—was so significant to him. It meant a lot. There was just something about it; it was almost like being a baby. You know how babies have to have that touch. And I think that I had to have that. I needed that. Not that I ever told her that. Because I didn't want her to think that she had to do that ever at any point. But it was important to me to have that, because you're so attached to the physical. Because you know she's going to be gone. And it's like you can't get enough physical interaction. It's like you just want to touch and be touched over and over and over. The last day—the night before she died—I was there the entire time. I was there when she died. I was holding her hand.

Many people are surprised at how much is revealed about emotions and relationships through nonverbal communication. Yet in close relationships, many messages are shared primarily through the nonverbal channel during health, illness, and death. Parents usually know when their little ones are sick because they are moving slower, their faces are grumpy, and their eyes look different; or they simply don't look or act like themselves. Siblings often let each other know when they are happy or angry with one other through a look, an expression, or a tone of voice. Romantic partners can tell each other that they love, trust, and need (or distrust and disrespect) each other through a touch or a look. Just as most people daily reveal their emotions, and express their feelings about their relationships through nonverbal expressions, the Living and the Dying do so at the end of life. This statement about the power and importance of nonverbal communication is not to suggest that words are useless—all communication is valuable, and there are certainly things that cannot be said without words. It's simply to point out the importance of nonverbal communication for those in close relationships. We want the Living to pay attention to *both* the verbal and nonverbal parts of their and the Dying's FC-talk so they can have the best possible communication.

Summary

What the Living Learned from Nonverbal Messages

Nonverbal communication is meaningful to the Living in part because there are so many unspoken ways to communicate or reinforce messages such as love, connection, fear, anger, and sadness. In fact, it's impossible to convincingly communicate positive feelings such as love, trust, or admiration to the Dying or, for that matter, negative feelings such as contempt or disrespect, without using nonverbal communication. Try it in your current relationships, and you'll see what we mean. We expect that many people get in trouble every day because they are communicating negative messages to their loved ones without intending to do so, or are failing to communicate positive messages adequately. A first step toward improving relationships is to increase awareness about the power and effects of nonverbal communication. And the last step in a "good" goodbye is likely to be an unspoken gesture or touch.

Messages that are sent nonverbally are powerful and poignant, and at times such messages seem more honest and real than any spoken word. People do *not* believe spoken emotions and relational messages like "I love you" unless the words are accompanied by appropriate nonverbal facial expressions, eye behavior, body movement, and voice. When in doubt, people generally trust nonverbal communication over the spoken word. Words can lie; but the face, the body, and the voice express feelings fairly directly. The Living who spoke to us believed and relied upon nonverbal communication to reveal the truth and to express for them what was too difficult to say adequately.

Perhaps **Grace**, who lost two husbands to heart disease, best captured the power and significance of nonverbal communication during FC-talk. The assurance of touch is the most important thing you can do [for both the Living and the Dying]. The reassurance of holding someone's hand, of having them there with you physically, is so vitally important. Even when there's silence, it's that reassurance of the human touch, which is the first thing we feel when we're born and, of course, the last thing we should feel when we die.

Advice from the Living

♥ Be nearby. Being physically close to the Dying is a powerful message of love as well as an indicator that you are open to participating in FC-talk without pressuring the Dying to do so.

♥ Time does matter. The more time you can spend with the Dying, the more FC-talk you will participate in, and ultimately, the more you will gain from the experience. But remember, the Dying get to choose who spends time with them and how much time is enough.

♥ A touch, a look, a sound of recognition can be worth a thousand words. Don't worry about what words to say. Open your heart; your feelings will show.

- ♥ Touch at the end of life brings comfort to the Dying and healing to the Living.

- ♥ Trust the nonverbal communication that you experience; it is as real, as powerful, and often as meaningful as spoken words.

CHAPTER 6

Heartache Released

Healing Damaged Relationships

*To do that for her—to give to her what she
had never given me—I didn't want to do it. But
I was kind of forced into this place, and it just
seemed like that was my assignment.*
[Katherine]

How do you have FC-talk with someone who has been mean and miserable to you? Why would you even consider inviting FC-talk and making yourself vulnerable again? Why would you want to be kind, considerate, and forgiving to the Dying, if they had never done so for you? The answer is provided by the Living: You do it for you, to survive. Not everyone has a happy, loving, or safe relationship with the Dying—but they're family. Sometimes, the Living are the only family available for the Dying, so they are expected to visit and possibly become a primary caregiver. And this can be a very uncomfortable duty.

Approximately 20% of the Living we spoke with had very difficult relationships with the Dying. We were fortunate that they were willing to talk to us, given the hurt they had to recall. In some cases, the Living simply faced challenges in a relationship that included both good and bad moments. In others, the Living had terrible relationships with the Dying; they described typical past interactions with the Dying as filled with criticism, defensiveness, guilt, manipulation, coldness, and even contempt.

These Living reported that their FC-talk focused primarily on the goal of "cleaning up" the mess they'd been dealing with for most of their lives. But it's more complicated than that. The Living look for ways to let go of their anger and resentment before it's too late. FC-talks offers a way to begin this difficult journey. The process of healing as "cleaning up" includes four areas of concentration:

1. The Living often must release negativity by forgiving and accepting their former nemesis.

2. The Living might hope for (but not expect) a surprising apology.

3. The Living may find a new kind of relationship with the Dying.

4. The Living, in general, did not want to make things worse than they had been prior to the terminal diagnosis.

Whatever the outcome, this special group of the Living were incredibly brave, and trusted that we knew what to do with their stories. We are extremely grateful for the stories they shared. We learned a great deal from them.

Cleaning Up the Mess

Katherine was 46 when she helped Linda, her 80-year-old mother, face death. For most of her life, she and Linda had not had a good relationship. Katherine had waited and waited for Linda to be the mother she wanted, the mother she hoped for. But she learned that as people near death, they rarely change. As they approach death, the Dying usually act as they have acted every day prior to their terminal diagnosis. We all become limited by our daily routines, our habitual ways of responding and communicating. As we near death, we know no other way to be. With this realization, Katherine came to see that it was going to be her job to clean up their relationship if she had any hope of bringing it to a resolution.

Katherine's mother, Linda, had been ill for a number of years. Linda first dealt with lymphoma, then with breast cancer and four years of chemotherapy. Finally, it became apparent that her life was slipping away, and Linda was angry and afraid. She continued her tendency to be ornery and difficult, and did not go easily from life. What she would say, how she would say it—she had less governing of it. In her life, she would control it—her sharp tongue and her statements—but as she got more ill, she didn't, and she just would say whatever she wanted to say. My dad and I tried to keep her at the apartment, keep her at home. At the end, we had her moved into hospice care; when you do that, you know that it's the end. She was on a lot of morphine. We got a nurse to come in to stay during the nights so that my dad could sleep on the couch. And she refused to let my father have any rest. He had to be with her every second. And if he wasn't there, it had to be me. And we would go back and forth between really tough love with her, really holding boundaries with her, and then the next minute realizing that this is a dying person: We need to be nice. I had a really hard time getting in her face about stuff and holding the line with her. And she just totally dominated everything.

Katherine felt the intense pull of these conflicting impulses: to hold the line for her own needs, and to be "nice" to her difficult, dying mother. That was very frustrating. I had a lot of anger. I did a lot of talking to friends and processing a lot of my resentment and anger towards her during that time. I think that's what came out of it for me . . . I cleaned up a lot of my stuff with her by taking care of her during that time when she was as mean as she could be. As difficult as she could be, I became the parent. I parented her through that. She became a little girl emotionally as she went down. And my father was just emotionally a wreck and worn down. And I parented him through that too. And then I would go to school and teach school all day, and go back to the nursing home as soon as I got out of school. I have a friend whose husband is a family counselor, so she's kind of like an assistant family counselor. She helped me process a whole lot of it. And we would talk and talk and talk and talk, as we both had similar mother-daughter relationships which were not at all warm and fuzzy and best friends. Not at all.

Because Katherine had a negative history with her mother, she had to make a conscious decision about how she wished to say goodbye. I remember saying to myself, "Be here. Don't check out emotionally." You know how you just go away emotionally and walk through it, but not feel it? I remember thinking, *Be aware of this. Be awake during this. Pay attention.*

I would have to say it took me days to get myself ready to tell her that I love her, and that seems like such a weird thing. It probably is just an amazing thing to people who say that all the time before they hang up the telephone. I knew it was my assignment, but it took me weeks of processing and going to the nursing home and not saying it, and going home and thinking, *Oh! I didn't do it.* You know? It seemed like this huge thing. It had just so much emotional baggage with it because she had never told me. I would be damned if I'm gonna be the one that reaches out there and does that . . . My friend was encouraging me, of course. And I knew that her days were numbered, and I knew intellectually that I would be so angry if I didn't get this done and she died. How wasteful. And so I felt a lot of pressure from myself to take care of that and at the same time, so much resistance: not doing it, not going there.

One evening she was just absolutely throwing a fit at when she didn't get her way. She had no strength, but she could throw her dinner tray across the room. You know? And she had done that, so it was a really high-level emotional situation. She was throwing a fit, and I needed to leave, I needed to get home. And there was just all this guilt and manipulation that she had used all of our lives, only very subtly. You know, I wasn't really surprised—I mean, this is my mom, I was used to it. I would just dance to the tune. Then this situation is different in that I'm the adult, and she's pretty much not really in control of herself . . . So I'm wrestling with *What do I owe her? Do I stay for her? Do I leave for my kids? Do I stay all night? Do I need* more than two hours' sleep? All that reality-check stuff. That evening, another lady was there, a friend of the family. The two of us were in the room, and I just began to talk to my mother from my emotional place of [acting as the] mom. And I was just listing: We're doing this, and we're doing this, and Dad and I've discussed how we can do this better. And we want you to feel safe, and we want you to be happy . . . I was just trying to calm her down and list all the things that we were doing to help her. And she was ranting about how nobody loves her . . . And it just laid itself out there. I just said, "Mom, I love you dearly. And I appreciate everything you've done for me all of my life."

My mother had never told me in my whole life that she loved me. Ever. And so I spent that last month reassuring her how much my father and I loved her. It took me a long time to be able to say it. I would say it to my friend Mary, who was helping me process this. I emotionally didn't want to do any of that; it seemed like this huge, big monster—to go there emotionally with my mother. But what it ended up being was a healing for me. I don't know what she got out of it. I don't even know if she was aware of enough. But I got to tell her that I loved her. And I got to thank her for taking care of my children when they were young. And it was really hard for me to do. It was really hard for me to do. To do that for her—to give to her what she had never given me—I didn't want to do it. But I was kind of forced into this place, and it just seemed like that was my assignment. That was my assignment. There was a strength gained by it; I don't know how you would get it any other way except mothering a child, I suppose. It's very similar to that. Hard, you know. And it's not fun. But that's what we did.

Katherine found strength in this new "assignment," in filling her final nurturing role with her mother, in opening her eyes to different expressions of love. She had a hard time accepting it— that people were coming, food was coming, gifts were coming—and she wouldn't allow herself to be loved. That was the lesson that I learned from it. I'd been single for fifteen years out of a divorce, and had a lot of questions about love and commitment . . . I watched my parents, watched my dad be there for her, and love her in that real nonverbal way. He never left her side. I learned a lot about their marriage that I had never paid attention to.

I had never really been aware of the way he dealt with her before her passing. And I would've told you that I respected my mother because she was my mother, but I did not love her. I probably would have told you that in my twenties and thirties, because I didn't think that I did. But going through this with my whole family—not just between her and me, but with my whole family. It changed my definition of what that is. Of course she loved me. And of course I loved her. How silly to spend half my life thinking that there wasn't love between us just because we didn't say the words. That was a lesson I learned.

I think that late, late, late, she told me that she loved me; but not more than once or twice during all that. She didn't know how to receive that. She knew how to cook, and she knew how to clean, and she knew how to go to work, and she knew how to sew, and she gave. I think back on the mothering job that she did: She gave constantly. It wasn't emotional, it was the doing. I began to understand why it was so hard for her just to lie there. It was hard for her to just lie there and be. It's a difficult emotional place to be. The heaviness of death, which none of us had ever talked about—none of us wanted to talk about it, but it forces your hand. It forces your hand to go to this emotional place. You have no choice about it. But you can deny it. It's like this huge thing in the room with you, which you're just ignoring. Which is basically what we did for the first years.

Katherine decided that during her FC-talk, she had to describe the ways that her mother was being loved. She wanted her mother to recognize and be open to the love in her life; just as Katherine was finally able to start opening herself to love. She began by telling her mother, "You know, there is this parade of people in and out of here, and flower and gifts . . . You are loved, people love you. Don't you see that?" And she couldn't see it. She could not receive that. That's the most powerful message to me because I am her daughter. And I have very similar things happening in my life. I mean, I had been alone, guttin' it out, doing it all by myself for fifteen years. And she had not been there for me. So that was when I pretty much laid it out there and told her I loved her.

I think I put down the baggage, anger, and resentment towards my mom that I'd been carrying all my life. I didn't like her very much. Doing for her what I wanted her to do for me cleaned that up. That was the interesting part of that . . . What cleaned it up was that I did it for her.

Katherine, in reversing roles and doing for her mother what her mother never did for her, healed much of the anger and resentment she had stored up from the need for mothering. And she began to perceive a *physical* component to this role switching. Her big, bad mother became smaller as Katherine expanded into her full adult stature. The first thing that comes to my mind is how small she got. She shrunk, and I got bigger. I probably really didn't change size. She probably literally changed size. But the first thing that comes to my mind is, I just would be astounded at how small this little lady was, and how fragile she was in this bed. The bed got huger, and she got smaller. And the other weird thing about that was that I was getting stronger, I was getting bigger as she got smaller. Well, that was the strength that I was getting. It was the first time I'd really dealt with her as an adult—not as her daughter, but as an adult.

Katherine felt a sense of achievement and esteem about accomplishing these difficult tasks: I was bigger than she was emotionally. I could do it. I could push through my own fear and do it anyway.

Katherine realized that she had grabbed the opportunity to clean up the mess, while her siblings had not. Everyone in my family, the three children that she had, suffer from very low self-esteem, my brothers especially . . . well, all of us. I took the opportunity to work out some of this stuff, and they did not. They're old, they're 63. And they are still beating that old drum of, "My mother didn't ever da-de-da." "My parents, my family didn't ever do this, and that's why I'm so screwed up." I can see that. And I'm hoping that I learned and cleaned up and can move on. That's what I'm hoping: that I'm not just carrying around that trailer full of history of "my family screwed me up."

Not only did Katherine surrender her negativity, she opened up to receiving love, just as she had asked her mother to do. The amazing thing is that, after both of my parents were gone, love came back into my life two months later. And I didn't know what to do with that, but I thought, *This doesn't come around a lot. I'm jumping in with both feet.* Well, that's a whole separate story, but I opened myself up to relationships and love in my life.

Katherine resolved to get herself clear of the negativity surrounding her relationship with her mother. And in so doing, she left herself with a clean slate for a new and wonderful love. Still, she acknowledges a legacy from her mother that she didn't expect: What's so funny is I'm in a real traditional Methodist church, and because of how I was raised, I know every song. My mother sang hymns when she worked, washed clothes, did cleaning tasks, whatever—and since she's been gone, I do that. That is weird. Even though she sees how differently from her mother she responds to life now, she recognizes a single, light-hearted similarity she can enjoy. Katherine's story is one of finally releasing the parent and coming into full maturity.

Sam described cleaning up the mess in terms of the need for the Living to own their part of the problem and stop the blame game. Sam revealed, My dad was the obvious problem person in the family, but the relationship I had the most trouble with was the relationship with my mother. I think what happened with her in those last couple of years was really some closure . . . I remember that scene from *On Golden Pond* . . . Jane Fonda is cursing about her dad to her mom. And her mom slaps her and says, "That son of a bitch is my husband." And you just basically grow up. You know? There comes a point when you can't blame your parents anymore for your life. Her death, and being with her leading up to her death, brought that to an end for me. I mean that was kind of the end of the blaming; there really was no longer any parental reason for any of my problems. I had to own them myself.

Laura W had a challenging relationship with her mother throughout most of her life. She decided that it was time to really spend some quality time with her mother before time ran out. Spending a lot of quality time together was totally out of character for Laura and her mother prior to the terminal illness. A middle-aged woman, Laura decided to have a "slumber party" with her dying mother—it turned out to be one of the best nights of their entire relationship.

I told her that we were going to have a slumber party. And she smiled at that. She couldn't really talk to me too much, but I spoke to her all night that night. I camped out on the floor, and I felt like there was something that I had to say to her. And I didn't know what it was. I couldn't figure out what it was. We had a really good time that night. It was almost like a girls' night out. I can't really explain it, but it's something that we had never done before. And I could see the tips of her mouth kind of curling up. You know? That I was there. And then I would stay all night with her. Not because I didn't believe that she wouldn't wake up in the morning, but that I just didn't want to miss anything.

I had been resentful at her; I had to just give myself permission to love her. Even though I was kind of like her punching bag. I really was. And I'm still working on all that. Laura also knew that there was something she wanted to say to her mother, but she wasn't sure what to say, or how. She asked her AA sponsor of twenty years— who had become like a second mother to her—what to say. There's just something I have to tell my mom . . . She says, "Just tell her you're sorry that you misunderstood her." And so the next time I went up there and she got really, really close this time, that's when I told her, "Mom, I'm really sorry. You know? That I misunderstood you." And for some reason, that just cleared the air. It kept my side of the street clean. My side of the street was clean, just from that one utterance.

Mom stayed awake purposefully that night. And I would say things to her. And I knew she knew what I was talking about. She didn't even have to try and say anything that night. She didn't have to do of any of her hashing out of things. It was almost like we were really connected at the hip that night. And I had forgiven her.

In the process of cleaning up the mess, the Living often have much to forgive. That act of forgiving is part of letting go of negative bonds created over a lifetime.

Letting Go: Forgiving, Accepting, and Acknowledging

Holland was angry with his mother, Pamela, for embracing death so willingly. On his 16th birthday, he discovered that Pamela had been diagnosed with hepatitis C and liver disease. Of course, he wanted to know what she could do about it. She simply responded that she would die, which she did about four years later. He had known of her alcoholism from a very young age, but she stopped drinking when he was 6 and resumed when he was 12. During that time, Holland got a sense of who she was as a person. He loved talking with her until she started drinking again after his stepfather left. At 13, he moved out. I was old enough to be on my own in her eyes. And I knew I wasn't; I mean, I still needed her, but she didn't need me. So I was left to deal with the rest of my growing up myself.

Holland's frustration and anger are still very real to him. He talked about the fact that his mother's selfishness was very difficult to understand. Holland told Pamela, "You kill yourself to end your pain, but in doing so, you're causing pain to so many others." I couldn't understand how someone could be so selfish as to do this to themselves. So I had a very hard time being impartial during our conversations. I was very self-righteous: "How can you do this? I would never do this. It doesn't make any sense." To this day, it still doesn't make any sense to me.

I remember a conversation we had in the truck, where it was almost like a parent to a child, a teenager. I was the parent, though.

"Why are you doing this?" She says, "You can't tell me what to do. I will *do* what I want when I want to do it. You don't have any force in my life." I said, "All you have to do is stop, and you can see me walk across the stage [for high school graduation]." And it wasn't that important to her, so she kept doing it. But she was so stubborn. The doctors on three separate occasions gave her less than a year to live. And every time she had an outbreak in the hospital, I'd get the phone call. I'd be the first one there, because there was no one else to call. And the doctor would tell me, "Your mom has six months, eight months to live . . . if she doesn't stop drinking, less time than that." And she would repeatedly beat [the death diagnosis]. They told her that she had no chance of living to see my high school graduation if she didn't stop drinking. She had less than two years to live. She stepped up her drinking and lived another five years. And that's why her death, to this day—I don't believe it. Because she was so stubborn, she thought that she wasn't going to die. She wasn't going to let someone have that kind of influence on her life—telling her when she was going to do something, that this one [her ultimate death] can't be real either.

Talking with someone who has caused tremendous pain in your life isn't easy for anyone, and it doesn't get any easier because someone is dying. The big difference is that the Living feel the urgency to have the talk—the talk has to happen now, before the person is dead. Holland needed a final showdown with his mother, and he recalled giving himself a pep talk. If you're angry, don't show it, don't feel it, because you don't want that to be the last impression she has. And I wasn't really angry so much anymore, just confused. So I was just talking with her and explaining to her that everything was okay. That she raised me just fine, and that I was the person I am today because of who she made me, and the values that she instilled in me in the time period we had together.

I knew her biggest fear was dying a failure because she didn't accomplish anything and she hadn't had a job in twenty-three years. But I was telling her that she succeeded in life through her children;

that I am the person I am because of her. And there are things that I accomplish because of her. So she can find success in my accomplishments. And [my brother] John was doing better; he will do something in his life, and he will be a good father. And she could find success in his love that he'll have for his children. And I explained to her that [my sister] Hillary was a great mother, because of the principles that she had. Hillary got these principles from seeing my mom and how my mom interacted with us. And she could find success in that. I told her that I would look after [my sister] Megan and make sure that Megan succeeded in her life. Because she instilled in us family principles: You always look after your family. She wasn't a failure in her life because she didn't succeed in accomplishments, because all of us are good people and true. Those are successes enough. And she doesn't have to fight it anymore. She doesn't have to deal with the pain that she had within her because if she was waiting to die until she had a success, then she could die in peace, because we were her successes. I held her hand, and I got to tell her I loved her. And she told me she loved me.

The negative effects of Pamela's choices will live on for some time in Holland's life, but his FC-talk was the beginning of awareness and a shift in his attitude. At some point in the last conversations, I went from being bitter about what she was telling me to accepting the fact that she wasn't telling me these things because she believed them; she was telling me all this because it helped her with her reality. And if that's what she needed, no matter what, I didn't have to believe it. I refused, and I live my life by my own saying, "I refuse to be a victim of circumstance." My mom was an alcoholic; it doesn't mean I have to be. I don't have to give in to drugs. Too many people I know are victims of circumstance. "I don't have the money, so I can't do this." Why not? You can do it if you just set your mind to it. So the conversations I had with my mom led to a lot of attitude adjustments within me.

But in the end, that final night I wasn't worried about anything she'd taken from me. I was just worried that she knew that it was okay, that despite everything I loved her. And that's forgiveness, I guess. If I learned anything, it's that no matter what someone does to you, there's always room for forgiveness. Everybody gets second chances.

Holland took a huge leap into the mess of his relationship with Pamela to accept her, acknowledge her, and finally forgive her. In so doing, he prepared himself to heal a lifetime of hurt and disappointment.

Sam's father had also been an alcoholic who had few kind words for young Sam. But adult Sam found himself able to say, "Dad, I love you. I forgive you for all the ways that you screwed up. I realize you're just a person. And you're not perfect." Sam explained why this was hard but necessary: A lot of his and my relationship from that point on was the relationship of me as caretaker with him. My dad, who had been throughout my childhood this kind of scary guy . . . my childhood memories of him were of a volatile guy. All of a sudden now, as he was dying, he became this big teddy bear guy, who was always so incredibly grateful . . . A lot of this was nonverbal. We could talk a little bit, but it was real hard for him to talk . . . The way he looked at me, he looked up to me. He looked up to me so much. He was incredibly proud of me, and that just exuded from him. In fact, people who knew him . . . were always coming up to me saying how proud my dad was of me. He would be apologetic sometimes for needing me to do things. But he was also very, very appreciative and grateful that I was there for him.

I had gotten over my whole co-dependency issues where I'd be resentful of him. Because he could be real manipulative prior to that . . . There was about a two-year period probably after my mom's death that he drank still very heavily. And then he started having problems with his liver, and he quit. He had about five years of sobriety. For the first time in his whole life, sobriety. I mean his whole adult life. So that was another thing, during these final conversations with my dad, it was almost like I was getting to know a different person than the person that I knew. I mean he was really—this was the guy underneath the guy that I knew. But during that period of drinking after my mom's death, again it was all about, in some ways, constructing boundaries. I got a phone call from him one time: "I'm gonna kill myself." Oh, you know, this drunk thing. And I said, "Okay." So I got on the phone, and I called the police. Ten minutes later, he calls me back: "Sam, would you please tell these police officers that it's okay for them to go?" I said, "Well, I don't know if it is or not. You said you were gonna kill yourself." He wanted me to drop everything and run over there. And I was saying no, this is not how you get me to come over and respond. But then obviously when he had the stroke, and he really did need help, I had just gotten over the whole thing. There was no longer a need to distance him or create boundaries because it was genuine. And I discovered or became aware of this sense of nobility. I felt like a noble person with him. It was because he was proud of me, and he just expressed that. This was a man who throughout my life hadn't really expressed that a lot.

Then I'm there with him. I'm holding his hand, and I'm whispering in his ear: "It's okay. You've lived a good life. You have no regrets. Try to relax. Imagine if you can that you're in a boat and you're floating down a river. And you can feel the warm sun on your face and . . . you're kind of dangling your hand into the cool water. And you can feel the cool water and the warm sun on your face. And you're just drifting slowly down the river. And you can smell the smell of lilacs in the air. And you're at peace, and it's very calm and very lazy." And as I'm telling him this, he dies.

Sam never would have guessed that he could have given this gift of peace to his father—this gift of helping him to let go and die peacefully. But in the process of his FC-talks and subsequent processing of his father's death, Sam realized that only through acceptance and acknowledgment could he and his father move forward. Because Sam told his father that he understood that he had done his best, that he forgave him, and that he loved him, his father was able to move to the next realm. These FC-talks also gave Sam's father an opportunity to accept and acknowledge Sam's gifts and successes. Witnessing his father's nonverbal behaviors, the pride on his father's face, and the way his father looked at him, Sam—a social worker and caregiver in his career—was able to accept the fact that he was a caregiver in this life. For years, being a caregiver meant to Sam that he was co-dependent. Originally, this seemed negative; Sam feared that he had let his father manipulate him, setting him up to be an "enabler." An enabler is someone who makes it possible for another to continue in self-destructive behavior (such as alcohol abuse) by providing excuses for the person, or by making it possible to avoid the consequences of such behavior. Following his FC-talks with his father, being a caregiver no longer had a negative connotation for Sam— it simply was one of his gifts.

There are times when the Living must accept the Dying and acknowledge their accomplishments, rather than pointing out all the ways that they have failed. And there are times when the Living need that same acceptance and acknowledgment from the Dying.

Blanca loved her father dearly, and while she did not have the horrible relationship that some of the Living had with a parent, she still had been hurt. She was relieved to resolve that pain before her dad died. All he said was, "You look just fine, you look just fine just the way you are." And he couldn't really see me because he was in and out, and his eyes were closed a lot.

It meant a lot to me because I had always felt like my sisters had more approval about their looks from him than I did. He would worry about me getting overweight because his sister had gone from Sophia Loren beautiful to very overweight—very overweight in my family, not very overweight to the rest of the world. But very overweight in my family. He wouldn't make cutting remarks or mean things like that, but he would comment on it. Mama and Daddy both would worry at different times about my weight. And it was kind of tiring. It hurt my feelings. And I always felt like I just wasn't good enough or something. So it just meant this huge amount that nobody else really gets in my family, because I, out of my whole family, I weigh the most . . . That acceptance of me as I am: I count. And not just like you're fine, you're okay. But you're beautiful as you are. You know, you are very beautiful. And it was just a release.

The aspect of approval of your father is so . . . People always talk about the mother and how everything was her fault; the child is good or bad because of the mother. But fathers are ridiculously important. Just as important and very powerful in a very different way. I know for daughters—I mean, I see it, I witness it—for daughters, they want their fathers to think they're pretty. It has to do with their relationships with men later on . . . Acceptance of you as you are—that was just as important for me as for anybody else. Realizing and acknowledging for myself how important my father's perception of me was, was really important. That final conversation solidified that part.

But that other part . . . Pretty is one thing, and being seen as a beautiful person is one thing, but I had always worked real hard for them to understand what I did for a living and value my intelligence. Daddy had had a hard time; he would just say I was book-smart. And that I was dressed book-smart . . . He had finally come to value what I did for a living and had come to understand me. Blanca is the first in her family to have a master's degree and is a counselor.

Not all FC-talk that offered relief occurred in a damaged relationship. Some of the Living simply mentioned bad moments or challenging issues between themselves and the Dying. In the next example, the relationship had been a loving one, but there were some areas of hurt that still needed to be released. FC-talk afforded the opportunity.

Victoria's FC-talk with her dying father acted as a bridge: between the ways they had previously handled their differences, and the new peace between them. Father and daughter found a way to acknowledge and accept their different ways of managing things and seeing the world. Victoria said that the transition began when her father first told her about his aneurysm and his grim prognosis. She said that, in his place, she would have accepted the inevitable. But her father wanted to fight death and to have a risky surgery that offered him a chance to live. Victoria's most meaningful FC-talk began with her father's decision: He said he wanted to try this, and he accepted the possibility of losing, and I did not disagree with him. He took control of his death. And it seemed like he was honoring me in telling me his reasons and not just saying, "None of your business." And I was honoring him by accepting it. Mutual respect was a big deal in my relationship with my father, and that conversation really played it out. I think all the conversations had echoes of that—where we sort of made decisions together along the way.

Unfortunately, Victoria's father had multiple complications following the risky surgery. It became clear that he was going to die, and one of the big things about the conversations in the last period was that I had had trouble with his long silences when we were younger, but now I sat in his room and did needlepoint, and was finally able to follow his pace and not feel rejected by the silences. That felt very good. The silences weren't because he was sick; that was just the way the man was. And I was very happy that before he died, I had reached an acceptance of that and no longer felt rejected by it. He was very grateful for my being there: my having taken time off from work to be there, my going down and getting him the Wall Street Journal or the strawberry ice cream that he wanted, all of that stuff during the period when he was doing well. And that felt really good to be able to be of help to him.

I always seem to know when death is imminent. And I just went and took his hand. I said, "I give you to the stars." And he died. I felt really good that even though he made a choice that was different than the choice I would have made, he did it on his terms. He lived on his terms, died on his terms. And again, because I went and stayed down there those six weeks and did the deal, I felt peaceful. I did what I could do for him, helped him go out. It felt pretty triumphant.

Releasing the emotional hold of a lifetime—or even a single instance—of negativity and hurt isn't easy. But it is possible. The

Living who acknowledge, accept, and forgive those who hurt them find freedom and peace.

Receiving the Surprise Apology

Sometimes, especially after the Living partner in a difficult relationship has found a way to release some of the pain, he or she receives a lovely reward—an apology.

Pinky was given the gift of an apology from her mother. She would never have received it if she hadn't given her mother something as well. Pinky was caring for her mother, perhaps mostly out of obligation. Despite cultural changes in gender roles, we still expect that mothers will take care of their babies, and more subtly, we still expect that daughters will take care of their dying parents. Pinky wasn't caring for her mother with the expectation that she would receive an apology; after all, she had never received an apology before. She was caring for her because she was supposed to do this job. Pinky begins her story by explaining a little about their relationship. My mom and I did not get along. My mom beat me. My father beat me . . . There was a lot of bad karma between my mom and me. [But during her final weeks and days] the wall kind of went down.

My mother had her chair that she sat in. And she'd point to her feet and ask, "Take them off, please." This was not my mother. My mother didn't say take them off. My mother wasn't this docile kind of a person, but now she was. She had these special shoes because she'd had some problems with her feet. So I would take off her shoes and massage her feet. That was a big deal for her. And she would just look at me. And I would just look at her. And again, this is somebody who—we didn't get along. We hadn't gotten along for a long time. A long time. But it didn't matter any more. I never massaged anybody's feet. And she had these calluses and whatnot . . . And I'd talk to her and just make conversation. I think it was kind of nervous at one point, and she said something like, "Tell me about your marriage." I thought, and I remembered she knew something wasn't right . . .

so I explained to her that it wasn't going well. And I cried. She just looked at me, and she said, "I'm sorry. I wish things were better. I'm sorry I wasn't a better mother." And that is worth 10,000 days of conversation.

We never had another conversation for the rest of my life or before—that was it. And that, more than anything, healed whatever was going on prior to any time . . . We did not have a good relationship for a lot of my life, but those simple words, "I'm sorry I wasn't a better mother" [made all the difference in the world]. My mother was the best mother that she could possibly be, given what she came into the world with. And I knew at that exact moment. I'm eternally grateful that I had that final conversation. Within a couple of days, she went into a coma. Although Pinky expected nothing in return for caring for her mother, she received a sincere apology that released her from the strictures of a lifetime of pain.

Laurie W also talked about a surprise resolution to a lifetime of strife between her and her mother. Laurie's mother, Mary, told her that she was sorry that she hadn't been there for me when I needed her. And we hadn't had the mother-daughter relationship that we could have had. And how nice it had been, we'd had the time lately after she'd stayed with me. And for me not to feel guilty for all the things that I had carried. And it was kind of a release. I knew she was going. I guess in my mind, I never thought this would ever be resolved.

In the end, it makes us wonder why saying the two simple words "I'm sorry" is so difficult for people, especially when there can be so much healing from those words. These messages of apology were long overdue, but at least they were finally given, and could contribute to the peace of the Living.

Closing a Door, Opening a Window

Not all family relationships are close, yet some people hope that impending death is the opportunity to set things right, and to make a family relationship what they want it to be. FC-talk may be seen as the last chance to get the relationship right. However, just because the Living one or the Dying one wants this to be so doesn't mean that it will happen. **Laurel's** experience shows that FC-talk does not satisfy all of one's wishes, but may create something new and unexpected. Laurel described her relationship with her brother, Reed, as one that had never been close, and they had become more alienated with time. I don't think we had an adverse—I mean, we didn't really hate each other or anything—but I don't ever remember being close with him . . . Reed had some—as I was older—some particular kind of grudge or something with me. And I don't know to this day really what it was . . . As his illness progressed, he began to get really crotchety.

During a visit, I noticed more and more that he was picking on me, and I tried to be mature about it . . . It became apparent that he was being mean especially to me. Not my sister, not my other sister, not my mom or anybody, but it was me. And I said one day to him, "I want to talk." I'd had enough and said, "I want to talk this out. I don't get why you're mad at me. What is this about?" Laurel reported that Reed didn't answer her and just grumbled at her some more.

However, he called her on the phone after she left the hospital. He said, "I don't want you to use psychology on me." And I wouldn't. I read such a point in my schooling, and my whole philosophy was that I was never going to do that . . . that it was invasive, and it was certainly unprofessional, and it was unkind—I just couldn't do that. I tried not to. I guess once in a while, it slips out when you're studying it all the time. I just wanted to talk to my brother about why he was being mean to me. He said, "I don't [want to talk about it]." So I explained that to him: "If I've ever come across that way, I'm sorry. I just want to know why you're treating me badly." He said, "Well, we've never been close." And I said, "Well, a lot of siblings aren't close. So what? That's not a big deal. I mean, it's one thing not to be close, but . . . I feel like you're being hostile towards me. And that's different. And I think it's unfortunately the case that a lot of siblings never really get close to each other. It's too bad, but it's not something you've never heard of." I tried to make that distinction and didn't try to dismiss what he said: that we were not close. "Because I know you're right. I haven't wanted it to be that way, and I don't know why it's that way." He said, "I just don't want to talk to you. Period. I just don't want to." . . . I can't remember what I said, but I just remember how deeply that hurt because it was so final.

I think he thought maybe it was phony. I do know this, that he thought that it's phony because people all of a sudden love you so much because you're sick. And he really didn't like phoniness of any kind. I didn't know what to say to that, because he was right. I probably wouldn't have been crying and making contact and trying to help and do what I could if he hadn't been so sick . . . so I didn't deny that or anything, but I was just saying, "Well, when things like this happen, it's like a wake-up call. And you do want to—maybe not fix relationships—but at least I want to show you some love, because I do love you. It's just not been, you know, expressed from either one of us." . . . He said, "I don't want to talk to you." So it was like a closing door.

Surprisingly, a month after her pleas to talk with him, Reed contacted Laurel. He called, and he said, "I don't want to talk to you." So that much didn't change. But he wanted to write his life story, because he knew he wouldn't meet his grandchildren because he wasn't going to survive it. We didn't know how it would end, so I was just so delighted that he made contact . . . I'm considered the writer of the family, and so I think that's why he came to me. But maybe it was in a way a sort of an apology . . . an offering . . . and I took it. I said, "I'd love to."

There were weeks when we met daily, and then there were weeks . . . I don't think there was a week that we met less than three times. We met a lot. And he would just talk about his life. And I'd record it. I'd prompt him. He's done some neat stuff . . . He was a metal sculptor. He was. And he actually made his own urn. A beautiful thing. I mean it was simple, ordinary, beautiful. And so, all of a sudden we were closer than we'd ever been. I really never could ask him what had happened between us because, I guess, I was just letting it, whatever it was, heal through this process. And it did to a great extent.

As Laurel and Reed demonstrate, some relationships find a way to create a new and even improved relationship at the end of life. This new relationship may be based on the needs and talents of both, rather than on duty, and it appears to be an unexpected, beautiful gift between the Dying and the Living. Regardless of the reason for these openings, we can almost hear a sigh of relief between the Living and the Dying as they experience a shift in their relationship.

Reed invited a new and different kind of relationship. Although he closed the door firmly on "fixing" the sibling bond, he opened a window by inviting Laurel to join him in forming a new bond between two creative people, based on their talents.

A different sort of opening is one that returns a relationship to a formerly healthy status. The door closed for Victoria and her mother, Josephine, as dementia took her mind. But a window opened during their last conversations, when Josephine displayed moments of surprising clarity. I think the important thing here is to know that my mother had been sinking into dementia for the last four or five years of her life . . . a lot of her last couple of years was pretty horrendous. And the conversations—it was really magical, or grace-filled to even have any conversations with her at all; most times she just didn't even talk. And when she did talk, a lot of it was really crazy. And then we would have interludes. I mean really crazy, like people were trying to kill her. Not just unusual, but really hallucinatory. So, this is really different from any of the other experiences I've had with people. I have had a number of experiences with people who'd been dying, and this is the only one in which the person had really been lost, for the most part, a good bit of the time before their death.

Mother was in a nursing home just a few blocks from my house. Every night, either my father or I went in and fed her supper. And the nights of the week I didn't feed her supper, I would go by for a good-night kiss. A lot of the time, there wasn't a whole lot that passed between us. But occasionally, there would be these spurts of lucidity. Mother and I had had a difficult relationship. I had never really been the daughter that she wanted. She wanted an extroverted cheerleader, someone who was pretty, someone really good in math and who went to medical school. I was too much the poet, too quiet. I think she worried about me a lot. She didn't understand how someone as unworldly as me would make it in the world. Yet as time passed, she became thankful for many of my qualities, even though she would say, "I don't understand this woman." But I married men that she would not have understood why I married. Many of my choices were very different. But in the end, she was proud. And I was very helpful to her a lot of times . . .

One [FC-talk that stands out] is the time that I spent the night with her when she was hospitalized for a bladder infection. She started talking about love and sex and passion, and the value of it. And how she was glad that I had that in my life even though she couldn't understand the choices I made in life. Victoria highlighted the most significant part of this FC-talk: when her mother talked about passion—it was just priceless because she hadn't said anything to me that had really made sense or reflected some of the more precious conversations that we had had when I was younger; it had been such a long time. And so that was like a last, totally unexpected gift. It was like our relationship used to be. So that was something that was really great to cherish and hold on to.

Laurel and Victoria each found a window to a better relationship with the Dying. For Laurel, it was something entirely new, and for Victoria, it was a return to a lovely, earlier version of the mother-daughter relationship. It may not have been what either woman expected, but it was what they each needed.

Don't Make It Worse

Let's say your relationship with the Dying was not terribly dysfunctional, but just irritating enough to fall into the normal range

of family spats. Often, the best you can do with a slightly negative, but not horrible, relationship is to not make it any worse.

Herschel had had his disagreements with his son, Douglas.
But now Douglas was dying of cancer, and Herschel knew they
needed to talk. *It's a chance to kind of make your peace and say your
final goodbyes . . . You want conversations. I guess in most cases, you
hope they end well. I would say that most of our conversations at the
end of his life were better than some of the conversations earlier,
when I'd get angry with him about things. So they didn't end in anger
or some other kind of unpleasant emotions. I wouldn't say it was all
pleasant—it certainly wasn't. But at least anger wasn't generally
present or saying something that you kind of regretted. I didn't have
too many of those.*

The group of Living who had troubled relationships with the
Dying talked about the importance of not making things worse.
A cynic might think that the Living don't want to add to their own
guilt by worsening the situation when someone is near death. But
the Living gave us the impression that they genuinely did not
want to be a part of any more hurt in these relationships. They did
what many of us can't do: They overcame their own anger and disappointment, and they did not demand an apology or a reckon-
ing of the Dying one's bad behavior. They risked being hurt again
by being vulnerable and open to FC-talk. In their vulnerability,
they were able to let go and release their heartache, thereby freeing themselves to move on without regrets, without the chains of
anger and pain that bound them to the Dying for so long.

Benefits of Heartache-Released Messages

Accepting and Forgiving

Many of the Living discovered that they needed to accept the
Dying for who they were—flawed, imperfect human beings who
made mistakes in their lives. By accepting that the Dying did the
best they could, the Living were able to forgive the hurt and pain

inflicted on them. Victoria states that the importance of her FC-talk with her mother had everything to do with *being able to be the one who was there at the end, to be able to put a cap on my forgiveness and acceptance of her.*

Similarly, **Wallace** accepted the reality of his marriage and the way that Marie, his wife, had treated him during their last years together. He spoke of the improvements in their relationship that followed the acceptance and forgiveness their FC-talk brought out. *Our relationship for the last, maybe two years, before we knew she was dying, was distant. And then there was a vast improvement once the doctors said, "You're done for." You know? She apologized for what she had done to our marriage and so on. And of course, I forgave her. I was never mad at her to begin with. I just couldn't understand it. Our relationship changed, and it was much better for the last four, four and a half months she lived after she was diagnosed with cancer.*

Letting Go

Hanging on to piles of anger and resentment makes for a heavy load. In their FC-talks, the Living found a way to release excess baggage collected over a lifetime of disappointment, hurt, and anger. Holland said, *It took a burden off my shoulders. Because by telling her I forgave her—I remember mentioning to her I forgave her for everything and there weren't any bad feelings—I was releasing a lot of the power she had over me and taking the burden off a lot of things she said, because even memories are burdens.*

When asked what the FC-talk did for her, Pinky replied that it was *sanitizing. It needed to happen. And I don't think it could've happened [without the impending death]. It had never happened before; we'd never approached that.*

Moving Forward

Difficult relationships have a way of keeping people stuck—stuck in the muck of resentment, rage, and rancor that can overwhelm us when those who are supposed to be closest to us have hurt us. Think back to a time when someone really hurt you. It was difficult to think about anything else, it was impossible to do the things you enjoyed, and it felt heavy on your body—like a ton of bricks. You may have felt stuck, simply immovable. You probably thought there was nothing you could do to make yourself feel better. And once you felt hopeless, the pain got tucked away to be joined by other insults later on. And so forth. Is it possible to avoid stuffing our duffels with negative emotion? You can't change the person who hurt you, but you *can* choose how you will react to hurtful situations—even if in those emotional moments, it doesn't feel like you can. You can choose to blame the other person and harbor resentment, or you can talk about how both parties fed the situation.

The Living who spoke to us recognized that the only way to move forward was to get out from under those heavy loads of negative emotion. Thankfully, they recognized that FC-talk was a last opportunity to get unstuck with the Dying. In the instances they described to us, although the Dying didn't initiate the conversations, they opened to cleansing and healing communication. Both the Dying and the Living were finally able to move on to their new paths.

Summary
FC-Talks and Heartache Released

Almost everyone has some kind of heartache to release. After all, almost every close relationship can be challenging from time to time. If, as the Living one, your relationship with the Dying one has not been consistently difficult, you can choose either to focus on the positive and not make it worse, or to clear the air of minor grievances. If on the other hand, you have had a very painful relationship with the Dying, you will find models among the Living who show compassion, forgiveness, and release in the face of death. They remind us what the human spirit is capable of accomplishing.

We aren't telling the Living that they **must** initiate FC-talk with someone who has hurt them. Each person has to decide what's possible or worth the risk. The Living who spoke with us were glad they did take the risk and did have the difficult talk. And based on our combined forty-four years of teaching interpersonal communication, we believe that for damaged relationships, the risk is worth the healing.

We're all aware that we fail each other at times. Some of the Living simply cannot be vulnerable to the Dying, ever again. And some FC-talks will probably fail miserably to achieve the Living's goals. We wish we could tell you without a doubt that all FC-talks are good and positive, but we can't make that guarantee. There are costs and benefits to every communication. Only you know the costs and benefits in your relationship. So only you can decide whether the possible benefits outweigh the probable costs.

Cleaning up messes is never fun. In reality, cleaning up is something that no one looks forward to doing, but the benefits are usually worth the trouble. Some of the Living experienced their FC-talks as healing acts. For others, FC-talk marked only the beginning of their healing journey. We guess that some FC-talks have resulted in negative, even costly outcomes for others of the Living. Since these people understandably chose not to tell us about their FC-talks—maybe because it hurt too much to relive them—we can't say for sure what these conversations were like.

Anger, hurt, and resentment are not uncommon feelings in families and close relationships. Those who are closest to us have the greatest opportunity to hurt us. What no one teaches us is that these negative emotions often hurt us more than they hurt the person who inflicted them. Letting go of this pain is the only way to move on to healthier relationships and happier lives. FC-talk at the end of life with the one who has caused the harm is one way for you to begin healing. If it is not possible, we strongly urge you to talk with a professional about the pain you still hold inside before it can cause any more damage.

Advice from the Living

♥ Release the power that your anger and resentment have over you by once and for all letting go of your baggage with the Dying.

♥ Be prepared for negativity. The Dying don't become angels just because they are at death's doorstep. Set some boundaries, if necessary, to protect yourself.

♥ Be fully present as much as you are able. Feel the emotions you want to express with the Dying. This is your chance to heal.

♥ Forgive. This decision is the most powerful one you can make in the face of hurt and pain. Forgive the Dying so they can let go; forgive them so you can move on.

♥ If you think that FC-talk will be too difficult for you or for the Dying, then your healing may have to begin after the Dying is gone. Get help.

♥ Don't be afraid to work with a grief counselor. FC-talk does not heal all wounds; it just begins the healing process for many of the Living.

♥ Set yourself up to look back with compassion and move forward with no regrets.

CHAPTER 7

Growing Up

Maturing Through Final Conversations

*I grew up really, really fast. I went from a
15-year-old girl to a 25-year-old woman
in a week . . . I was just in such a different
place from everybody else, emotionally and
spiritually . . . It was a crash course in
adulthood, really. [Karen]*

Talking with someone who is dying changes you. It changes the
way you view your own mortality, and it changes your sense of the
stability of relationships. It can change the way you view yourself
in the world.

- *Children* have a very difficult time understanding the finality
  of death. They often feel that the inevitable abandonment by
  the Dying is somehow their fault. They require special assistance in coping with the death of a loving caregiver.

- *Teenagers* understand the nature of death better than younger
  children do, but they must make a real effort to empathize
  with the Dying's need for closeness and closure. When they
  do make that effort, they are rewarded with changes in their
  perception of themselves and others.

- *Older teens and new adults* are facing their own challenges of
  serious relationships, continuing education, and beginning
  careers and families. Although the concerns of the Dying are

normally far from their thoughts, the Living young adults who engage with the Dying find that they can gain new insights into their own character and into what kind of adults they want to be.

- For *mature adults,* death is increasingly something to consider, for themselves and their friends. Older Living ones who take on FC-talk with the Dying learn not only about the dying process, but also about how they want to live the rest of their days.

Children's Final Conversations with the Dying: Being Real

Children don't know much about death; they gradually get clues about it and begin to consider it more seriously at puberty. Most of us don't have to consider how death affects us early in life. But some do. In today's ocean of electronic media, young children flounder with the task of separating the real from the make-believe, particularly when faced with media images of violence and death. Children who live with a dying relative every day have the opportunity to learn that hard reality early in life.

Ruth's father died when she was 5. Now, at 21, she recalls his care for her as he died of cancer. What's critical to very young children is their bond of trust with parents. Ruth's father, Kerry, seemed to know intuitively that to die without explaining his leaving could destroy this trust: It could greatly damage Ruth's ability to form later relationships. Ruth recalled the last time she spoke with him. He essentially just said to me that he wanted to die. Not because he wanted to leave us or anything, but because he wasn't afraid to die. I just remember him being really, really, really, really happy to be alive, and really, really not all that upset to be dying . . . just like it was the next natural step. I remember at the very end he would say things like, "I want to die. I don't want to leave you. I'm not scared. You don't need to be scared, everything's natural." It was like he was trying to free me of being angry at God. And I don't know why I didn't get angry at Dad. Now I would think, "Oh, you want to die. You bastard." But I didn't; I just thought, "OK, that's the way it's supposed to be. Sure." And that was just totally natural—him telling me he was going to die. I don't remember being told he had cancer, I don't remember knowing it was coming—it was just like every day had been the way Dad had said it was supposed to be. And this was the next thing Daddy said was supposed to happen.

Ruth trusted her father to know how the world worked. Her father was at peace with his life and his death. Ruth explained how she felt. I felt happy. I mean I felt happy, I felt hugged, kept secure. My dad was essentially telling me he'd always be there permanently, and it wasn't until I was a teenager that I figured out my dad dying was weird. So at that point, I didn't know it was weird, I didn't know it was bad. He just gave it to me so factually: "I'm going to die, and it's okay," that he decided it was okay and I just felt that from him; I thought it was fine. I felt content with that.

As she reflected now at the age of 21, Ruth was grateful for her father's ability to take care of her as he died in dignity. I'm amazed. He was a great dad when he was alive. And he was a great dad when he was dying, and I feel like that was the exact right thing for him to say. And I think he really meant it too; I don't think he was faking it. I'm just ultimately impressed that he was protecting us until the end. There was like an absolute lack of guilt, which I think is kind of odd now as an adult. I would almost have to apologize to my child, "I'm sorry I'm dying, I'm sorry I'm going to leave you alone." And he didn't do that. I've been trying to figure out what that means the last three or four years. I guess it feels like an ultimate vote of confidence that he thought we'd be okay. I got the sense that he was in awe of us and impressed by us, and that we were magic, and that he would be there.

Ruth told us several times that her father did everything to let her know that his death was not her doing. He was wise to do so. Young children, in their egocentrism, often feel responsible for the things that happen around them and affect their world, such as one parent leaving (for whatever reason, e.g., divorce, career, illness). And because children are so willing to fulfill a loving parent's expectations, feeling some guilt following the death of a parent—*for* the death of the parent—is almost inevitable.

The remembered impressions and residual expectations of a deceased parent can no longer change over time, as a living parent's expectations can. Later in her life, Ruth would feel some guilt for not living up to her father's view of her as his wonderful child: My perceptions about me weren't greatly impacted at the time because he did a lot of ego reassurance. "You're wonderful, you're wonderful, you're wonderful." And now, I guess there's still a little 5-year-old part of me that still thinks that way. I know my daddy loves me and is so proud of me, but I know it gave me huge trouble when I was a teenager. We were all being bad, horrid, mean, selfish things when we were teenagers, and I always thought, Oh my God, my dad's looking down from heaven right now. He wouldn't even recognize me. I would so disappoint him, and I'm not a little girl with ribbons in my hair. And I'd be crying and crying and crying and crying. Because I'd let down my dad. So I guess that final conversation gave me this huge expectation to live up to. Which is kind of interesting. I mean, I don't think he meant it as a final guilt trip. But it kind of was. I felt a lot of guilt for not remembering him more.

When a young child loses a parent, there are inevitable repercussions in later life, such as distrust of enduring relationships or confusion about how to be what the absent parent expected. As Ruth said, Everything changes when your father dies when you're 5. If you're 5 and your father dies, you should feel completely like your world is rocked and everything is shaken and you no longer are in the way that you've come to expect life to be. But because of the things he said to me—he said, "It's time for me to die, and I want to die, and I'm curious about dying, and I'm going to go be a good father to other people, and help them die and help them be born"—I didn't feel bad, I didn't feel broken, I didn't feel like our lives had been inalterably changed in a bad way. So as a result of his conversation, I expected it. But as a result of his death, I only had one parent. Death itself does change a child's life. The best that the Dying can do is love and talk until the end, and assure the child that he or she will be surrounded by love and support from the remaining caregivers after the Dying is gone.

Dana W also lost her father, but a little later in her life. He was first diagnosed with a brain tumor when Dana was 8, and he finally lost his battle when she was 12. She had quite a lot of time to prepare for his death. Eventually, her father's disease worsened to the point where he couldn't talk but could still interact. Dana visited him regularly in the hospital, and as she related to us, these unusual interactions became the norm for her. She recalled feeling duty-bound and experiencing some resentment about missing out on childhood's usual freedoms. *The information revolved around "I love you." And I always thanked him for how much he taught me. I always told him that I would never forget him. That I would always remember him. And after doing it every Sunday, and usually a night during the week, and sometimes on Saturdays, it became really rote. Especially for an 11- or 12-year-old, when you have to learn something and you do it again and again, it's like a script. I remember many times thinking [SIGH], This could be the last time I'm talking with my dad and I sound like a script. Because I knew what a script was. I'd been in plays and memorized my lines to the Dancing Pumpkin, and that's not how I wanted it to be. My capacity for word choice was limited, and I didn't know exactly what I wanted to say. And then there were times where I thought, Okay, if I could just say goodbye to my dad now, I get to go home and meet my friends for ice cream later. There were some feelings of resentment because I was missing out on my some of my socialization with my friends.*

Dana's feeling of "missing out" on things that other kids her age were doing is fairly common for a child who is losing a parent. Such loss involves the child emotionally, and in doing so, it interrupts her young life. It can be difficult for children to admit—or effectively deal with—the frustration they may experience during a long journey towards death. Fortunately, Dana's mother, Ellen, had asked counselors about the best way to prepare her children for their father's death. Ellen (who also told us her story) made sure her children knew that interaction with their father was important, even after interaction became challenging. Dana said, *My mom was, and is, very focused on communication, and talking, and the process. We were little, and we were getting, "This is important, and this is why it's important," and the value of "having these final words with your father because you never know when he is going to die."* So Dana continued, even though the interactions were difficult and repetitive for a pre-teen, and the meaning of her script at times seemed to fade. Today, as an adult, Dana can acknowledge her childhood frustrations with parts of the FC-talk, yet she is very grateful for the communication that her mother encouraged.

Dana described more of the challenges she and her dad had to overcome in their FC-talk. *My dad listened a lot, and I did more of the talking, especially when he was sicker and couldn't talk. And then he had a tracheotomy and had a device—it was just a toy from the toy store that made a mechanical robotic sounding voice. And so we still communicated. And then it was pictures. He had a laminated sheet of icons and numerals and the alphabet, and common words and phrases. He would point, and I would talk.*

For a while, I just felt like I did a lot of "I'll always remember you, I'll always take you with me wherever I go. Thank you so much for all I've learned, I'll try to keep your values in my heart." And I just felt like I sounded like a repeating tape. Because it was so often. So I tried to vary it because I knew that if it felt insincere, then it probably was. Not that I didn't mean those messages, but that what I was saying—it was true—but it sounded the same week after week. It didn't have the initial meaning that it had the first time I said it. So I tried to think of new things to say. Especially when Mom would say, "Okay, guys, we're going to be leaving in ten or fifteen minutes. Make sure you each have your time with Dad." At that point, I already was thinking, Okay, I have to remember, say something new so that Dad remembers something new. And the final conversations consisted of "Hey, Dad, I got an A on the big paper"—the type of information that is timely for an 11- or 12-year-old.

Dana's father made a point of telling her what she meant to him. This was crucial for her, poised as she was at the brink of adolescence. Dana recalled vividly her dad's messages: *He thanked me for being me, for being a blessing for him. That was really special because, even though I heard it also from my family, I knew that my dad would not always be with me. And so, hearing that from my father was extremely important, especially as a child and a pre-teen.*

Dana was left with healthy feelings about herself, about her father, and about death. *Not to be morbid, but when each day is going to be our last . . . I mean you always hear people say, "Well, you don't know when you're going to die—you could get hit by a truck." Yeah, knock on wood, we're not getting hit by trucks, but you don't know. Because life is so uncertain, and it's so precious simultaneously. I had the chance to say goodbye to my father. Many people don't. To a lover, a parent, a child, a sibling, a best friend, a lot of times it just happens. You're here, and then all of a sudden an accident arises or "Oh my God, they're in a coma!" and you didn't get the opportunity to say goodbye. So even though I only had twelve years with my father, I wouldn't trade them for some of the relationships my friends have with their parents now. Because I had twelve really strong, solid years.*

I said a really, really good goodbye. I said what I meant. I told him I loved him. And that I'll always love him—that I'll keep him in my heart. That was something, a phrase I always used. I felt like if he passed away in the night or the next day and I didn't see him, then I would still know that I was complete. That feeling of completeness aided in my grief tremendously, because we had months and months of preparation that he was going to die.

Dana not only had the support of her parents, she benefited from professional counseling as well. There, she was helped to prepare to have no regrets about her goodbyes to her father. *I was in* therapy with a little support group of eight other 12-year-olds who all lost or were losing their fathers. And we all had to talk about it. My brother was in art-and-play therapy with little 3- and 4-year-olds. So we talked about it, and we talked about it, and we talked about it. Until we were back talking about it again. Because there had been so much of that emotional communication, I was prepared when he passed away. And I always felt like that final conversation could be my last, so I needed to take it. I didn't want to feel guilty or upset that *Oh, I should*—I didn't want any *should'ves*. At 12, that was very important. I didn't want *should'ves*. Because I knew, I may not have them at 12 or 15 or 20, and I don't want *should'ves* when I'm 50 or 60 or 70. Mom would say, "Say it. You're not going to hurt anybody's feelings. Say what's on your mind. Speak your mind." And so I did.

When asked about the lessons she took away from those conversations, Dana recalled, The main one was about being happy. And the other one was about living life to its fullest. Because life is so precious. I think that I try to always acknowledge people, because during that final conversation I had to continually acknowledge him, and who I am, and who he is, and what his meaning is to me and vice versa. Because Dana had the gifts of time and loving adult support, she came through her father's death with good memories of him and a healthy sense of herself and her place in the world. She will come through life's challenges, such as job interviews and marriage, by seeing herself through her father's eyes.

Jeanette was 18 when she recalled for us the death of her Grandfather Weber six years earlier. He was much more than a typical grandfather to her. After her father left the family, it expanded to include her maternal grandparents. On the face of it, this new living situation was established so Jeanette's mother could help care for her own mother, who had multiple sclerosis. But the fortunate side effect was that Grandfather Weber became the father figure that Jeanette and her sister needed. My grandfather spent half the time with us and the other half in his house in L.A. And then every summer I'd go to L.A. with him. So we were very close.

Then, when Jeanette was 12, her grandfather was suddenly sick. One night he couldn't walk. His breathing was getting so bad. My mom took him to the hospital, and he died in the hospital a month later. He was very upset that it happened that way. But I know I was sort of glad because if I hadn't had that month . . . I'd go to school in the morning and then I'd come to the hospital and sit with him. I just wanted him to know that he'd been really important in my life. I mean, I'd always known that he was that important to me. I think it more affected my relationship with my father, because I actually had to come to terms with the fact that he wasn't as important in my life.

On the brink of puberty, Jeanette began to realize how special her grandfather was to her, and that it was up to her to let him know. He was very quiet and sort of stoic. He said that he loved you, but he didn't elaborate. I think it was the first time that I got to tell him how much he meant to me. I mean, he knew, but I really wanted him to know just how much he'd done for me. As a teenager looking back, Jeanette is grateful for that opportunity to say what she felt, because she has already recognized that you hide feelings from yourself.

One distinctly personal outcome that Jeanette noted from this experience was the insecurity it produced in her. I know that it made me look at my grandmother, who had been getting even worse, and I started thinking, What have I told her? And then, my mother and my sister. Especially since it happened so suddenly—I hadn't known at all that he was sick—I started thinking, What's going to happen to everyone else that I love?

Children will react in a variety of ways to the death of a loved one, depending on their age, their relationship to the Dying, and the experience they are allowed to have of the death. For some, the death of someone so close may produce insecurity and guilt. But children who have time with the Dying, and who receive affirmations of love from them, can gain new appreciation for the relationship they had and for the self they are becoming.

Teens' Final Conversations: A Crash Course in Adulthood

Teenagers are typically ego-centered. And that's a good thing. They are finding out who they are, what they think, how they feel, and what they want to do about it. But teens faced with the death of a dear one are challenged to consider someone else before themselves. Unlike young children, teens have considered the meaning of death and mortality. If they do rise to the occasion and wish to interact with their loved one, they can feel resentful about the time and effort it takes to engage in FC-talk. If they don't communicate, they can feel guilty. Either way, it's stressful and life-changing, and can propel teens into maturity before their time.

Karen was 38 years old when she talked with us, but she remembered clearly her father's death from lymphoma when she was a teen. Eight months after his diagnosis, his pain was so great that he knew he'd have to go back to the hospital to die. I was 15 at the time . . . My dad was in the bed, and we all wanted to sit down and say goodbye. And it was so nice that we were in our home, that it smelled like home, and it felt like home, and it didn't smell like a hospital. I don't remember how long the whole experience lasted. I do remember my father saying that he loved us and how proud he was of us. For Karen, this message stayed with her through the ensuing decades and greatly influenced her own beliefs about love and faith. I guess I've got a lot of my self-esteem from knowing how much my dad loved me. Even though he wasn't with me anymore, I have that. I remember in college, every girl's got some kind of daddy issue. They didn't get enough affection—and my issue was my dad died, and he was no longer there. But in the time that he was with me, I got so much of what I needed.

Karen admitted that losing her father interrupted her adolescence and propelled her toward premature adulthood. And that experience gave her a perspective that differed from her peers'. I grew up really, really fast. I went from a 15-year-old girl to a 25-year-old woman in a week. It was just at the end of my freshman year of high school. I can remember sitting at football games and stuff, and looking at the cheerleader girls going, "Daddy, Daddy, take my picture." And I'm thinking, *You just don't know . . . you just don't know what you have.* I was just in such a different place from everybody else, emotionally and spiritually, having gone through this experience. It was a crash course in adulthood, really.

Following her father's death, Karen became a bit wild during her teen years and was thankful that she didn't suffer any negative consequences from her rebellious acts. She still believes that it was the death that propelled her into her wild actions, but she also believes it was the FC-talk that helped her find her eventual peace. As Karen wrote to us after the interview, FC-talk is not a prophylactic for reactive behavior, but it can offer some comfort in the moment and upon reflection in the years that follow. Her father's legacy of love sustained Karen through her abbreviated adolescence and propelled her toward feeling older and wiser, but perhaps a bit cheated of her teen years.

Claire, now 26, was 17 when her Uncle Matthew died of AIDS. She vividly recalled being a typical, self-involved teenager. And, as clearly, she remembered her uncle's forgiveness and wisdom. Matthew had been an energetic psychiatric nurse before the disease began to incapacitate him. He had wanted to make a special event of Claire's completion of a bike ride for charity. But it wasn't meant to be. When we came across the finish line, he was there along with our parents, and that was a happy time. But I remember focusing in on him. For the first time, I had seen him not being positive. He really was in pain. I remember he lay down on this little bench, and he was complaining, "Oh, I'm in so much pain." And it was horrible because my mom and I were both frustrated. We didn't know how to respond to it. Anger was the first thing that came out instead of sympathy. Here it was a happy time, but instead it was like, "You should be in bed; you need to be resting." And it wasn't the right reaction at all. I remember he wanted to do everything perfect. He got a room at the Hyatt Regency downtown and wanted us all to spend the night. We went to the hotel, and he was upstairs. I didn't even go up there, but my mom had gone up to speak to him. And I will always regret that I never went up there to talk to him.

Claire's uncle had some insight into the mindset of a teenager and made sure he spoke with her later about the botched party. Undoubtedly, his background in psychology helped him to understand, but it was his affection for his niece that led him to forgive her for the failed celebration. Instead of me bringing it up and saying, "Oh, Uncle Matt, you know, I'm so sorry about this," he was the one who brought it up. He was very strong about it. He wasn't tiptoeing around the subject; he just said, "You know, I don't know what happened back there, but I don't want you to have any guilt. I'm going to be gone, and you're going to have to go on. So I just want to tell you whatever happens, you remember, I don't want you to have any guilt." He was more than understanding: "Well, you know, you're young, and I understand." After that, I had told him, "I am just so sorry. I'm sorry." And he said, "I don't want to hear that. I forgive you. It's okay."

Matthew knew that youngsters can hang on to guilt about their real and imagined failings, so he nipped Claire's in the bud. He went on to share with her a slice of his value system, including self-acceptance, strength, and a deep belief in the value of education. Claire remembered, I was 17, and my insecurities were about being pretty enough, or too fat, you know? I don't think there's ever been another person that talked to me about that. He says, "I'm glad you're talking to me about these things. Because nobody is going to be as blunt with you as I am. And I hope that you remember what I have to tell you. Because I am the only one that can leave you with this." And he said, "You have your whole life to live. Look at me! I don't have the rest of my life. And if I can leave you with any of these things, I want you to find happiness in life, and not to spend so much time worrying." He would always say, "You're worrying way too much. You're wasting your life away by worrying." And I truly am my own worst enemy. I think it just ate him up that he saw so much potential and . . . these are his words: "You're killing yourself. You know, I don't think you even have any idea how beautiful you are. And it just makes me sick to see you doing this to yourself."

Matthew pointed out the flaws in Claire's self-perceptions and then set her up to take over for him: "Well, honey, you know you have to be your own best friend. You have to." Those words are so powerful, but yet, I don't follow. I try to sometimes. But that was probably the most important, because it is something that I have to deal with every day. I could send myself into a frenzy if I allowed myself to, and so I always think, *Well, what would Uncle Matthew say?* I know what he would say: "Don't you ever get your breasts butchered." One time he said, "Go stand in the mirror right now." And he said, "Look at yourself. You are beautiful. You have beautiful breasts. You have to stop this. Stop this self-destruction." He said, "You know, I was dyslexic. When I was in elementary school, they would tell me I was dumb and I couldn't read. Well, look at me now. I'm a registered nurse. I work in the psychiatric department. And honey, I failed that class three times. I forced myself to read." He said, "So, you know, you've got it easy. And whenever you feel like you can't do something, you have to make up your mind. You have to force yourself to do it. Because you're telling yourself you can't do it."

Which messages have stayed with Claire from Uncle Matthew? "Don't feel guilty about feeling good" and "You can never learn too much." She clearly has been affected greatly by them. Claire didn't have the best self-esteem, but her uncle wanted to change that. And he had some success in shifting her self-awareness. In fact, she acknowledged during our interview that she has continued almost daily to reflect on what he said. I believe that for him, it wasn't just about looks—it was about anything that I did. One of his dreams was to take me to Paris. He wanted us to open up our eyes and be educated. He wanted us to know about different foods, about different art. He would always say, "You can never learn too much. You're always learning." He would, I know, be very angry with me if, number one, if I said, "I can't," and number two, if I was embarrassed for something that I should be proud of. Claire's self-image has continued to improve on the basis of the gifts of approval and encouragement that Matthew gave her.

Teenagers may be self-involved, but they are also immersed in a time of great personal change and sensitivity to the uniqueness of others. Indeed, the death of a loved one can compel them to look at the world from the Dying's viewpoint. They may have regrets about what they did or didn't do during the dying process. But they will remember the needs of the Dying that they were able to meet, and they will remember their own needs that were met by the Dying. And they will come to see themselves as different from their carefree peers, but grateful for the chance to participate in the Dying's end time.

New Adults' Final Conversations: Challenges in Changing Times

Perhaps the busiest and most challenging time of life, early adulthood is a time of action, reflection, and change. Typically, as teens graduate from secondary school, they move on to higher education, training, or a job. No matter what path is taken, the challenge is mastery—of skills, of concepts, of a body of knowledge. With mastery comes accomplishment; with accomplishment comes responsibility; and, of course, with responsibility comes reflection on how to make good decisions. New adults are challenged to figure out what they will stand for. They are building character, and they can be merciless perfectionists. This makes having FC-talk—something they most likely have never practiced or studied—a daunting prospect. But those new adults who do it anyway may discover that being perfect isn't as important as being human.

Tory was 21 when her 19-year-old brother, Jacob, died. The diagnosis of leukemia had been a long time coming after months of symptoms. The leukemia was actually in remission when he suffered a brain hemorrhage from the effects of chemotherapy. Even though he was the younger sibling, Tory looked up to her brother as smart, generous, and forgiving. One tangible reason for her admiration is that Jacob had fathered a son when he was 16, and had nurtured and loved his young family until his death. Tory spent as much time as she could with Jacob during his last months, including hours talking together on her bed.

I asked, "So, what are you going to miss about me?" And he said, "I am going to miss the fact that . . .," he goes, "well, I'm not really going to miss you because I'll be able to see you anyway." But he went on, "The fact that you don't understand jokes. You don't get the punch line. I'm not sure you have common sense, Tory," he would always tell me. And I said, "If you explain it to me, I will." He says, "That's not the point about a joke—you're supposed to get it. I shouldn't have to explain it to you." I said, "Well, sorry, I'm a little slow" and "Well, that's not really something deep or emotional." He goes, "I'm going to miss the fact that you always have a Band-Aid for my wounds." And that's what he told me. And I was kind of stopped. I said, "I didn't realize that I did anything like that for you."

The fact that he said that I was the bandage for his wounds . . . I think that was the most meaningful part of that conversation because all that time, I had thought that I was more needy of him than he was of me. I would always show him my vulnerability more than he would show me his, I guess because he thought he had to be the pillar of strength. He would always say that he was my big-little brother, because he was taller than me. So I think that he really wanted to take on that role. And I think that's why it was more mean-ingful that he said that.

He also said that he was the only one born the appropriate race. We are full-blooded Hispanic, Mexican-American. He said, "Tory should have been a blond-headed white girl, because she never gets the joke. She has to have everything organized. And she wants to have the Better-Homes-and-Gardens life when she grows up." And my sister Rebecca—we call her Becca—"she should just have been black, because she's so ghetto." So, that was his theory on our family. He was the only one born the appropriate race. And, of course, we all had our input on that, all the time. And when one of us would fall into that category, he'd be like, "I told you so."

Tory the perfectionist became Tory the nurturer. When she saw herself reflected in her brother's perceptual mirror, Tory discovered several things about herself: That I'm not as cold-hearted as I may seem. That I'm a good listener. I think that he would be proud to know that I try so hard to take care of his child. I think he would be glad to know that he picked a good person to be his son's godparent. I try to talk to his son about him. I think he felt better that if something happened to him, things wouldn't be that chaotic.

Now 25, Tory is still being changed by this relationship. I think I have more to say. I think I share more. I think I love more. I think I'm not as reserved. Her brother still has a profound effect on who she is . . . and she wants to preserve that influence for as long as she can. Tory has also remained faithful to her vow to help watch over Jacob's son. She is active in his life on a weekly—sometimes daily—basis, and she continues to keep her brother alive in his son's eyes through the stories that she tells him and through her reflection of his character.

Breanna was 25 when she said goodbye to her 76-year-old grandmother, Imogene. Breanna was a favorite of her doting Nana, so she did her best to care for her during her decline. Breanna spoke about her relationship with Imogene during their FC-talks: I think in a way it cemented what I thought—how special we were, and had that bond that we had with each other. It's a huge family. There's like fifteen grandchildren. And it was special to me to know that I was special to her out of all of those. You know? I felt some guilt because she did so much for me. I feel like I should've taken care of her more. No, I mean physically be there, take care of her. Because I had problems with my parents when I was in high school, and I lived with her for a while. And she bought me a car and took care of me. And I wouldn't have finished high school if it wasn't for her. She believed in me when nobody else did. And my mom—I think that my mom knew that I was feeling that way because she said, "Tell her whatever you want to tell her, because it's okay and she'll understand."

But there were so many things I really wanted to say. And then I felt self-conscious because there were other people in the room. It was like I never got a chance, but things would go through my mind that I wouldn't say. And I kept thinking, *Why didn't I say that?* And then I'd think, *Well, the next day. When she wakes up, I'll say it.*

Breanna admitted that she kept putting off what she really felt was right in order to present a particular impression. Young adults are quite concerned with their place in the community, and how they fit in. Usually they find their unique voice later in life. But Breanna recognized the need to break out of her passive response at this critical time. I think I saw myself as being a little bit timid because I wouldn't assert myself to say what I wanted to say, or even want to take my place beside her when somebody else was there . . . feeling like maybe I'm not so important, and I need to leave the room so that somebody else can be with her. But inside I was thinking, *I want to be right with her the whole time. I don't want to leave.* Other people might say, "No, I'm not going to leave," or "I'm not going to move," when I would be the one that says, "Okay, do whatever you want."

Breanna recalled a history of being teased by her family for being "prissy." She explained that the teasing bothered her, even though she admitted she had earned the reputation by being particular. But Imogene defended and soothed her in a way that no one else did. I don't really want to see myself as being picky and prissy, and "this is the way I want it." When I was young, I got this Strawberry Shortcake little sleeping bag for Christmas. All my cousins were sitting on it, and they were video recording us sitting there. I was telling everybody to "get off my sleeping bag. Get off. You're gonna mess it up. You're gonna ruin it." But, through all that, Nana was always taking up for me. She always said, "Oh, it's okay, don't worry." I remember telling my mom after she died, "Who's going to stick up for me? Who's going to understand me in the way that she understood me?" And my mom said something about, "Oh, well, I'm going to have to be a better mother." I said, "No, you're a great mother. That's not the point." It's just that she always made me feel better. Imogene left a hole in Breanna's life that she had to learn to fill for herself. Still age 25 when she spoke with us, Breanna is now defending her rights and her character just as her grandmother used to do for her.

New adults are often hard on themselves for their lack of "perfection" in handling FC-talk. This response is understandable, given how important it is to them to see themselves positively in relationship to the Dying, and indeed to anyone. The Living new adults saw themselves more clearly in the mirrors of their loved ones and felt shifts in their self-images.

Mature Adults' Final Conversations: Role Changes and Getting Real (Again)

Adulthood covers a range of ages and changes, but most of the mature adults we spoke with were middle-aged when they talked with a dying child, spouse, or parent. Middle-aged adults know who they are; they have faced many of life's challenges already. But they may not have faced the loss of one so dear to them. And what they found was that the process forced them not only to shift their view of the relationship, but also to shift their view of who they are and how they want to spend the rest of their days.

Remember Tory, who lost her 19-year-old brother, Jacob? We also heard from **Gloria**, who is Tory's mother. She recalled how Jacob helped her to see some of her talents and capabilities. He said, "Mom, I want you to go back to school . . . That's where you belong." He says, "You and I need to be lawyers. So that way, we can help people, help children, help women." He said, "I want you to go back to school." And I told him, "With everything that's happened, Jacob, I don't know if I can." He says, "Mom, just go. What did you tell me, Mom? When we first found out that I have leukemia, you said we're fighters. You're a fighter, Mom."

Near the end of Jacob's time, he was affected by seizures. This last bad sign destroyed Gloria's composure. "What's wrong?!" His hand started shaking, and he started laughing. And then he went into a seizure. I'm one of those people that has to be in control. I have to be on top of things. But I lost it. Rebecca [Gloria's second daughter] was four months pregnant, and she was sitting there holding his hand, and she said, "Mom, snap out of it." And I ran out into the street and I screamed. I knew what to do, because my little daughter is mentally retarded and had seizures. I knew what to do. But I couldn't do it. And I just cried, and I was mad . . . and I hated myself for being so not in control.

I had to sit there and watch my son die. And there was nothing I could do. I couldn't take care of the "owie" this time, like I used to. Gloria gave voice to every mother's worst fear: that her child will be taken from her. As a dear friend said after her son's death, "No mother should have to bury her child." Gloria agreed: I don't wish for anyone to understand the loss of a child. It is tremendous. I lost my dad when I was 21, but to lose my boy is far worse. I think it was telling me that to be a mom is special. And to have a child, to be able to share [his death] with him was a very strong indication to me that my role is what it should be. That I was there for a reason. That all these years, from the time he was born up until then, this is what I was destined to do. And that my role as a mother was important to him and to me . . . I don't think it ever was so strong as at that very point. I was meant to be a mom, and it was very evident at that time.

As each mother must consider at some point, Gloria's child was like her. And in being like Gloria, Jacob had taken a portion of her reflection with him into death. I think he was a mirror of me, in essence. Because there were times we would butt heads. He was a devil's advocate in my opinion. And I am kind of that way too. I didn't realize how much he was like me until after he died. The things that he would do, things he would say. The fact that he would laugh because I have no forehead. And he had no forehead. You know he was always laughing, "You have no forehead, Mom. Look—you have nothing there." I'd say, "Have you taken a look at yourself lately?" You know, "Look in the mirror, Son. You're kind of like your mom there."

I guess Jacob and I were helpers. My girls are too; don't get me wrong. But Jacob and I were—I almost consider him my soul mate. I guess there was a reaffirmation for me about what I did to help people, what I do as a friend, that it was okay. That's who I am. Because that is who he was. You know, someone could stab him in the back and be ugly to him, and he could pick their friendship, their relationship, right back up. And I'm kind of like that. You know people can be ugly, and we exchange words, but then we're okay. You know, they're my friends, they're my family. I think it was for me a reaffirmation that what I do in my life is—it's not bad. It's okay. You know, Tory will tell you, I'm very vocal, I'm very opinionated. She calls me "two cents." She does. "Nobody asked you to put your two cents in." I say, "I give it freely. And so, take it for what it's worth."

Gloria now feels that some of her own principles have been strengthened since Jacob's death, and that she sees herself more clearly now. It's important to say what you feel. To share that emotion at that time. Never be afraid. Never. I don't think I could ever be afraid of anything anymore. Nobody intimidates me. I have no fear. I will always have a part of me gone, always; that part I will never retrieve, ever. And my son taught me. He was my teacher as well as the one who learned. For me, he taught me the importance of always saying what you feel. And just to say what you think. Some people don't want to hear it, but he would say it. And it would make sense.

Definitely, I'm a stronger person, but weak at the same time. Imperfect, a great deal of imperfect. Rebecca was laughing after he had passed away—months had passed by—and she said, "Tory, I wish you could have seen Mom out there. Ms. Control out in the street screaming her head off. She was out of control, Tory. Jacob would have been laughing because Mother was not in control." And I know that now. I cannot be in control of everything. I can't cure everything. All I can do is try to do the best I can. I couldn't make—like I would tell them—I couldn't make your "owie" go away, baby. This is the one time I couldn't make it better. And in that I thought I was a failure, but I wasn't. Gloria hung on to her strength and her opinions, but she let go of her need to feel control. Her son—her teacher—led her to the fearless expression of her truth.

Susan's relationship with her mother, Molly, like many mother-daughter relationships, was rocky at times. But at 52, Susan pulled through for her mother as emphysema took her. Although Molly had been judgmental throughout her life, Susan was determined not to follow suit and to stand up to her primary critic. Susan began by describing a bit of her relationship with her mother as it led up to their own FC-talk. Susan's grandmother had died, and Susan accompanied Molly to help her close down her grandmother's empty home. Standing up to her mother for the first time would become a turning point for Susan.

I was not built like her at all, and she always complained about my shape. I was rounder than she was. I had rounder hips. And she had no bottom at all. In those ten days I was there, she took five different shots at me about how big my bottom was. Finally one day I looked at her and said, "Mom, I'm 49 years old. I'm a grandmother. I wear a size six. How big could I possibly be? Do you think we could give this a rest?" She looked at me, and she never took another one of those shots again. So I have to think that maybe by standing up to her, I wasn't quite who she thought I was. Later on, another time when I was visiting her, we were sitting at the dinner table and, for some reason, talking about religious matters. I'd been in a Bible study for years. She had her own views and was sure that her way was the only way. She looked at me and said, "Well, I hope that you're not one of those fundamentalists." And I looked at her and said, "You know, I probably am." The basic Christian concepts were very clear to me. And she had some really far-out-there, off-the-path kind of ideas, but for the first time in my life, I was speaking for myself.

Susan's new ability to defend herself evidently led her mother finally to see her as an adult. Susan discovered her own voice, which resulted in a shift in Molly's perspective. That changed their relationship enough to allow the two of them to participate in FC-talk. And FC-talk, in turn, encouraged Susan to own her beauty and convictions, to be confident in the woman she had become, and to nurture Molly through her final days.

Susan went to visit for her mother's birthday, but when she arrived at Molly's house, she found her in bed and very ill. She took Molly to the hospital, and they were told by the doctor that Molly was dying. Her pulmonary specialist came to us and said, "There is really nothing more I can do for her. We can either put her on a respirator or just let nature take its course. We can keep her comfortable." And Mom resigned herself.

One of the FC-talks between Susan and her mother concerned Molly's admission that she had wronged Susan. Molly's apology went a long way toward telling Susan that she mattered to her mother. My father died when I was 4. And that was another one of the things that we talked about during those dying times. She said to me that she was sorry that she had not taken me to the funeral because she thought now that it would've helped me to grieve him. That was very meaningful to me, because I was never encouraged to remember him or to grieve him. And in fact, years later, I went to therapy in order to move through my abusive first marriage, because I was stuck in that grief. And so for her to say that really meant a lot. It was almost an apology. I mean it was an apology because she said, "I'm sorry I didn't." And my mother almost never apologized. So, that was very big. It was like, "How you feel matters to me, and that I did you a disservice is something that I regret."

I had never been allowed to grieve my father. And even though I did it as an adult, the fact that she recognized how important it was gave me more credibility in her eyes. I always felt that I was a disappointment to her until those last few years, when I was the one that showed up. And she really did appreciate me, but it helped to make up for all those years when I felt like I was not good enough.

In a way, I felt that I had become her mother. It was a caregiving thing. There was no turning away. I felt comfortable doing it. Poor

Mom, she had terrible teeth, so she had dentures. And so we'd have to do the denture bit. It became so clear to me that this is just body stuff. You know? You can get through this stuff. Hopefully some day, somebody will be kind to me and not go "yuck" [LAUGHING] when I have these old lady problems. But I think it was a gift I could give to her.

I think that because of our earlier relationship and my poor choice of my first husband, I didn't have a lot of confidence in myself. I didn't see myself as very bright or very capable. Over the years, I'd had some therapy, and that had improved some, but this was almost like my coming-out time. Even though I was almost 50 and other people saw me as a grown-up, this was the proof to me that I really was capable and emotionally mature enough to handle something like this and hold the whole family together. I don't mean to say that like I think I'm big, because I don't feel that way at all. But it really did verify that I was an adult.

Susan moved beyond the early influences on her self-esteem to become a fully functioning adult, secure in her abilities and maturity. And her decision to find closure with her mother was pivotal in that growth. As Susan's story demonstrates, seemingly small verbal acts can make for large shifts in relationships and self-image.

Although it may seem to younger people that mature adults have no more growing to do, we older adults know that the habits formed in a lifetime of less-than-perfect relationships can weigh heavily. The mature Living partners who engaged in FC-talk found that they could heal challenging relationships, forgive old insults, switch roles with parents, and receive the gifts of feeling their own strength and confirming their adult status.

Benefits of FC-Talk in Developing a Self

Discovering Aspects of Self: Through Their Eyes

Most people who study human development agree that we develop a sense of self by discovering how others see us. The way the Dying one sees, in the fullness of personal truth, can change the Living one who is seen. For instance, **Victoria** described an emotional exchange between herself and her young dying husband, Kerry: I screamed at him, "You can't die! I can't live without you!" And I remember that he was still strong enough, he grabbed me by the shoulders, and flung me around, and just right in my face were these really gleaming ice-blue eyes, and said, "Yes you can. Yes you can if you have to. And you will do it well." And that was a first. Victoria said that she grew up at that moment. She has gone on to live a productive and fulfilling life.

What Would They Do? Many of the Living told us: "In difficult times when I don't know what to do, I ask what my beloved would do." As Tory put it, If I'm not sure, I'm thinking, *What would he have done? What would Jacob have done had he been here?* Or I'll talk to him, saying, "What do I do? What do I do?" Or you know, if I'm having a big pity party, I'm thinking, *Why aren't you here? Why did you leave me?* You know, I think about him every day. Every day, at some point, if not every moment of each day, I think about him. But Tory now doesn't just think about her brother, she believes she has taken on some of his characteristics. I just think people look at me now and think I'm a better friend. I'm a better person—I don't lie, I don't try and keep anything. You know, I don't think I have as big a heart as he did, but I think I'm working my way to get there.

What Would They Say? Claire remembered exactly what her Uncle Matthew said: "Well, honey, you know you have to be your own best friend. You have to." As Claire told us a few pages back, when she is feeling frenzied, she wonders what Uncle Matthew would say. And she realizes that she already knows. If I had to think about a final conversation that was the most important, it would be that. He knew me so well. He knew how I was going to be, how I was going to continue to lack confidence and self-esteem. So I think that whenever we were together, he was always treating me like a princess or telling me I'm beautiful.

Looking in the Mirror

Some of the Living revealed to us the reflections of self they found in the Dying. **Greg** said of his grandfather, I look inside myself more, to maybe see if God did bless me with just a little piece of my grandfather somewhere. I could draw strength from that when I needed it.

Laura W, a college professor and community activist, spoke of her aunt's pride in her service work: It was nice to see how she saw me. I think almost all of her friends and most of her family do some sort of service or community work. Mom's a nurse, my sister worked in nonprofit, teaching . . . So it was nice to see how she saw me through her eyes. She was very, very proud of all the education that I had received. She was just really proud of her family. It was nice to be seen in those ways.

Seeing self through a loved one's eyes is a primary way we develop a self-image. It's also the way we change and adjust that self throughout life. The roles we play, though, often change with the demands made upon us. We have children, so we become parents. Sometimes we take over a role the Dying has filled, such as parenting, as they become incapable of performing it.

Switching Roles with the Dying: "Who's the Parent Now?"

Many of the Living who spoke to us were called upon to nurture the Dying through the failing of their bodies. Although this isn't the only kind of role-switching that takes place, it is quite common. You might recall that a sibling can become "the strong one" or a mother becomes the "out-of-control one." But most often, certain parenting roles are switched. If you have this experience, remember that this kind of role-switching allows each party to experience the other from a different position. This not only gives insight into your loved one, but builds confidence in your own abilities to do what you aren't used to doing.

"I became the parent." At 46, **Katherine** was telling her difficult mother goodbye and found that it called for more than she bar-

gained for. But she also found that she came to some peace with her mother as a result. *So those last days when I could talk to her, I pretty much mothered her in the same way that you would mother a 2-year-old that was irrationally afraid of the monsters under the bed or whatever. Because you can't logically talk them out of that. You just have to comfort them . . . That was my assignment. I'm very glad now.*

"She didn't have to be my mother any more." For Susan, this process meant that she was finally an adult in her mother's eyes. *She didn't have to be my mother anymore. I mean, she didn't have to be in charge. And she didn't have to tell me how to respond or what to do. She finally saw me as an adult. I was probably almost 50 by then, but oh well, better late than never* [LAUGHING] *. . . And so, I just kind of became the mother. Without taking away her dignity, I could be loving and gentle with her.*

Accepting Self and Pursuing Life

We'll hear more about this benefit of FC-talk in Chapter 8; some of the Living who share their stories in this chapter will continue them there. For now, let's say that FC-talk helped the Living look at themselves and accept some truths about what they really wanted. And that hard look at the self either confirmed what they had been doing, or led them in a different direction.

"Her death made me want to take hospice training." **Emily** lost a best friend at 50, but gained a new vocation. *Everyone needs to have those conversations. She needed it to go on to her other life. I needed it to survive. And in a small way perhaps, help somebody else. Because over and over, she would say to me—this was the new chemo they were just checking into at the time—"If I can help one other human being by taking this, it'll be worthwhile." She looked at it in that manner. I looked at it in this sense: I saw the need [for hospice care]. I wished that we had a hospice so that she could've had more assistance with her death than I could give her. Her death made me really want to take the hospice training.*

"It just made me more the person I am." **Mandy** said goodbye to her grandfather when she was 22. She said this about their FC-talk: It confirms how you feel. It's him acknowledging back at me. It makes me feel like he knows that I love him. And he just acknowledged it by shaking his head . . . It just made me more the person I am. It makes me a huge family person. And that just confirmed that that's what's important to me.

"What I believed was really true." As a young adult, **Lucia** lost her mother, Engeline, to complications of depression. You may recall that she had an amazing nonverbal experience with her catatonic mother before the death. On a walk, Engeline had shown no signs of involvement, but then looked up and pointed to a bird perched on a tree branch. Then she looked to Lucia. Although others did not see the significance of Engeline's actions, and denied that she could communicate, Lucia knew: It just helped me confirm that what I believed was really true. That's the best way for me to summarize it. It definitely fueled my idealism. You know? It did. And also the philosophy I had that love can transcend anything . . . But really, caring is a good thing. I can use it in my teaching—really care about the kids.

Just knowing that you're appreciated the way you are is sufficient payoff for having FC-talk. And for some of the Living, this knowledge brings new and clearer self-awareness.

Summary
How the Living Grew Through FC-Talk

The way that children handle death depends greatly on the responses of the caregivers around them. If a child is not allowed to see the Dying, there is a risk of lasting damage. Children who lose a loved one suddenly and with no explanation are likely to believe that it's their fault that the Dying abandoned them. On the other hand, children who participate in FC-talk begin to understand that nothing they can do will alter the outcome. They are also given the chance to express their feelings and to hear how the Dying feels about them. Even children who do have FC-talks may feel resentment about the shifts in their lives, and later, feel some guilt about not living up to what they perceived as the standard set by the dead loved one. But they are also more likely to feel closure with the loved one *at the same time* that they continue to feel some relationship to the Dying. They feel the love of another beyond death.

Teenagers grow up physically, while their emotional maturity often lags behind. They learn about the viewpoints of others, but are still wrapped up in their own perspectives. The risk of losing a loved one to death is the risk of losing a critical adult role model during a stressful time. Teens who had FC-talks learned a great deal about themselves. They found that they could put aside their own concerns in order to focus on another person, and even recognized how petty those concerns can be. They learned to feel good about themselves, indeed, to see themselves as the Dying saw them. And they remembered messages of encouragement, admiration, and love, incorporating that feedback into their still-developing identities.

Young adults face multiple challenges to their decision-making abilities. As they complete their education, start jobs, and create families of their own, they must figure out for themselves what is right, what is moral, and what they want their character to be. Those who had FC-talks found themselves questioning aspects of their identity. They had to decide whether they had a right to express themselves honestly. They had to consider whether the Dying's feedback was accurate. And, if they chose to accept the self-image the Dying reflected to them, they often had to change their sense of self to conform more closely to the way the Dying saw them. Indeed, several took over the function of the Dying in their lives, becoming their own best supporters and cheerleaders.

Mature adults often think they're done with development, that they are who they are. But those who participate in FC-talks find that these talks can change them in unexpected ways. FC-talk can change the Living from children into parents, as in the case of the living child who nurtures the dying mother or father. FC-talk can also change parents into peers. Recall Gloria, who found that she and her son were "soul mates"—two like minds—and that she was left to carry on his legacy and work. Indeed, FC-talks often change what the Living choose to do with their remaining years, as we'll see in the next chapter.

Advice from the Living

On the basis of the Living's experiences of growth and development through FC-talk, we can make a few suggestions for those of you interested in noting the effects of FC-talk either on yourself or on a child or teen close to you who may need assistance in processing their own FC-talk.

- Not everyone will find that FC-talk leads to dramatic identity shifts or self-discovery. You can't force a particular topic on the Dying; nor can you get exactly what you want or expect from it. And you may not be in the right place in your life to personally take in FC-talk.

- Children experiencing the death of a loved one need to be told directly that it's not their fault. Discussions of death and its inevitability may be simple and direct. Invite questions about illness, and reassure them about the health of the other members of their family network. Get children professional counseling if possible.

- Children should be encouraged to express their feelings about the death and the Dying. Some feelings may be expressions of love; but some may be feelings of resentment and anger that could be better received by another loving adult. This doesn't have to be the Dying, but could be a parent or counselor.

♥ Allow yourself to be touched by the Dying. You're fortunate to be in the presence of someone who doesn't have to be careful about what they say. The Dying can offer some truths about you, your potential, or your life. Listen. Take it in. Decide what you want to do with it.

♥ Paraphrase what you have heard or understood the Dying to say. Then listen for any corrections or additions. You may not have a second chance to get this feedback, so be sure you receive it accurately. Try not to change the Dying's words to suit your needs, but really hear their intention. (See Chapter 9 for details.) Others close to you can often see you more accurately than you can see yourself.

♥ Give yourself time to take in what you receive, whether it confirms what you already know or offers a new perspective on who you are. You don't have to decide today how you will use this information. If it's news to you, it will take time to really receive the news, and decide what it means for your life.

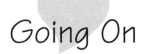

CHAPTER 8

Going On

New Directions for the Living

*Life goes on . . . Those conversations with
Steve always reminded me that life does get
better, and life does go on. [Sondra]*

In the previous chapter, you heard from those who were changed
on a very personal level by their FC-talks. If you've ever experienced a profound change in the way you perceive yourself, as a
result of either the words of a loved and trusted friend or a belief-
challenging event, you know that your behavior and plans often
shift as well. In this chapter, the Living share their changes in attitude and their new life directions.

A New Attitude: Lessons Learned

A brush with death often leaves the Living with a renewed zest for
life. FC-talk can change the Living's vision of the rest of life. **Ruth,**
who lost her dad when she was 5 years old, is now a grown
woman, married, and hoping to start a family of her own soon.
She said it well: *It makes me constantly aware that every day could
possibly be our last day—that we have to live it to the fullest. And I
hate that phrase, it's so cliché. Except that we **should** live each day
like it's our last . . . Being real is better than being perfect. Just be
open. Be open to messages from other people, and be open to share
what you have on your plate and on your mind. Don't put up walls for
the sake of propriety or to save for tomorrow, 'cause there may not
be one.*

FC-talk can act as a simple reminder for the Living about their own mortality. **Sam** described a lesson he received from his mother. Something that is significant about our talks, and really a gift that she gave me, was the opportunity to be with somebody that's dealing with their own mortality. I had never really been around that before, and it really made me very aware of my own mortality.

"More life!" Joy, Energy, Spirit

This recognition of personal mortality leaves the Living firmly in the present moment. They don't want to waste a minute. **Judy Q** explained it this way: After this experience . . . you know, on a nice day we'll go hiking, or if someone calls me up and says, "I haven't seen you in forever," I'll say, "Let's get together now." Yeah. [LAUGHING] "I'm free this afternoon. What are you doing?" Judy's joy and appreciation for life after her last interactions with her grandfather is contagious and enviable.

Others of the Living took a more philosophical view of this personal shift in their value systems. For **Derrick**, the gift of "more life" was an energetic one. He understood his change to be the result of the energy that his grandfather left behind. I think that every action has a reaction, and I think that my reaction to his dying was more life. You know what I mean, more energy. It has to go somewhere. And I didn't think about this logically; I am just thinking in retrospect. The energy lying there in the bed—this life form, his spirit—is not dying; his soul is not dying. He is around. He's gone to where souls go. But the actual form of energy that is physical was dying. Well, it has to go somewhere, and if I can claim it and take it on—psychologically or physically or physiologically or whatnot—if I can take that away and do something with it, then why not! And even if it is psychologically, well if it helps, take it.

Derrick explained what this energy did for him. Energy can be used in many ways, [including as] a nurturing strength for [one's] future. I learned something from it of course; seeing a person die is an experience. So you can take that experience on with you, and it is going to make you stronger in some way. We all thrive on psychological strength anyway in our lives. If I can take that strength away and just tell myself the reason I am going forward, the reason I have strength to do the things I want to do, is for the success of the future and my kids, and that I want to leave behind a legacy—so be it. Then that is what I'll take. We'll hear from Derrick again later in the chapter as he tells us about the new direction his life has taken.

Dana W also received a new philosophy, but hers came as a directive from her father, Michael, that she was happy to follow. He told me how wonderful I was, and that he wanted me to continue living life. Not differently . . . that I didn't have to be different just because I was a young child without a dad. And basically—he never said it in these words—but continue on his little happy philosophy about life: If you're not happy, find something that makes you happy. And that's something I really took to heart. I heard it over and over again as a youth, but now as an adult, I'm able to apply it directly to my life.

FC-talk seems to help the Living learn about life and death in a very positive way. As **Sondra** pointed out, the Living who find themselves debilitated by grief and depression have most likely *not* been participants in FC-talk with the Dying for whom they grieve. Sondra knew that her husband wanted her to move on and love again after his death. Too many of the Living either do not receive this message from the Dying, or cannot hear it even if it is spoken. Sondra said, I'm aware, much more aware, of other people when they go through the grief process of losing their husband or losing their parent or whatever. I wanna shake 'em, especially when it goes past two or three years of grieving. Then I want to say, "Life goes on. You don't have to stay in that state of bitterness and mourning. Is that what your mother would've wanted? Is that what your husband or your wife would've wanted?

Sometimes I get a little impatient with others because maybe they didn't have a conversation with the person that they lost. And it would've been a good idea if they had, so they could have had a life that was happy and fulfilled. And I think too, I understand more of how people go into depression. A lot of depression is caused by losing a spouse, or losing a parent or child—because they're not getting past the grief. But I don't take what they say while they're going through that depression as what they really, really mean. I take it as that's their depression voices speaking rather than what they really believe. So it's made me a lot more aware of what other people suffer. But I wish they would've had that assurance from someone before that person went. Sondra acknowledged that the Living not only feel grief, but often feel guilt at living beyond their loved one's time. They need permission to go on living and be free of guilt to find life's joy.

Recall again **Lucia's** story from Chapter 2. Her catatonic mother gave her the gift of shared delight in a bird perched high in a tree that they passed on their regular walk together. In this small gesture, Lucia was enabled to said goodbye to her debilitated mother, and she also found joy and hope in the spiritual nature of human connection. It just made me feel like maybe I could show my daughter a bird one day. You know? I was affected by Mom, and somehow that was real healing for me. That she was still—it's hard, it's weird to say it but—still alive. You know her spirit or something was still alive . . .

I learned that I don't have to let go of that spiritual connection. I don't need to suffer. I don't need to do things, like hang out with a man that I'm not really in love with. If my daughter doesn't visit me some day when I'm ill, I can still see a bird with somebody. For Lucia, "seeing a bird" became a metaphor for that beautiful, unspoken spiritual connection that never dies.

Near his death, **Roxanne's** father had squeezed her hand in a meaningful way, despite his dementia, to cement the bond of love between them. Roxanne felt that her own spiritual and behavioral changes since her father's death have been a result of this last connection with him. It's made me a whole lot less judgmental. My actions, a whole lot more compassionate. I'm much more open because I've experienced something that was really not rational. I think it's made me much more spiritual and much more open. I don't know if that's reflected in how I deal with others, but it's reflected in what I do and my goals and what I choose to read; and my music, and . . . from inside out, I think, I'm still unfolding from that.

Joy, energy, spirit—the Living find so much more life when they have taken the time and effort for FC-talk.

Take the Time

Blanca was the one to bring attention to something we probably assumed—that it takes time to have these FC-talks. And there probably are no people on earth who complain as much as Americans do about having "no time!" How many people have felt resentment about demands on their time? And that includes the time it takes to be with the Dying, who may be approaching their deaths at the most inconvenient times for the Living.

Blanca reminded us to take time, but also admitted that she was fortunate to be able to do so without too much disruption of her life. Taking the time to be with people in these times is crucial. It's more important than anything else. I'm lucky because I'm a therapist and I work for a therapist. My boss is the kindest, most wonderful human being. I mean, he is just a genuinely wonderful and wise human being. And I would come to his office and say, "I've got to go to the hospital." He'd say, "Go. Take as much time as you need. These times are important, and you need to spend time." He told me, "You will never regret spending a lot of time. You will regret if you don't." He's completely right, and I'm so grateful for having a work environment where I had that privilege. Because that is a privilege. Not everybody has that. I wasn't fired. I didn't lose money. I was given the space, and people covered my slack without retaliation. And I needed that. I needed to be there. So that's the most important thing: I got to be with him.

This need for time echoed throughout our interviews. Judy Q, who lived across the continent from her grandfather, confessed that after his death, she was definitely depressed, because I always thought that there'd be more time. I've lived in California for five years now, so I always assumed when I got back, oh there'd still be a little bit more time. He's going to live to 80. I think my mindset gave me that extra time. Every time I went home for holidays or the summer, I would always go and visit him. That was definitely one of my first stops on the way. The last trip there, I think it finally hit me that there really is such a thing as time. And not everybody has it. Value the time you have with people.

Jim also found himself sad and depressed following his father's death. He regretted what he described as his selfishness regarding his father. Many children feel this way after a parent's death—that they expected to get more than they gave in that relationship. And of course, we do. That's what parent-child relationships are about for so long. Jim said, I thought What am I going to get out of this relationship? What's he going to give me next? Where's the check in the envelope? Stuff like that, rather than thinking, Oh my God, I want more time with him.

I want more time. I hadn't thought that before. I hadn't thought. I thought, You get together two or three days at a time, twice a year. That's fine. Talk on the phone once a month. Father's Day, Christmas gifts, birthday gifts, and that was good. I didn't want more than that. All of a sudden, I wanted a lot more. Unfortunately, we often fail to see that it's our time to give back—until it's too late. Jim's new awareness spurred him to feel more intensely. I've managed to change direction since he died. I value my mother more, my brother. I got more sensitive and more [in touch with my] feelings . . . to others' too, but mostly to my own. Jim couldn't have any more time with his father, but he can make that time now for other loved ones.

You may have noticed that many of these examples about the value of spending time with the Dying came from women. In this culture, as in many others, nurturing the sick and elderly is considered "women's work." Although a number of men in this project were actively involved in caring for the Dying, we still caution men not to leave the care of the Dying to their female relatives. As Jim just demonstrated, some men regret the fact that they didn't spend more time with the Dying. Jim's realization came too late for his relationship with his father. Fortunately, Jim is now taking the steps to insure that things are different in the future for those he loves.

Although the nurturing and caretaking role of women is based on a stereotype, stereotypes are often based on the actual state of affairs. Don't let that stop you from defying the stereotype. At the end of life, both men and women can effectively offer care and nurturance to the Dying. Yet until men realize that they can manage some of the burden at the end of life, the stereotype will remain. Men must be the ones to change this image by taking on some of the nurturing role in families; the end of life is a perfect opportunity to do so. By leaving the caretaking of the sick and dying to women, men miss out on many opportunities for FC-talk—and for the gifts it brings.

Stop Walking on Eggshells

The Living often approach FC-talk with fears that they may overstep their bounds, they may offend the Dying, or they may talk about things that will cause discomfort. But they eventually realize that "walking on eggshells" is just using up the precious time they have left without making the real connection they crave.

Sam was trying to figure out how to help his mother have a good death. They had a lot of talks during the last year of her life. He realized that he and his mother could both be alone in their thoughts and fears about her death, or they could take the journey together. What I remember the most about my mom's illness when we found out that she was terminally ill with ovarian cancer was that she really would have gone through that whole process, I believe, in silence if we had let her do that. She really couldn't talk to my dad about what it was like to be dying, to be facing her own death, because it was just too painful for him. He really was having a great deal of difficulty dealing with it.

After six months of conversation focused on chemotherapy and other "safe" topics, Sam finally decided to be bold one day and simply ask his mom a question about dying to see if she might want to talk about her death journey. "Are you afraid of dying?" And that was really all it took for her to kind of open up. I gave her permission to talk about how she felt. It really made me realize that people who are facing their own death certainly aren't thinking about anything else during the day. And so many times people kind of walk on eggshells around them, and you don't want to bring it up. And it's like the gigantic elephant in the room that nobody talks about. And [I think that most of the Dying] really want to talk about it. So in asking her questions like how she felt, she could open up and reveal how she was feeling. She would cry and I would cry.

As Sam demonstrated, there is nothing wrong with crying; in fact, at times it may be the only way to let out some of the pain and fear. Finally being able to talk about what is really in the hearts and minds of the Living and Dying is freeing. Being emotionally cautious is exhausting, and once people realize that life doesn't have to be that way, they usually experience a tremendous feeling of relief. Walking on eggshells in a relationship—any relationship—is not healthy. The Living and the Dying first need to recognize it in their relationship and then, second, find a way to break the taboo on talk about death. The lessons learned in the midst of FC-talk can carry over into the rest of the Living's life. Breaking the rules about death can lead to even more freedom from other stifling norms.

"Break the rules!"

Jo's father was a highly controlling person who ruled every aspect of his wife's life. He had rules not only for Mary, but for his children too, including Jo. Jo knew that her mother was dying, although her father refused to accept her condition and insisted on tests and more tests. I went down to see her. I had seen her a few times during that year. My father was saying that he was about to schedule a bunch more tests for her because he was certain there was some specific thing wrong, that they could find out what it was, and that they could cure her and she would be fine.

So he was telling us about the tests that they were going to do. And I said, "Well, what does she want?" And he said, "Well, that doesn't matter." And I said, "Well, yeah, it does." I said, "I just think it matters at this point what she wants, and she should get to say it." And he said, "No." And I said, "Why?" And he said, "She's not in her right mind. She hallucinates, and she doesn't understand." And I said, "You know, Dad, I've never seen her hallucinate, and I've never seen her not in her right mind. I think it's strange that it never happens when I'm around." He tried to forbid me to talk to her. He said, "I don't want you to talk to her anymore." And he tried to physically stop me. Because it was not allowed, I had never talked to her seriously.

So I went over, and I got up on the bed, and I got kind of close to her on her bed because she couldn't see very well. She had macular degeneration in one eye and shingles in the other. I said, "You know, we're having this conversation. Dad wants you to have more tests. He feels he's going to find out what's wrong and cure you. And I feel like you should be left alone, and you should be able to die in peace and not have to be pulled out and be given a test every day."

I said, "But the real important thing's what do you want. What do you want, Mom?" And she said, "I don't want any more doctors. I don't want any more tests. It's over." She fell back on her pillows and looked over at him and went, "I got you good."

It was astonishing to me; I'd never broken the rule before. This was frightening. And she broke it too. There was nothing he could do. And she died ten days later. She died very early in the morning of the day that he had scheduled tests.

Jo had believed, from her experiences with her father, that if I broke these rules I would die. And because I broke them and I didn't die, I would say to others, "Don't wait so long." Given the abuse that both Mary and Jo received, their triumph together not only provided the connection Jo longed for before Mary's death, but released her from the tyranny of arbitrary family rules.

Perhaps more reasonable are the tacit rules of polite, civilized people in normal circumstances. But still these are rules that are sometimes meant to be broken. One of those times is when they suppress what must be exchanged between the Living and Dying. **Breanna,** a young woman accustomed to deferring to her elders, regretted being so well-mannered. There were unspoken norms of how to act in the hospital room. When somebody else comes in, you give up your chair sitting beside her and go sit somewhere else. And if older people come in, you get up and let them sit. I wanna be like, "Forget you guys, I wanna sit here and hold her hand. I wanna talk to her." Breanna gave evidence that she knows better now. She voiced a plan for the future, when another loved one may face death: I won't let anybody else tell me what to do. When it comes to my own mom or somebody else like that, I'm going to be the one saying, "I want my time with her." Once you decide to find the time and break the rules, what will you do with that open space? Find your feelings.

Know Your Feelings, Then Speak Them

When **Jeanette** said goodbye to her grandfather, even at the tender age of 12, she knew that this was her last chance to say how she felt. She had time to think about this, as he was in the hospital for a while before his death. If he died suddenly, I think I wouldn't have been able to say that to him [that he was important in my life and I loved him]. And I still would've felt it, you know? I think actually being able to tell him that made it a little bit easier to deal with his loss. I'm not saying that I would say everything that I feel to everyone right now, but at least know how you feel yourself. Don't hide things from yourself. Because you know you do, you hide feelings from yourself. Yes, especially when feelings are intense and tender, we often hide them from ourselves, particularly when the object of those affections may leave. As the Living will tell you, though, it's much easier and more fulfilling to feel the immensity of that love with the one who needs to know it than it is to feel it all alone when they are gone.

Gloria, who lost her young son, can tell you more eloquently than we can. It's important to say what you feel, to share that emotion at that time. Never be afraid. Never! I don't think I could ever be afraid of anything any more. Nobody intimidates me. I have no fear. Life is good. I will always have a part of me gone, always. That part I will never retrieve, ever. And my son taught me. He was my teacher as well as the one who learned. He taught me the importance of always saying what you feel . . . to say what you think.

As we know from Chapter 6, FC-talk isn't always sweet and positive. Sometimes you have to say the hard things as well. And it's still worth it, as Blanca told it: Well, you can't keep having crap between you and expect to take care of it later. And when you have those explosions, those explosions are opportunities. They're difficult. Conflict is difficult, so we avoid it. I cried my eyes out in some of those conversations. Working that conflict out with Daddy allowed me to have a beautiful connection and peace at his death. I didn't regret; I didn't say, "Oh, the last thing I said was awful" or "We never talked about this" or anything like that.

Blanca found a way to face the conflict and use it. Opportunities arise all the time for conflict resolution. It doesn't mean that you always get to do it . . . you have to have two parties working towards it. He didn't like to not have the final word, but I worked with that. I worked that. He wanted to have the final word . . . and I'd throw in something else so we couldn't end the conversation. I knew exactly what I was doing. And Daddy loved me enough to not hang up on me. And that's a gift too, because not everybody is capable. So it was Daddy's strength too. It was my persistence and his strength. Blanca's wisdom was in realizing that she could not plan for the perfect resolution; she had to go through the muck of conflict with her father and allow him his say. But because she could let go of trying to control the "crap" between them, she could come to feel peace about their relationship.

Release Control: Let It Unfold

People want to do well. In fact, most people would prefer to do things perfectly if possible. But what is a perfect death? And what is a perfect goodbye? We'd love it if we could give you ten easy steps to have the perfect FC-talk. And even though we share advice at the end of each chapter and will give you some basic communication skills in Chapter 9, we have to be honest: We don't have a formula for the perfect farewell. Because there isn't one; there are many. And each FC-talk will look and sound different. What the Living who speak in these chapters propose is to accept what you can do and what your loved one can do. No matter what you expect, the actual experience will always unfold differently than your expectations. **Bill**, like everyone else, had some idea of how dying should go. But she showed me that that path can be something greater than you would imagine, because of the way that she herself handled it. Bill's mother was strong and spiritual. And Bill now hopes to go the same way, with no complaints, no fears, and no expectations of how it "should" happen.

Emily echoes this sentiment. She had an idea of how everyone else "should" behave as her best friend, Jeanette, died. There is no right way or wrong way to die or to say anything. You know, for a while I was kind of aggravated with her family, but everyone handles things differently. And it doesn't mean that there's a right way and a wrong way. And as aggravated as I got with Jeanette's husband, I know now that was just him. I couldn't chastise him for not—I tried to in the beginning—I'd think, Well, why, why can't he see that? But I've learned that all people see things differently, and it doesn't necessarily mean that this one's right and that one's wrong. Indeed, everyone around the Dying will respond in his or her own way, which may not be your way.

According to **Laurie W**, it simply isn't your plan to make. And the best you can do is to just deal with the way it all rolls out. Work and all the things in my world that I thought were so incredibly important and couldn't wait—so I didn't have time to do various family things, phone calls or conversation—were just so irrelevant and not important. It means a lot to take time to visit with those that you love. And even though I had prepared, knowing she was dying, I could tell anyone this: You could prepare in your mind, but it never, ever goes how you think it's going to go. In fact, it's worse if you prepare because then, when it doesn't happen the way you thought it should, you don't know how to react because it's not going according to your plan.

Laurie then told us about how her plan fell apart. Nothing went according to plan. It just didn't. I had specifically told my mother that I didn't want to see an open casket. And we talked about this when she was in the hospital on a previous visit some time before. And she said this: "You know, I never wanted to see my mother either, but I did. And afterwards, I visited with several of her friends, and her friends said how comforting it was for them to see her one last time and to say goodbye." And I do remember this conversation real specifically because I answered back very quickly, "Well, that was great for them, but as I'm saying, it's not what I want to do."

Then the time came; her mother died, and Laurie had to make arrangements for her funeral. So I had picked up her clothes and sent them with my brother to the funeral home. And they had called and said, "Do you want to come down and see how all the clothes worked out?" And I had a hat—she looked like she was going to the races with a big, big black hat. She looked very elegant. I said, "Sure, I'll go down." And so, Charles and I go down to the funeral home. And I walk into this room where there's an open casket, and I turn and walk out. I said, "No, no, no. I didn't say that I was going to look at her in the clothes. I just wanted to see how the clothes laid out." And they said, "Well, that's what this is about. You need to do this." Charles said, "If you don't want to, I'll take care of it." And I said, "No, I want to see how she looks. I picked out the clothes. I want to know." And I went up, and she looked beautiful. And I'm glad I did it, because she looked so bad in her last few days. It wasn't how she would've want- ed anyone to remember her. She looked amazing. There were a couple of things that weren't right. Her lipstick wasn't right. So I took a lip liner out of my purse and touched it up 'cause that's how she wore her lipstick.

For a woman who never wanted to see her mother after her death, Laurie did a complete turnabout, actually assisting with her makeup and clothes. Once you can release the need for control that is often born of fear, it becomes possible to allow yourself the privilege of just assisting in the process as you are needed. This kind of release is not only a gift to the Dying, it's a blessing for the Living.

No Fear, No Regrets

One fairly typical response to FC-talk is a decrease in the amount of fear the Living carry about death. Her grandmother's death not only emboldened Breanna to place her own needs in a priority position above others, it changed her feelings about death. I'm not afraid of death anymore. I wasn't afraid of being near her or what was happening—I mean I was afraid, but it just seemed natural. And I was there when she died, and that made a big, big impact on me. Because she died, and I was there right beside her, and it didn't seem scary at all. It seemed almost beautiful in the way that it happened. And I think that changes you. I was very happy that I had been with her the last two days. For some reason, that meant a lot to me. So I'm still afraid of death. I think everybody is, but it was more accepting it . . . it's not so horrific.

Particularly for those who may not say all they need to say in their FC-talks, or for those who fail to have the talks at all, regrets can loom large after the Dying is gone. What should I have said? What should I have expressed? Did they die as they wanted? **Grace** had begun to have these thoughts about her husband's death, but upon reflection, she found no reason for regret. As any person in a situation where you're the final caregiver, you question whether or not you did enough. You question your own actions. You question your own conversations. You question whether you told them enough that they were loved, and whether you listened enough to their feelings, and whether you were projecting your feelings onto them more than you should have. And I think that gave me some self-doubt. I had to sit down and examine what I had done and what I should have done. And that caused me to eliminate the word "should" from my conversations with anybody or from my thoughts. I came to the conclusion that I had done the best I could at the moment. What I thought was the best I could give. And there was nothing that I should've done, that I could've done otherwise.

Changes in attitude often lead to changes in behavior. For some of the Living, these shifts lead them to new ways of thinking about, and acting in, relationships. For others, changes in attitude may lead to new directions in education or career, or personal passions to contribute to society and serve others.

New Plans, New Paths

Judy W's stepfather, Frank, was the true father who had taken care of her and her sister and provided a home for them. When Judy's sister decided in middle age to take their birth father's last name, Judy saw this as an insult to Frank. So she wrote Frank a long letter expressing all the things she appreciated about him. She took the opportunity to express her gratitude before his health began to fail. After fifty-eight years of parenting from Frank, now he was dying, and she began to feel like an orphaned adult. Both of Judy's birth parents died before Frank, and she feared losing him. But she need not have. As she expressed it, That's my last parent to die. Well, I've always thought that would be really scary, but he lived so long, and I lived so long with him, that for me, it's like I'm not alone. It's a freedom to continue. It's not like there's nothing between me and death. It's more like, it's up to me to take charge of my life. He's always there in the back of my mind. Judy felt a new impetus to move into full adulthood with Frank's death. She was truly independent now and answerable only to herself.

When you no longer have someone watching over your life, you have to care enough about yourself to finally do what others may have urged you to do before—do well in school, choose a career, practice a hobby, earn fulfillment, find love.

Relationships: Who Knew How Important?

In our culture, it's commonplace to take relationships for granted. We work ourselves silly, assuming that friends and family will be there waiting for us when we're done—if ever we're done. When Sam's mother died, he learned something about that whole idea of living your life with anticipation of checking out of this world. Not in the sense of the afterlife, like earning a place in heaven or anything like that, but that at the end of your life, you can be facing your death with fear, or denial, or a feeling of emptiness or loneliness . . . I mean, there's all kinds of ways that you can die. And the way you prepare yourself is by making decisions in life leading up to that. Integrity and decisions that you make about what's really important, like family—spending time with family versus things like money—that's probably the biggest part of it. And I think if I were summarizing all of the reminiscing—the things that she remembered in the end of her life, some of which were very mundane, all centered around certain themes—those were the things that were really important. It was family, it was relationships. That was really it. Sam was 30 when he learned this lesson.

Kasey was 25 when she learned a similar lesson, one that a number of our elders have yet to embrace. Value your loved ones, keep them close. Keep them real close. I'll tell you what I've learned, and this is it. My dad, we hadn't spoken to him for years. He just decided a long time ago that he didn't want to . . . I don't know so much that **he** decided that or **we** did for him. We just didn't want to talk to him anymore. I mean, he owed my mom like fifty-some thousand in back child support for us. He just kind of stopped, at one point in time, taking care of us. So we just totally didn't talk to him at all. And that's one thing I'll always feel bad about.

Angie (my sister who died) wanted to talk to him, but see, my mom—it's weird—my mom doesn't want him to know where she lives at all, period. So the only way we can get hold of him is by paging him. Angie was never allowed to page him and then to have him call back. Because then that would mean that he would have my mom's number. So I always felt bad for my dad that he just heard through me, "Angie's sick." I didn't really get hold of him for the longest time, until I realized, she's sick. I really never had this strong desire to really have a relationship with my father. But what I've learned is that you can't hold grudges, that you've gotta love. I mean, this is your family, no matter what. So I've built a relationship with my dad, and now I talk to him like every Sunday. Kasey recognized the disservice that had been done to her sister; she had not been allowed to have a relationship with her father. Kasey is now determined to fill that gap as well as she can.

The Dying often know better than those they leave behind just how much the Living will need close relationships. Although no one is replaceable, especially intimates, spouses seem especially concerned that the Living love again. Sondra's husband made it clear that he wanted her to remarry after his death. Life goes on. There is certainly a human time that you do miss that person. And gosh, the loneliness I felt after that was extreme. But those conversations with Steve always reminded me that life does get better, and life does go on. I knew that for me to remarry was what he wanted. And that conversation definitely had an impact. The man I'm married to now, Glen, he had a very similar conversation with his late wife: I want you to remarry. And I think even with both of us today, we both know that we had the blessing of our previous spouses, our late spouses. And that conversation made a big impact on why we don't have that bitterness, or don't have that mourning and grief. Yeah, there's times when we miss them and those memories do come back. But their spouses made it possible for these Living to go on, to love again, and to benefit from the closest of relationships.

For **Sandra**, the experience of FC-talk meant that she had to give in to the emotional demands and discomforts inherent in close relationships. I let my wall down. Before it was like, "I don't want to get hurt. I don't." You know, "What if . . . what if this or what if that." And I gave in to a certain point, and then I held back. And after that [FC-talk], I didn't. I learned that I need to let people in; that I need to find the balance. To be able to still be the strong person that I am, but that I need to also appreciate everybody around me and let them be closer to me, because when it comes down to it, when you die, you don't take anything with you. Your relationships with people are the most important thing.

Carol agreed that FC-talk opens the Living to people in general and family in particular: I tried since then to be more honest about what I'm thinking or feeling with those that I love and care about. And not to let things go. What I learned has to do with, Why waste all that time not being close? I think, in general, I am a lot more open with everyone that I care about, whether it's my husband or my brothers, or especially my nieces. Or even just good friends. I tend to be more open and straight with people up front.

I tend to be a pretty private person, I think. But in the last year, I've seen a shift where I'll talk more openly about a whole realm of things that I would not have a year earlier. It's because I want to know people better, and I have, I think, more realization that I might not have another opportunity to.

The young adults who spoke to us often felt a shift of family responsibility to their shoulders. **Lori** felt that she was no longer the cared-for child. I guess I learned that they were not always going to be there, and that the torch was being passed. And that I had to, whether I wanted to or not, grow up and deal with it. That I couldn't be the kid anymore, and that nobody was going to be there to bail me out. That whatever I did from then on out was up to me. That scared me, but I thought: *How can I continue this man's legacy, this man I admire so much?* I felt like it was a torch passing, that I was the new head of the family, what family there was. And that I had to live up to his image. And I'm not sure that I do, but I try. Lori, ready or not, recognized that she was now in the position to head the family.

Similarly, **Michael** felt that it was up to him to be the kind of family man his grandfather had been. I perceived that I could do what I really wanted to do because he did. I can't take relationships for granted. He married the one woman that he loved. And he made a great living. He had a good life. He saw at least half, if not more than half, of the world with his travels and his business. He had good kids. They went on to do good things and have good families. And then good grandchildren, for whom—I use this analogy—he was much like The Godfather. He kind of held the whole thing together. He offered assistance when possible. So I like to think that I could do that same thing. And have maybe one, if not multiple, relationships with my grandchildren where they could all come and see me when I'm about to die. Michael, at 22, is beginning to plan the rest of his life; his grandfather had a great influence on the shape that future is taking.

B.J., a mature woman, seemed somewhat surprised by the influence her FC-talk with her mother-in-law, Sylvia, had on her own family relationships. We'd known for the last year and a half that she was fading. And we were going to Pittsburgh more frequently to make sure that we spent more time with her. I had been very disconnected from my family, who also live in Pittsburgh. I had not seen any of my family for years; this disturbed Sylvia very much. In that she wasn't that family oriented herself, it really disturbed her that I was so disconnected from my family. She'd always ask, "Well, are you gonna see your brother?" I'd say, "Well, I don't know. I don't know."

Last summer, for the first time in almost twenty years, my brother and his wife invited us to their house. We went to their house and then we went to dinner at their country club with a bunch of my cousins and their husbands. It was like a family reunion. And I went to visit an aunt I hadn't seen in years. I reconnected with my family. It was almost—this may sound stupid—but it was almost like I did it for Sylvia. Even though, of course, it benefited me, it was like she was the impetus for me. I came back from that trip feeling better than I had in a long time about my family. The Living find that FC-talk reminds them of the importance of close relationships in their lives, focuses them on their good fortune in having family or new responsibilities to family, and motivates them to reconnect with family they have neglected. Some of the same Living also found new directions for their personal achievements.

Personal Goals: New Directions in Education

Not all the Living who spoke of their renewed dedication to study were traditional, college-age students. After her son died—a young man who never got the chance to continue his education—Gloria went back to school. In part, she credited her son for her inspiration. He said, "I want you to go back to school. So then, I can go back to school." I said, "But Jacob, you're always wanting to be a coach and a math teacher." He says, "Well, maybe I'll do that, and then later on I'll become a lawyer. And I'll come with you." But he said, "You need to be a lawyer, Mom."

Gloria has just completed her bachelor's degree with a major in political science. She worked and attended school at the same time. She is now thinking of pursuing a master's degree or law school. When asked if part of her motivation was Jacob's urging, Gloria replied, Part of that, yes. And part of it is that there are a lot of women and children who need defending, a lot of minorities. A lot of situations come up, and they feel like the door is closed. I just feel like I can be a part of that and help in some way. I always think that if I helped one person, maybe that I'll make a difference. Jacob and his mother were alike in many ways, particularly in their willingness to serve others. And in some way, Jacob's idealism will live in his mother's work.

Some of the young adults who spoke to us also mentioned a shift in their enthusiasm and drive for education. Derrick admitted to a lack of focus earlier in his college career: Well, I've never sat down and said, "This is my goal for two years from now, or I want to have this degree in this year, or I want to go on to study this." I've never thought of it like that. But I think on a more short-term basis, the things I've set out to do, I've done. For instance, I will be graduating in December. Last year, or a year and a half ago, I didn't know when I was going to graduate or what classes I was going to take to get there. But along the way, I was more decisive about what I felt like I should do. When it came to registration time, and when it came to advising time, everything was more clear to me. I was less distracted. Derrick finally found his motivation: His grandfather's death changed his sense of purpose and drive to achieve. After the death of my grandfather, I knew that I just had a few things that I had to do, and graduation was one of them. And I've kept on that straight path since then.

For Michael, his grandfather's death affected not only the way he now values family, but also the way he values the link between education and achievement. School now is a little bit more important for me because of him. Not so much because of my parents or anything like that, but because he wanted me [to get the degree]. It seemed like he was the second father. I guess that's why they call them "grandfathers." But life was just pushed up the next notch, letting me know that it is more important than I was considering it to be. I took more focus—not that I was slacking off in school—but I definitely took more initiative to do better. [My lessons are] just realizing things I want to do more. Write more music. Because I don't want to lie in my bed dying, just wondering, What the heck did I do with all that time? The degree to which his grandfather, William, was a success, both in work and in relationships, led Michael to question his own life and begin to consider what he really wanted to do with it.

Personal Goals: New Directions for Work

The Living may continue in their jobs with a new view of how they want to do them; or they may quit doing what they have no passion for, and create new paths. After her mother's death, Laurie W slowed down the pace of her stressful life and embarked on work that would allow her to be more aware and present than she had been. I try to be a little more mindful and have a little more time to—I don't know—meditate, for lack of a better word. Just quietly think about what's going on. It's a good lesson. I was very caught up in my life.

It did change how I view work. I quit working for corporate America and went out on my own. It's been scary, but the way things happened with my mother still provides me a little income that got me over something I never could've done without that. Not only did her mother's death spur Laurie to consider more carefully how she was spending her life, it also provided the means for her to do so. Perhaps not everyone will be as fortunate, but everyone can consider whether the work they do suits their life goals.

Several of the Living were inspired to assist others in the death process. For **Victoria**, her young husband's death led her to her work as a grief counselor. You might remember her story about accompanying Kerry on his journey past death. After his vision, he came back briefly to tell Victoria of his experience and of their continuing work together. He came back down the mountain [of his vision], and he said that they had told him that what he would be doing next would be midwifing people who were dying. And that I should be doing it from one side, and he would be doing it from the other. And that whenever anybody was afraid about dying, that I was supposed to tell them to ask for Kerry. And there's actually a funny story about that. I've been treating Ken's wife, Martha, since May. So it's going to be hilarious because she's going to be a really old woman, and she's going to be dying in a context where nobody knows anything about her history. She's going to be lying there in the bed screaming, "Kerry, Kerry, Kerry, Kerry." [LAUGHTER] Somebody's going to think she has a secret lover. [MORE LAUGHTER]

Immediately after Kerry died, there was a real sense of peace. Kerry deserves the credit because I was so okay in the weeks after his death. But after that, it got real hard, because I had to rebuild. I'd never really been a grown-up without him. But I think those final conversations and spirit made the immediate period around this time not so hard. Victoria still works with the dying and their families, and of course, with Kerry as her partner.

Emily said goodbye to her best friend, Jeanette, twenty-five years ago. And she has done hospice work for the last sixteen. Jeanette didn't have the kind of support Emily wanted for her, so Emily searched for help and learned about the beginnings of the hospice movement in this country. Now she counsels the Living to have FC-talks with the Dying. I wished that we had had a hospice so that she could've had more assistance with her death than I could give her. Her death made me really want to take the hospice training. And the minute that it came here—it took me about three years before I had the time to go ahead and take the training—I knew I was going to do it. After she completed her training and began to work, Emily started having experiences that told her she was doing the right thing; her work aligned with her passion and talent.

Emily saw the need and recognized her own place in the world. She continues her work today. Absolutely . . . that's exactly why I chose to. Because I could see the need. I had read a little bit about hospice, but it was fairly new in the United States at that time. And it started in England. I made up my mind after Jeanette, when I saw the need was so great for her. And I know now how much hospice can really help. I made up my mind then, directly because of Jeanette, that if and when [hospice] ever comes here, I will take it. Emily honored her friend's memory by volunteering with hospice for the past sixteen years. In this work, she clearly finds delight and fulfillment, and a way to keep the memory of her friend alive.

Benefits of Going On

This chapter has been a bit different from the rest: It's **all** about what the Living learned for their own use. Everything they report here has to do with the benefits of FC-talk for those who continue life. And these benefits basically come down to two: (1) loosening up and (2) resetting life's defaults.

Loosening Up

Yes, that's a pretty broad statement. "Loosening up" means taking yourself and every single limitation you perceive in your life less seriously. The Living learned to stop walking on eggshells and to say what they needed to say. They learned to take the time from their serious daily lives to be with the Dying. They learned to break the rules—the cultural norms and the family regulations—in order to do what they felt they had to do. And they learned to let go of control, both over the process of dying and over their own emotions and actions. Isn't this all about loosening up and letting it happen? Sure. Is it easy to do? No, but take hope from those who were able to do it. You'll be reminded of your own mortality. And you'll be able to give yourself permission to do what your heart tells you to do.

Resetting Life's Defaults

People walk through many of their days on automatic pilot. And that is functional. We'd never get through repetitive daily tasks without default settings—the automatic drive that allows us to do things without thinking about them. Take driving to work: Aren't there days when you're scarcely conscious of where you've been until you pull into the employee parking lot? But if there's an accident along the way, you have no trouble switching to a highly conscious mode of thinking. In that case, you can vividly describe to your spouse or a friend that night what happened and your responses to it.

Similarly, the walk through life can get pretty programmed. You're supposed to go to school, you're supposed to make a good living, you're supposed to keep in touch—at least minimally—with family. So you do. But if you sleepwalk through life—and most of us do, to some extent—a day will arrive when you're jogged out of that sleep into an awareness that this life may come to an end tomorrow. That's when the sleepwalking ends, at least for a while. The Living tell us that after you engage in FC-talk with someone you've counted on to be there, you are forced to think about your loss. And that leads you to rethink your family relationships, your friends, your loves. It leads you to value them more, and take them for granted less. It may lead you to make changes in your relationship choices, and in what you expect from a close relationship. For many, it will mean re-evaluating the way you spend your days; consequently, it may lead you to change occupations, go back to school, or revise the time you spend making money. In other words, FC-talk can lead to resetting the defaults of life.

Summary
What the Living Learned About Going On

The Living experienced shifts in their life force and joy, in their willingness to take time out and to break some commonplace rules for their loved ones. They found that they had to know their own feelings, and to let go of the need to control. Once they allowed FC-talk to unfold, the Living also released much of their fear of death and any need for regrets.

Affected profoundly by their FC-talks, many of the Living went through deep shifts in their values and attitudes. Changes in attitude often lead to changes in behavior. As a result, some Living reconnected with family, cherished their friends more, or found a new love. Others focused more on their educational pursuits, transformed their careers, or embarked on new paths to follow their passions. Those who allow FC-talk to affect them will feel shifts in their outlook. And for each, the shift will lead to unique, personalized responses. Find yours. And benefit from those who have gone before you. Here you'll find some advice to prepare you for gaining the most from your FC-talk, and advice to prepare you to be open to changes in your life after your FC-talk. The death of your loved one is going to change you and your life; FC-talk simply gives you an opportunity to have some say in the changes that occur.

Advice from the Living

Before the Death

♥ Do whatever is necessary to spend time with the Dying. Speak with your boss, your colleagues, your friends and family to see if they can help you break away from your daily schedule.

♥ Break the rules! Defy ordinary conventions or habitual norms, and say what you need to say. Dying is not an ordinary, everyday experience for you or your loved one. Find your feelings, and then find your voice.

♥ Confront your fear of death. FC-talks will help dissipate that fear.

♥ Let FC-talk unfold as it will. It isn't yours to control, or even to prepare. Just prepare yourself to *be* there. Keep this in mind: "Half of success is just showing up" (a quote from Woody Allen). The other half of success in FC-talk may be just listening. (See Chapter 9 for details.)

After the Death

♥ Give yourself permission to grieve and then to go on. If you're having difficulty moving through the grief, seek a grief counselor you feel comfortable with.

♥ If you're comfortable sharing personal stories about your FC-talk with others you trust—especially after you have done your grief work—do so. Sharing is a way to learn more about the messages after you have some time for reflection.

♥ Value your own spirit as well as others'. Don't put off treating yourself and others compassionately.

♥ Find life's joy. It is unlimited, but your life is not.

♥ See where your own shifts in attitude take you. Follow your own good impulses.

CHAPTER 9

You Can Too
Communication Skills for
Final Conversations

*However long or short someone's FC-talks
are—they make a world of difference for the
person that has to go on living. [Cathy]*

While we don't have a ten-step program for the perfect FC-talk, we are going to suggest ten communication skills to recognize, practice, and improve for more fulfilling communication with loved ones. Here you'll find suggestions for any FC-talk, rather than a blueprint for the ideal FC-talk. Perhaps you'll also learn some tips for more satisfying communication with those you love, every day of your life.

We wish we could give you a prescription to guarantee perfect FC-talk, but we don't have that formula because it doesn't exist. Like snowflakes, no two FC-talks are the same. Some are uplifting, beautiful, exhilarating, and life-changing; others are sad, frustrating, mundane, or gut-wrenching. No FC-talk will fulfill your every expectation, but each will deliver unexpected gifts. Your FC-talk is unique because it is (or was) created by you and your dying loved one, making it irreplaceable. We believe that you can face your FC-talk with the confidence that you will say and feel what you need to say and feel.

We two authors have spent our lives teaching young adults about interpersonal communication: What is it? How does it develop? With whom do people choose to relate? When can people expect to face communication challenges? Why is it easy to communicate with some people and not with others? Which communication patterns work, and which do not? But although we can make educated guesses about relationship-talk, we can never predict for sure what will happen in any particular conversation. Human beings are unpredictable, have free will, and communicate in the moment based on all of their prior experiences. Communication during periods of stress and high emotion is often complicated, frustrating, surprising, and in the best of moments, uplifting and life-changing.

Your perceptions of events *are* your reality for what occurs in any given conversation. The way you perceive and react to those events is shaped by many factors. For instance, your gender can affect the way you hear and react to messages. Have you ever been frustrated or shocked when you've found out how the opposite sex interpreted your words or facial expression? Age and past experience also affect your reactions to events: You can accept that a 3-year-old is having a temper tantrum in the grocery store, but find the same behavior unacceptable for a 30-year-old. Your mood, your health, and your self-esteem can all influence your communication. If you're in a bad mood, then you probably react in a way that's grumpier than normal; if you're in pain, then you probably have a shorter fuse; and if you're feeling insecure or inadequate, you probably interpret innocent comments as personal attacks.

For example, you've probably had the experience of anticipating an important conversation and planning out everything you want to say. The issue at stake could be breaking up with an intimate partner, or sharing the news that you've been offered a job promotion that means longer hours and a move to another state. Yet when the conversation actually began, you faced a real, live person who reacted, interrupted, cried, asked questions, and foiled your well-rehearsed plan altogether. You likely never got to say half of what you had planned. You may not even have ended up breaking up with your partner, or you may have found that your partner wasn't as thrilled as you were about the promotion because of the anticipated stress and upheaval to the family. How you respond during an interaction arises from multiple factors. Every person has the potential to respond differently on any given day, depending on the circumstances surrounding the particular conversation.

Of course, as you get to know someone, you find it easier to predict how he or she will respond to you. But whenever you get two people together to truly dialogue—exchange and listen to each other deeply—something new is created: a relationship in which to learn and grow. That's why FC-talk can be life-changing. If ever you are going to be true to yourself and, at the same time, deeply concerned with your partner, FC-talk is the last opportunity to do it. We want to prepare you for that dialogue in the hope that you will have a more satisfying conversation with the Dying, and perhaps also carry the skills into your other relationships. We will walk you through the gifts of FC-talk, tell you how to prepare for it, explain how to listen, suggest what you might want to say, and advise you about when to ask for help.

Why Engage in Final Conversations?

First, there's the altruistic side of FC-talk: Giving the gift of your presence to the Dying reflects a clean, pure motivation. The Dying often do want to talk—about death itself, about preparations with which they need help, or about how much they will miss you and life. If you can be the person who allows the Dying to talk freely without fear of causing you pain or discomfort, then you will be blessed. That brings us to the second motivation, which might be considered the selfish side of FC-talk: Receiving the gifts that FC-talk brings is all about *you*. We encourage you to consider these gifts well earned, however. Any motivation to communicate can be perceived as "selfish" in the sense that you benefit in some way from the interaction . . . but so does your partner. In the case of FC-talk, the gifts to the Dying will ease their passing; the gifts to the Living will endure for the rest of their lives.

FC-talk leaves both tangible and intangible rewards that help keep the memories vivid and may expand your view of your place and purpose in this life. Many of you will receive memorable messages of love and caring that make you feel valued and worthwhile. Some of you will find resolution to difficult or challenging relationships and enjoy subsequent peace of mind. Most of you will learn to live with greater joy, and some will see your self-image shift in a positive way. This kind of personal growth can lead you to change your life's purpose and path.

The gifts that the Living receive are numerous and often positive, but as with all gifts, some of the things received during FC-talk are not welcome. FC-talks aren't always positive, and they can be challenging. But most worthwhile things in life do challenge us. We are suggesting that you participate in FC-talk, if it's possible, because the potential for benefits outweighs the costs. The costs include your time, your energy, and your increased vulnerability to getting hurt and feeling disappointed. FC-talk can be difficult and painful, and it may not meet your expectations. But in the long run, even a challenging FC-talk will reward you.

The gifts that you receive from FC-talk will vary according to your awareness of what you need and what you can understand in the moment. You may realize the worth of FC-talk only long after the Dying are gone. In the midst of your grief, it's often difficult to see or feel anything but grief; but the lessons and gifts of FC-talk have been given to you to be opened and realized later, upon reflection.

Remember, it's often the things that we *don't* do that we regret later. The Living told us overwhelmingly that they are pleased to have had FC-talk with the Dying, and that they would do it again, given the opportunity. If you're willing to take the chance to grow and be open to what might happen during FC-talk, please read on for suggestions about doing it in the best way possible. Take our advice based on what feels right for you and for your unique situation, but remember that doing something for the first time always causes some uneasiness. Our advice is founded on what we have been privileged to learn from the Living, and on our combined forty-four years of teaching interpersonal communication to thousands of students.

How to Get Ready for Final Conversations

As we were told by the Living, don't set too many expectations for how you think it will go. Just be ready to listen carefully, and follow your FC-talk where it leads you. We'll show you a few skills you can practice. But first, let's set the stage.

If you know that your loved one has a terminal diagnosis, begin by looking into the optimal *amount of time* you can put aside to spend with the Dying. Check with your boss, family, and friends to see how they can help you free yourself from daily responsibilities for a while.

Once your free time is set aside, figure out the best possible *time and place* for the Dying to engage with you. Talking sooner rather than later is best. The sooner your FC-talks begin, the more FC-talks you may be able to share with the Dying. The closer the Dying is to death, the less likely it is that they can interact.

Ask the primary caregiver, medical practitioners, or hospice workers about the best time to talk with the Dying. For example, if it's likely that the Dying will sleep immediately after pain medication is administered, then that time should be ruled out. Find out when the Dying is most alert and able to focus.

Surroundings and situations can make a world of difference in the nature and tone of FC-talk. Is there a favorite place where the two of you have been together? This could be a simple and easy-to-reach location, such as a backyard patio, garden, or somewhere a short drive away that holds special meaning for the two of you. You may not have the option to go anywhere other than the

Dying's room, but it's something to consider if you can. People tend to open up and talk when they are in a familiar and comfortable place—this is true for both the Dying and the Living. Remember that FC-talk can occur at any time; it doesn't have to be the last conversation that occurs just hours before the death of the loved one. Take advantage of the time that's available. Have FC-talks early and in places that make both of you relaxed and happy.

Consider the physical location of the actual FC-talk. How will it work for a *private* conversation? If it's a home, who else visits and when? Can the door be closed? If it's a hospital, is it a shared room? How noisy is it? When are visiting hours? How many people are likely to visit, and when? To ensure an optimum FC-talk, choose times when it's more likely that you'll be alone with the Dying. Privacy is not necessary, but it often makes a difference. People self-disclose and share more openly when there is safety and privacy.

Make sure that you *arrive on time, and go as often as is allowed.* There are gatekeepers at the end of life, and it will be their job to limit the amount of interaction that the Dying has with others. The Dying may have requested limited access, and you have to respect their wishes—this is their time. It's an honor and a privilege to be given space and time with the Dying; please treat it as such.

Keep in mind that the Dying is losing energy every day, and that communication takes energy. Your FC-talk could tire your loved one, so be sensitive about the length of your FC-talk. Be aware of the Dying's nonverbal communication, which indicates how your loved one is doing. Unless you are one of the caregivers, it's never a good idea to stay for hours unless you have been invited to stay. You may need to keep your visits brief—take your clues from the Dying and from the caregivers. You should be prepared to simply sit at the Dying's side and perhaps hold his or her hand quietly if that's all that is possible on a particular visit.

The primary caregiver has more rights than someone who is only visiting. Try to honor those rights; he or she may be exhausted and seem unreasonable. Be compassionate: Is there anything you can do to help? Perhaps the caregiver can go out for a break while you visit with the Dying. The primary caregiver is usually well aware of the Dying's capability on any given day or hour. You won't know what the Dying has asked the caregiver to say or do—perhaps even to be the "heavy" in the situation. How do you know who has requested the limited access—was this the Dying's wish, or the wish of a controlling caregiver? Honestly, you don't know, and it may be difficult to find out the truth! It's helpful to think about your relationship with the Dying and the caregiver in order to make sense out of the requests or restrictions being presented to you. If they seem unreasonable, then try to get some insight from a third party: How can you get more time and access to the Dying? You may also want to consider your own behavior. Are you helping the situation, or are you causing more tension in the environment?

One more thing you must ask the Dying's caregivers: Are there any *limitations* to your interactions? That possibility increases as death nears. Can the Dying still hear and speak? Does the Dying recognize people? What kind of touch is okay, and what kind may cause discomfort? Armed with this information, you can feel well prepared to meet the needs of the Dying and to engage in the best FC-talk possible. Later in this chapter, we'll give you details on handling such limitations.

How to Communicate Skillfully

There are two halves to communication: listening and speaking. Sometimes the halves are out of balance. Every human is a natural speaker. But listening is a different matter. Unless you have a driving self-interest in hearing what another has to say, you often tune out all but what you expect to hear. Listening is a critical skill in all interactions, but it's absolutely necessary when you interact with a special someone who may be talking with you for the last time. We recommend that you first practice the skill of listening with other people who are important to you. It can't hurt, and you'll be more comfortable with your listening skills by the time you really need them. Go ahead and share what you are doing with your practice partners. They'll be thrilled with the extra attention, and you may hear something you never expected.

But you may say, "I'm in the process of saying goodbye now; I don't have time to practice," or "My life is too busy—I don't have time to learn new skills." If you feel that you can't practice, at least read through the list below so you know that these skills exist, and you can start to become aware of them. A few of the skills below need no practice at all. But no matter what, do engage in FC-talk with your loved one, regardless of whether you feel prepared. Most of the Living who contributed their stories to this book had no special training. Your own good sense will serve you. If you have time, these skills can help you feel more prepared and help you gain more from your experience.

1. *Give yourself a reason to listen carefully.* Hearing is different from listening. Hearing really never shuts down. But words can just amount to background noise if you aren't truly paying attention. Practice thinking about what could be important to you about the words your partner might say. And then make it a habit to try to find meaning in those words. Now let's say that you are visiting your favorite uncle, who is in his final days. What might he be thinking? Perhaps he wants to tell you how much he loves you and what your visits have meant to him. However, if you are talking and not listening, he won't have the opportunity, and his sentiment could be lost to you.

2. *Be other-centered.* When you focus on what the other person needs and wants in a conversation, instead of focusing on yourself, the talk often goes better. Communication acts like

a mirror. If you treat your partner as you would like to be treated, listened to, responded to, then your partner often does the same.

3. *Stop talking.* Yes, this one seems obvious. But humans love the sound of their own voices. Once you have a reason to listen—and practice will reinforce your success—try to get comfortable with silence. After you have exchanged greetings and pleasantries, stop talking and see what develops. Imagine that you will be relating this talk to someone later on.

4. *Get out of your own head.* Are you really listening, or are you preoccupied with thinking about what you want to say next? Be careful—you may miss something precious and important because you're caught up in your own mind. Are you becoming defensive, perhaps thinking about ways to argue with the Dying about some point? Being "right" isn't important. When you are "right," someone you love is wrong, and your relationship suffers. Are you so caught up in your own fears and grief that you are running those messages in your head instead of really listening to the Dying? Acknowledge the fear and grief beforehand, and try to put it aside temporarily so you don't miss out on this special moment with the Dying.

5. *Ask a question.* If you've allowed a silence, and the Dying hasn't spoken, you might try a question. But do allow a reasonable silence. Count to at least twenty. Meanwhile, smile, make eye contact, hold a hand . . . act friendly and interested. Then, if it seems right, you can start with simple questions that require little effort: "How are they treating you here?" or "Can I do anything for you?" Then move to open-ended questions that allow the Dying to talk for a while and perhaps move to topics they want to pursue. For example, you could ask, "What have you been thinking about lately?" or even make specific requests: "Can you tell me again how you and Aunt Jean met?" These kinds of questions not only

show your interest in hearing what the Dying has to say, but give the Dying a chance to talk at length and get to a topic of importance.

If you ask only closed-ended questions, such as, "Are you too cold with that window open?" then you will likely get only one-word replies that lead nowhere. However, if the answers to your open-ended questions remain brief, you may want to go a bit deeper. But again, leave your questions fairly open so the Dying has some choice about how to respond. For example, "Is there anything in particular you'd like to talk about?" The Dying may just want to reminisce for a while about old times. On the other hand, he or she may want to talk about fears of death.

Sometimes the Dying give you hints; at other times, you'll get no such help. If your relationship is good, you can be fairly direct if you suspect the need to approach a particular topic. **Sam** was able to say bluntly to his mother, "Do you want to talk about dying?" and she was able to jump right in and do so. At the same time, once you've asked, if the Dying changes the subject or looks uncomfortable, then let it go. Try not to pressure the Dying into conversations that they don't want.

6. *Paraphrase your partner's statement.* The paraphrase is the hallmark of good listening. To paraphrase is to say in your own words what your partner has just told you. It isn't mimicry, but rather a demonstration of your understanding. Paraphrasing not only lets the speaker know that she has been heard, but helps the listener clarify her understanding and remember the gist of what has been said.

Let's say your mother has just told you, "I'm afraid it's going to hurt." If you repeat that exactly, word for word, she may wonder what's wrong. However, if you offer your interpretation—how you have made sense of it—she will recognize that you are checking your understanding of her words, rather than checking your hearing or mimicking her. For example, you could say, "I understand that you are scared that death will be painful."

Again, practice this with friends. You might feel awkward at first, but you'll find it really helps your ability to focus on people and understand them; it also becomes easier and feels more natural the more you use this communication skill. As a bonus, your partners will appreciate being understood—unless, of course, your interpretation wasn't quite accurate. In the earlier case of a dying mother, she could then clarify her meaning. For example, "No, I don't think it will physically hurt to die. I'm afraid it will hurt too much to leave you." Paraphrasing is really an opportunity to let the other person feel understood.

7. *Pay attention to nonverbal communication.* Watch the Dying's nonverbal communication. It's amazing what you can observe if you listen with your eyes as well as your ears. With an increased awareness of nonverbal communication, you'll notice more and more as you practice this skill—and it is a skill. Believe it or not, you're probably already an expert on the nonverbal communication of people closest to you.

8. *Do perception checks.* Both verbal and nonverbal communication can be ambiguous and may lead to misunderstandings. Doing a perception check simply means giving the other person two choices about your interpretation of the message. For instance, "Your voice sounds angry. Are you mad at what I just said, or are you in pain?" or "You just told me that you are afraid. Are you afraid of dying, or are you afraid of being in pain?" By offering two choices (even if both are wrong), you are telling your partner that you want to truly understand, not misunderstand, the message. But don't do this all the time, because if perception checking is overused, it can be very annoying. Perception checking is best done when there is potential for confusion, and when clarification is needed.

9. *Say what you feel.* Over and over, the Living told us, "Say what you feel. Don't leave anything unsaid." Definitely leave the door open for the Dying to express their feelings, but allow yourself the opportunity to speak your mind and heart as well.

   a. In a difficult relationship, this may mean putting tough topics on the table, allowing the Dying to speak, and then allowing yourself a say. Even so, the Living taught us that the end of life is not the time to kick the Dying. They found a way to talk with the Dying, and to say what they needed to say, without threatening, accusing, or insulting. Causing more hurt won't help the Living heal or move on. All of the Living who had difficult relationships with the Dying stressed that they needed to express their thoughts and feelings to the Dying as a path to their own healing.

   b. In clearer relationships, simply expressing what is felt at the time will serve. For example, "I'm feeling at a loss to know what to do," or "I love you so much and will miss you forever," or merely, "I'm uncomfortable with the silence." When the Dying one is unable to speak, this may be an opening for the Living to simply express feelings. Remember that you can also use nonverbal communication to express what you're feeling. A touch can often express what is too difficult to say in words.

10. *Be there.* A time will come when all has been said and done; all that's left to do is to be present in the moment. If both the Dying and the Living are at peace with the leave-taking they've done, then merely being there is what's required. Being there can include hugs, kisses, caresses, deep eye contact . . . all the many ways we have to express our caring and closeness without talking. Playing music, reading poetry, watching a meaningful movie . . . all these pastimes can constitute being there too. What the two of you choose is limit-

ed only by your imagination and the physical comfort of the Dying.

Is it always easy to be a good listener and engage in true dialogue? Obviously not, since so many people complain about communication problems. It takes energy and focus. You learn to talk before you are 2 years old, but very few people think they are excellent communicators. Communication is a set of skills that we learn, either by trial and error or by formal training. You can simply talk with people in a variety of contexts and see what works, or you can take a communication class. Just the experience of having FC-talk will make you a better communicator. Awareness of your own communication is an important starting point.

When to Ask for Help

At times you may need to rely on professionals. When you are walking alongside the Dying, you will probably have to consult medical personnel and caregivers. You may need suggestions about how to communicate with the Dying whose communication abilities are diminished. When your loved one is gone—or even before—you may also wish to contact a grief counselor.

Medical and Caregiving Professionals

You will find that the Dying's caregivers, nurses, social workers, and other professionals—doctors too, but often they are not easily available for conversations—have a lot of information about the Dying that can help you have the best interaction possible. They look busy, and they are. But don't let that stop you from trying to find out about the Dying's physical strength, medical regimen, or daily routine. When these people have a minute, explain who you are and why you are asking—that you want to maximize your last interactions with the Dying. If you're not a family member, doctors will be reluctant to speak to you about some aspects of the Dying's medical status. Indeed, confidentiality rules prevent them from giving you specific information.

Despite legalities, you may ask about the basics: When is the Dying most likely to be alert and pain-free? Is it okay to touch and hug her? When is the best time to have a private conversation? The answers should be sufficient to give you the best chance to optimize your FC-talk.

Caregivers' services run the gamut, from simple assistance with grooming and feeding to highly specialized nursing or end-of-life care. If the Dying one has in-home care, that professional may be a nurse who can answer some medical questions, as well as questions about general care and nurturing. You should ask general care questions especially if you want to do something special for the Dying. For example, if Dad always had sore feet, and you occasionally gave him footbaths and pedicures, you may want to follow your impulse to share that closeness again, yet you don't want to interfere with his caregiver's duties. Ask the caregiver if it would be appropriate for you to perform this duty while she does some other task. Remember to ask if there is any possible danger to the Dying, such as infection, bleeding, or discomfort, with this or any other procedure.

Other questions become more pertinent as death approaches: "Can she still hear me?" or "Is he in pain?" Those who work with the Dying, and the Living who had FC-talk with the "unresponsive" Dying, suspect that hearing is often the last sense still active in the final stages of the dying process. Therefore, they encourage you to continue talking even when it seems that the Dying cannot hear. Go ahead. You'll feel some closure, and there's a good chance that your words could comfort the Dying and assist them in crossing over without fear.

Be sensitive to the possibility that even the unresponsive Dying may want some peace and quiet. Say what you need to, but be wary of chattering. Present a calming presence. For instance, **Maureen's** mother was in a coma. For some reason, many family members were in the room surrounding her at that point and quietly talking among themselves, but around her and in her space.

Someone looked around and suggested that Pat may need some quiet. Maureen remembers looking up as she and the others were walking out of the room, and Pat was nodding her head yes. She did need it to be quiet and peaceful. She lived for two more days. Everyone made sure that the house was very calm and quiet for the remaining hours. Pat was never alone, however; one person was always at her side as she passed the final days of her life.

Limited FC-Talk: How to Interact When the Dying's Senses Are Impaired

Some of you will want FC-talk with Dying whose communication abilities have become limited. These loved ones may not be able to speak because of paralysis, throat cancer, or a brain tumor; to hear because of advanced age or disease; or to respond normally because of dementia or a coma. What can you do? We can give you some general suggestions, but your best bet again is to consult with the medical professionals. They know the extent of the impairment and the range of possible adaptations you could try.

For example, if you know that Aunt Rae's hearing has deteriorated, we suggest that you talk in short sentences, and speak a bit slower, clearer, and louder. She may be able to hear you well enough as long as background noise is minimal and you articulate your words well. If you're tempted to shout—stop. Shouting can be perceived as a sign of anger, so it's not an effective remedy for hearing difficulties.

Although the technologies to assist those with communication deficits improve almost daily, you may find that they are not available to your loved one. If death is imminent, then costly and training-intensive technologies may not be considered feasible. However, if your loved one has trouble speaking or hearing, it's worth asking if any support is possible, and how you can best communicate with the Dying in the absence of such help.

Pain may be a constant companion to the Dying. If you've ever had a really bad toothache or discomfort after surgery, you know it's difficult even to think straight—never mind carry on a calm, intimate conversation. The right pain medication makes a world of difference for those with limited time remaining. It can mean the difference between having a long, heartfelt FC-talk and an abbreviated one punctuated by gasps of pain. The attending professionals will know when the Dying experience their pain-free peak, when the medication is beginning to fail, and when it's just best to "be there" if the pain cannot be eased.

Finally, some of the Dying are unresponsive. For **Lucia's** mother, this was a persistent condition; for many, it's a brief stage before death. In any case, it is still not known whether people who don't respond are unaware of their surroundings. You will never convince Lucia that her mother's last gesture was just an accident of which she was unaware. Some healthcare professionals believe that even those in a coma can be reached; that they can still take in information even if they don't respond. So, don't give up and walk away if your loved one goes into a coma. Although you may never know for sure, you can still express what you need to through words and touch. Remember **Holland** talking with his mother, who was in a coma? The fact that she squeezed his hand at just the right time in their conversation had special meaning for Holland. Say what you need for yourself, and you just may be saying it for the Dying as well.

Getting Through the Grief

It's almost impossible to grasp the gifts that come with FC-talk if you are buried in grief. Losing someone you love hurts, and you'll grieve even as you participate in FC-talk. We believe, and were told by the Living, that FC-talk helps people deal more effectively with their grief and bereavement, but it's not a cure-all. Everyone needs help at some point. Rather than live with the tragedy of depression, the misery of failed relationships, or the pain of loneliness, people seek counselors and therapists. Yet with death, many feel that grief is inevitable and simply must be endured. To some extent this is true. Grief is inevitable, but *how long* must it be endured? Grief can be intense, and it can come and go for years. But it does come and go; life does continue. When grief becomes depression, it's a constant companion.

What if you just can't go on? What if the grief of losing your dearest friend, your spouse, or your child is just debilitating? And what if the grief isn't just yours? What if, after your spouse's death, your children don't talk to anyone? They withdraw, their grades deteriorate, and their friendships wither? If you are just too sad to make them talk about it, don't continue suffering or let them suffer. There are people—some of them shared their personal FC-talk with us in this book—who specialize in grief counseling. It's what they know; it's what they've experienced; it's why they have great compassion for the grieving. They have been well trained and often work with hospice facilities. Seek them out, and use their expertise. They can help you feel whatever you need to feel and then come back into the bright light of a full life.

The FC-talk shared with the Dying will return to the Living in waves—waves of memories, waves of inspiration, and waves of love—but only if the Living can dig themselves out of the depths of grief. These waves can last for years, perhaps forever. Some of the Living who talked with us recalled FC-talk from a long time ago. We interviewed **Roy** twenty-seven years after the death of his mother, and he still recalled his conversation with her vividly and fondly. Words . . . looks . . . touches . . . live on long after the Dying are gone.

Summary

Communication Skills for Final Conversations

Although there is no "ideal" FC-talk, some interactions are more fulfilling than others. Many of the Living intuited the right communication skills to employ. You don't have to guess or to fear failure. You can prepare and practice. Preparation includes setting aside time, finding the right time and place for private visits with the Dying, and respecting the Dying's preferences when you follow through with the visits.

Your communication skills may be quite adequate for everyday tasks, yet you find your confidence flagging as you approach FC-talk. We urge you to practice being a good communicator: Know when to be silent, when to speak, and what to say. After years of teaching these skills, we know that they can become second-nature with practice.

If you are currently in the midst of accompanying a loved one on his or her death journey, and you don't have the time or energy to practice communication skills, then realize that you have already become more aware of them by reading the Living's stories in this book. Go ahead and do it! The time you spend with the Dying will be better than you think; you'll do better than you give yourself credit for.

Know when to seek help. You will be more comfortable with FC-talk if you know what to expect about the Dying's communication capacities.

Finally, take care of yourself. You can't receive fully the gifts of FC-talk if you are paralyzed by grief. Get the support you need to walk back into your full and beautiful life.

The most important thing to remember: Showing up is the bigger part of success. Often the Dying don't care what you say; they care that you are there.

Final Thoughts and Reflections

The Cultural Experience of Dying

Death was hidden away for about half of the past century. Now, with death increasingly postponed by medical advances in diagnosis, treatment, and pain management, it's time for death to return to its proper place: as a part of life. More now than at any time since the early twentieth century, dying may be done in the comfort and company of loved ones.

Making death a medical issue and bringing it into hospitals led to a blackout of death for most of us. As a result, the Living who face the death of a loved one often don't know how to be present or why that might be important. We, Maureen and Julie, want to bring death back to the Living—to retrain the Living in the skills needed to relate to the Dying, and to bring death back into view of the Living. We want to share our belief that communication is an effective tool for dealing with the death of a loved one, for continuing the relationship with the Dying until the very end of life, and for improving all relationships.

We know, from professional and personal experience, that relationships are the source of our humanity and joy. But good relationships don't just happen. They must be pursued, nourished, and valued. And this commitment to build fulfilling relationships does not end with approaching death. If you continue your commitment to the Dying, your humanity and joy will grow.

We have shown how FC-talk functions to strengthen relationships, reach closure, release old pain, and lead to shifts in identity and life direction for the Living. Now, we will share with you how the process of doing this work has affected us.

Our Gifts

As we were writing about the many blessings the Living received from their FC-talks, we realized that we were also blessed by the process of collecting and sharing these stories.

- We have greater respect for the process of dying, as well as for the Living and their bravery in facing the intensity of telling us their stories.

- We learned that we want to write from our own passion; we want to make a difference by applying what we know.

- We learned that being productive doesn't have to be painful; indeed, it is often a joy . . . if we are doing what we love.

- We learned to listen to the voice of intuition and not to question the truth or validity of that voice.

- We learned to trust that things happen when they are supposed to. Sometimes we have to let go; we cannot control everything.

- We learned not to fear death, for it truly is a natural part of life.

- Finally, we learned to love and trust ourselves and each other.

Our Wish for You

We embarked on this project so that more people would enter joyfully and comfortably into their interactions with the Dying. We wish for you the unique gifts that only you can receive from your loved one as you converse in the final months, weeks, days, or hours that you have together. Although the stories told in this book are amazing and inspiring, none of them will be your story. Live your own story. Follow your own path as you turn to say goodbye . . . and facing forward again, you will move on.

Research Participants and Graphics

How Did We Get This Material?

We asked people who had one or more FC-talks with the Dying to share their stories with us. The FC-talk could have taken place at any time between the diagnosis of terminal illness and the moment of death. The Living heard about our project primarily by word of mouth from our students, colleagues, and friends, but they may also have found out about it from a flyer, newspaper article, or website. We wanted to make sure that participation was voluntary, so each person who shared a story took the initiative to contact one of us.

No one received money or other compensation to talk with us. These wonderful people wanted to help us learn more about FC-talk. Most of the Living appreciated the chance to share their experiences. They hoped that sharing their stories might encourage you to make your own memories from FC-talk.

We did not interview anyone who was going through the death process at the time of the interview because we didn't want to create any additional stress or pain during an already difficult situation. For most people we interviewed, our discussions of their FC-talk happened within five years of their loved one dying (although the actual time that had passed ranged from as short as three months to as long as twenty-seven years). We spent a long time with each of the Living, allowing every story to unfold. The majority of people who shared a story told us that it was a cathartic and positive experience in spite of the intense emotion involved.

Chapter 1 contains an overview of our research. The statistical charts in this Appendix provide basic information about the Living who gave us their stories and about aspects of these Living's FC-talks such as location and timing.

Who Talked with Us About Their FC-Talk?

We heard stories from eighty-two people, most of whom were female. That isn't surprising, given the fact that traditionally, women are the nurturers and caregivers in the family. Indeed, many of these women spent a lot of time caring for the Dying.

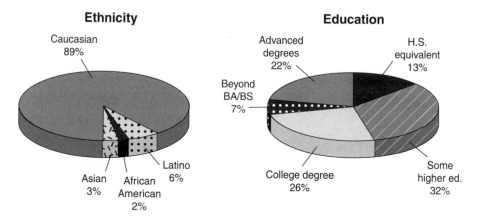

Ethnicity

Caucasian 89%

Asian 3%

African American 2%

Latino 6%

Education

Advanced degrees 22%

H.S. equivalent 13%

Beyond BA/BS 7%

College degree 26%

Some higher ed. 32%

Most of our volunteers were Caucasian and well educated, probably because we conducted the interviews in or near college towns. However, we believe that communication at the end of life is important for all people, regardless of ethnicity, culture, education level, or level of income. We hope that men as well as women, and people throughout the ethnic spectrum, will recognize themselves in these stories and gain the courage to have a final conversation with the Dying. While we know that there are major differences in the way various cultures deal with death, we believe that the communication issues surrounding death are not limited to one sex, race, or culture. Many commonalities can be found, and this book offers a good place to start learning about end-of-life communication.

The Living

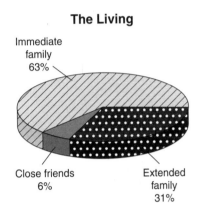

Immediate family 63%

Close friends 6%

Extended family 31%

Not surprisingly, most of the people who participated in final conversations were family members or the sort of friends who considered themselves to be members of the family. Over half were immediate family members: a spouse or life partner, child, sibling, or parent of the Dying. Another third were extended family members of the Dying: a grandparent, grandchild, aunt, uncle, niece, or nephew. The remaining were close friends who were considered family, and so received access to the Dying at the end of their lives. Many of these friends told us that they felt that in some ways, they were closer than family members because their relationships were based on choice, not family ties. In fact, their FC-talks with the Dying cemented their family status because they were one of a select few or, at times, the only non-family member to be privileged with an end-of-life interaction.

Who Started the FC-Talk?

Many variables affect who begins FC-talk: comfort level, needs, opportunity, goals for the interaction, and so forth. Most of the time, the Living reported that both partners in FC-talk initiated

Initiator of Talk

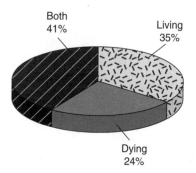

the interaction. Clearly, initiating FC-talk is not the sole job of either the Dying or the Living, but is shared by both participants. One cautionary note: You can't force FC-talk on anyone, but you can invite it. If your effort to initiate a final conversation is rejected, you may have another opportunity in the future.

Who Did Most of the Talking?

As you might expect of people trying to have good conversations, many of the FC-talk participants engaged about equally in the talk: 40% of our interviewees thought the amount of talk was about equal for each party; 35% thought they, the Living, had done more talking; and 24% remembered the Dying as doing more of the talking.

Amount of Talk

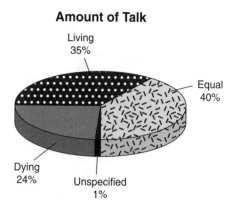

When Did the Conversations Occur?

Most of the people who shared their stories with us had their FC-talk in the afternoons and/or evenings. The Living often visited the Dying during lunch, following a day of work, or later in the evening after their children were settled. The Living who acted as the primary caregivers of the Dying may have had more opportunity for conversations in the middle of the night when the Dying couldn't sleep, or in the morning after rest. The Living who had other obligations, and spent time with their loved ones as visitors, were more likely to have conversations in the late afternoon and/or evening. The timing of FC-talk appears to be related to when the Living are able to visit, and to the primary role of the Living—as caregiver or visitor.

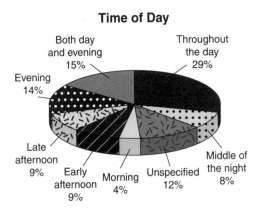

Time of Day

Both day and evening 15%

Throughout the day 29%

Evening 14%

Late afternoon 9%

Early afternoon 9%

Morning 4%

Unspecified 12%

Middle of the night 8%

Between diagnosis and death, few conversations occurred soon after diagnosis, and even fewer occurred within hours of death. Between these two extremes lie the rest. It makes sense that relatively few FC-talks occur within hours of death because as the Dying near death, they usually sleep more, have difficulty speaking, and show numerous signs that their bodies are shutting down. As people near death, their physical capacity for a conversation is diminished. This leads us to suggest that the Living should be encouraged to participate in FC-talk while the loved one is still capable of being an active participant. This is not to imply that the

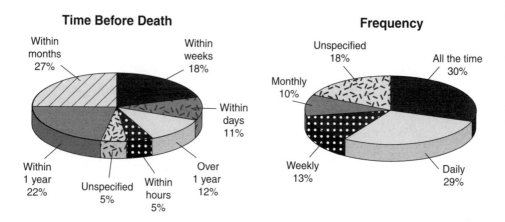

later final interactions are without meaning. These last moments, filled with a final touch or a momentary look, can be extremely meaningful and powerful for the Living.

The timing of FC-talk is related to the amount of contact that the Living one has with the Dying one. The majority of the Living said that they had multiple conversations with the Dying; almost 60% had at least daily interactions. The fewer days you have available, the more intense the time crunch will be. However, if you begin having these talks far in advance of the end, you can afford to spread them out over time.

Where Did the Living and the Dying Talk?

The location of FC-talk usually depends on the Dying's condition at the time of the conversation. The top three locations in order were (1) home, (2) both home and hospital, and (3) hospital. (Note that our participants generally bucked the trend of dying in the hospital, although it's possible that these talks happened much before the actual death. But we suspect that dying at home will become more common for those with long disease courses, as more people learn of their options and wish to have these last private interactions at home.) Interestingly, 10% of the FC-talk took place over the phone, which illustrates how mobile and spread out our society is today. While some of the Living resided in the same town, others lived a state away, across the country, or even across

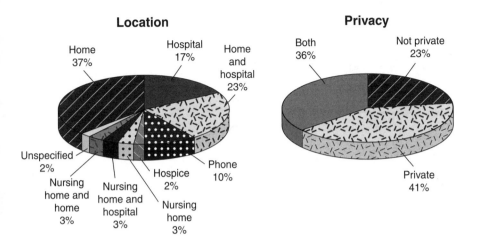

Location

Home 37%

Hospital 17%

Home and hospital 23%

Unspecified 2%

Nursing home and home 3%

Nursing home and hospital 3%

Nursing home 3%

Hospice 2%

Phone 10%

Privacy

Both 36%

Not private 23%

Private 41%

the world. In the end, the most important criterion for the location of the final conversations depended on where the Dying were most comfortable—we must go to them. It appears that FC-talk most likely just happens.

It should be no surprise that the majority of final conversations occurred when the Living were alone with the Dying. Most people need privacy to open up and be honest in revealing how they're feeling and what they're thinking. Of those who had FC-talks while others were present, over half were in the presence of other family members; the rest were with a nurse or caregiver.

Suggested Readings and Resources

This is not an exhaustive list by any means, but we wanted to give you somewhere else to look for information, and we found these books helpful.

Aiken, L. R. *Dying, Death, and Bereavement.* 4th ed. Mahwah, NJ: Lawrence Erlbaum, 2001.

Bateson, M. C. *Composing a Life.* New York: Penguin/Plume, 1990.

Callanan, M., and P. Kelley. *Final Gifts: Understanding the Special Awareness, Needs, and Communications of the Dying.* New York: Bantam Books, 1992.

Doyle, D. *Caring for a Dying Relative: A Guide for Families.* Oxford: Oxford University Press, 1994.

Foster, E. *Communicating at the End of Life: Finding Magic in the Mundane.* Mahwah, NJ: Lawrence Erlbaum, 2006.

Glick, I. O., R. S. Weiss, and C. M. Parkes. *The First Year of Bereavement.* New York: John Wiley and Sons, 1974.

Gottman, J. M. *The Relationship Cure.* New York: Crown Publishers, 2001.

Harter, L. M., P. M. Japp, and C. S. Beck. *Narratives, Health, and Healing: Communication Theory, Research, and Practice.* Mahwah, NJ: Lawrence Erlbaum, 2005.

Heinz, D. *The Last Passage.* New York: Oxford University Press, 1999.

Kübler-Ross, E. *On Death and Dying.* New York: Touchstone, 1969.

Kübler-Ross, E. *Living with Death and Dying.* New York: Simon and Schuster, 1997.

Levine, S. *Meetings at the Edge: Dialogues with the Grieving and the Dying, the Healing and the Healed.* New York: Doubleday, 1984.

Linde, C. *Life Stories: The Creation of Coherence.* New York: Oxford University Press, 1993.

Lynn, J., and J. Harrold. *Handbook for Mortals: Guidance for People Facing Serious Illness.* Oxford: University Press, 1999.

Moller, D. W. *Confronting Death: Values, Institutions, and Human Morality.* New York: Oxford University Press, 1996.

Nussbaum, J. F., L. L. Pecchioni, J. D. Robinson, and T. L. Thompson. *Communication and Aging.* 2nd ed. Mahwah, NJ: Lawrence Erlbaum, 2000.

Parkes, C. M., and R. S. Weiss. *Recovery from Bereavement.* New York: Basic Books, 1983.

Shames, L., and P. Barton. *Not Fade Away: A Short Life Well Lived.* New York: Rodale, 2003. Distributed by St. Martin's Press.

Wills, M. *Communicating Spirituality in Health Care.* Cresskill, NJ: Hampton Press, 2007.

Wood, J. T., and S. Duck. *Composing Relationships: Communication in Everyday Life.* Belmont, CA: Wadsworth, 2006.

Yingling, J. *A Lifetime of Communication.* Mahwah, NJ: Lawrence Erlbaum, 2004.

Pertinent Publications by the Authors

Keeley, M. P. "Turning Toward Death Together: The Functions of Messages During Final Conversations in Close Relationships." *Journal of Social and Personal Relationships* 24 (2007): 122–152.

Keeley, M. P. "Comfort and Community: Two Emergent Communication Themes of Religious Faith and Spirituality Evident During Final Conversations." In *Communicating Spirituality in Health Care,* edited by M. Wills. Creskill, NJ: Hampton Press Health Communication Series, 2007.

Keeley, M. P. "Final Conversations: Messages of Love." *Qualitative Research Reports* 5 (2004): 48–57.

Keeley, M. P. "Final Conversations: Survivors' Memorable Messages Concerning Religious Faith and Spirituality." *Health Communication* 16, no. 1 (2004): 87–104.

Keeley, M. P. "The Nonverbal Perception Scale." In *Beyond Words: A Sourcebook of Methods for Measuring Nonverbal Cues,* edited by V. Manusov, 586–610. Mahwah, NJ: Lawrence Erlbaum, 2004.

Keeley, M. P. "Social Support and Breast Cancer: Why Do We Talk and Who Do We Talk To?" In *Evaluating Women's Health Messages,* edited by R. Parrott and C. Condit, 293–306. Beverly Hills, CA: Sage, 1996.

Keeley, M. P., and A. Hart. "Nonverbal Behavior in Dyadic Interactions." In *The Dynamics of Relationships,* edited by S. Duck, 135–162. Beverly Hills, CA: Sage, 1994.

Keeley, M. P., and J. Koenig Kellas. "Constructing Life and Death Through Final Conversations Narrative." In *Narratives, Health, and Healing: Communication Theory, Research, and Practice,* edited by L. M. Harter, P. M. Japp, and C. S. Beck, 365–390. Mahwah, NJ: Lawrence Erlbaum Associates, 2005.

Yingling, J. *A Lifetime of Communication: Transformations Through Relational Dialogues.* Mahwah, NJ: Lawrence Erlbaum, 2004.

Yingling, J. "Verbal Responses of Children and Their Support Providers in a Pediatric Oncology Unit." In *Journal of Health Communication* 5, no. 4 (2000): 371–377.

Yingling, J. "The First Relationship: Infant-Parent Communication." In *Parents, Children and Communication: Frontiers of Theory and Research,* edited by T. J. Socha and G. H. Stamp, 23–41. Hillsdale, NJ: Lawrence Erlbaum Associates, 1995.

Yingling, J. "Constituting Friendship in Talk and Metatalk." *Journal of Social and Personal Relationships* 11, no. 3 (1994): 411–426.

Yingling, J., and M. Keeley. "A Failure to Communicate: Let's Get Real About Improving Communication at the End of Life." *American Journal of Hospice and Palliative Medicine* 24, no. 2 (2007): 1–3.

Index to the Living

We honor the many people who spoke with us, regardless of whether we were able to use their contributions in this book (NDQ=no direct quotes). If you wish to find all the contributions from one of the Living, the appropriate chapters are listed next to each name.

Name	Chapter(s)	Name	Chapter(s)	Name	Chapter(s)
April	2	Jeanette	2, 7, 8	Mary Jo	3, 4
Betty Lynn	4	Jennifer Q	4	Maureen	3, 4, 5, 9
Bev	4	Jennifer W	5	Meaghan	NDQ
Bill	4, 8	Jim	3, 5, 8	Melissa Q	2, 3, 4
B.J.	2, 5, 8	Jo	8	Melissa W	NDQ
Blanca	2, 5, 6, 8	Joseph	2	Michael	8
Bob	NDQ	Josey	NDQ	Nancy	3, 4
Breanna	3, 7, 8	Judy Q	3, 8	Nick	NDQ
Brenda	1, 3	Judy W	3, 8	Patti	2, 3, 5
Cara	3	Jules	5	Pinky	5, 6
Carol	5, 8	Karen	4, 7	Roxanne	2, 8
Cathy	2, 3, 5, 9	Kasey	2, 5, 8	Roy	1, 4, 9
Claire	7	Katherine	3, 5, 6, 7	Ruth	5, 7, 8
Dana Q	3	Katie	NDQ	Ryan	3, 5
Dana W	1, 2, 3, 5, 7, 8	Ken	NDQ	Sam	2, 3, 6, 8, 9
Darrell	2, 3	Laura Q	3	Sandra	2, 8
Debbie	5	Laura W	5, 6, 7	Sarah	3
Derrick	8	Laurel	6	Sondra	2, 8
Ellen	1, 2, 4, 5	Laurie Q	2, 3	Stan	5
Emily	3, 5, 7, 8	Laurie W	3, 6, 8	Susan	3, 4, 5, 7
Erin	3, 5	Leeann	3	Tory	3, 4, 5, 7
Gloria	4, 5, 7, 8	Lilly	NDQ	Victoria	1, 2, 4, 5, 6, 7, 8
Grace	2, 3, 5, 8	Linda	3		
Greg	3, 7	Lindsey	NDQ	Wallace	6
Herschel	2, 3, 6	Lisa	NDQ	Waltraud	5
Holland	3, 5, 6, 9	Lori	1, 2, 4, 5, 8	William	2, 4, 5
Jack	3	Lucia	2, 7, 8, 9		
Jarrod	2, 4, 5	Mandy	2, 7		

Index